The Taming of Solitude

Psychoanalysts would argue that at the root of anxiety about loneliness, which commonly brings people into analysis, lies anxiety about separation, unresolved since childhood. When re-experienced in analysis, the painful awareness of solitude – the sense of being a separate person – can be better tolerated and can become a rich source of personal creativity. Many analysts have written about such anxieties and in *The Taming of Solitude* Jean-Michel Quinodoz brings together the views of Freud, Klein, Hanna Segal, W.R.D. Fairbairn, D.W. Winnicott, Anna Freud, Margaret Mahler, Heinz Kohut, John Bowlby and others, presenting a comprehensive approach to the experience of loneliness, a universal phenomenon which can be observed in everyday life and in any therapeutic situation.

In the first part of the book the author uses a clinical example to illustrate how a patient expresses various forms of separation anxiety, and how such anxiety can be transformed during the psychoanalytic process. The second part carefully examines the major psychoanalytic views on the topic and the third part explores several technical and clinical aspects of the problems which arise from the interpretation of separation anxiety. Finally, the author introduces a new concept, 'buoyancy', to express how a successful working through of separation anxiety can lead to a capacity to 'carry' oneself at the end of an analysis.

Written with clarity and simplicity, *The Taming of Solitude* will be of great interest to all psychoanalysts and therapists.

Jean-Michel Quinodoz is a psychoanalyst in private practice and Consultant Psychiatrist at the Department of Psychiatry, University of Geneva. He is also Editor for Europe of the *International Journal of Psycho-Analysis*.

THE NEW LIBRARY OF PSYCHOANALYSIS

The New Library of Psychoanalysis was launched in 1987 in association with the Institute of Psycho-Analysis, London. Its purpose is to facilitate a greater and more widespread appreciation of what psychoanalysis is really about and to provide a forum for increasing mutual understanding between psychoanalysts and those working in other disciplines such as history, linguistics, literature, medicine, philosophy, psychology, and the social sciences. It is intended that the titles selected for publication in the series should deepen and develop psychoanalytic thinking and technique, contribute to psychoanalysis from outside, or contribute to other disciplines from a psychoanalytical perspective.

The Institute, together with the British Psycho-Analytical Society, runs a low-fee psychoanalytic clinic, organizes lectures and scientific events concerned with psychoanalysis, publishes the *International Journal of Psycho-Analysis* and the *International Review of Psycho-Analysis*, and runs the only training course in the UK in psychoanalysis leading to membership of the International Psychoanalytical Association – the body which preserves internationally agreed standards of training, of professional entry, and of professional ethics and practice for psychoanalysis as initiated and developed by Sigmund Freud. Distinguished members of the Institute have included Michael Balint, Wilfred Bion, Ronald Fairbairn, Anna Freud, Ernest Jones, Melanie Klein, John Rickman, and Donald Winnicott.

Volumes 1–11 in the series have been prepared under the general editorship of David Tuckett, with Ronald Britton and Eglé Laufer as associate editors. Subsequent volumes are under the general editorship of Elizabeth Bott Spillius, with, from Volume 17, Donald Campbell, Michael Parsons, Rosine Jozef Perelberg and David Taylor as associate editors.

ALSO IN THIS SERIES

'Qu'est-ce que signifie "apprivoiser"?

– C'est une chose trop oubliée, dit le renard. Ça signifie "créer des liens. . . "

– Créer des liens?

– Bien sûr, dit le renard. Tu n'es encore pour moi qu'un petit garçon semblable à cent mille petits garçons. Et je n'ai pas besoin de toi. Et tu n'as pas besoin de moi non plus. Je ne suis pour toi qu'un renard semblable à cent mille renards. Mais, si tu m'apprivoises, nous aurons besoin l'un de l'autre. Tu seras pour moi unique au monde. Je serai pour toi unique au monde . . .

– Je commence à comprendre, dit le petit prince. Il y a une fleur . . . Je crois qu'elle m'a apprivoisé . . . '

'What does "tame" mean?'

'It is something that is too often forgotten,' said the fox. 'It means "to forge links . . . "'

'To forge links?'

'Yes, of course,' said the fox. 'To me, you are still just a little boy no different from a hundred thousand other little boys. And I don't need you. Nor do you need me. To you, I am merely a fox that is no different from a hundred thousand foxes. But if you tame me, we shall need each other. You will be unique in the whole world for me. And I shall be unique in the whole world for you . . . '

'I am beginning to understand,' said the Little Prince. 'There is a flower . . . I do believe it has tamed me . . . '

Antoine de Saint-Exupéry, *Le Petit Prince*, p. 68

NEW LIBRARY OF PSYCHOANALYSIS
20

General editor: Elizabeth Bott Spillius

The Taming of Solitude

Separation Anxiety in Psychoanalysis

JEAN-MICHEL QUINODOZ

Foreword by Hanna Segal

Translated by Philip Slotkin

LONDON AND NEW YORK

First published as *La Solitude apprivoisée* by Presses Universitaires de France in 1991

English language edition first published 1993
by Routledge
11 New Fetter Lane, London EC4P 4EE

Simultaneously published in the USA and Canada
by Routledge
29 West 35th Street, New York, NY 10001

© 1993 Jean-Michel Quinodoz

Typeset in Bembo by LaserScript Limited, Mitcham, Surrey
Printed and bound in Great Britain by
Mackays of Chatham PLC, Chatham, Kent

British Library Cataloguing in Publication Data
A catalogue record for this book is available from the British Library

Library of Congress Cataloging in Publication Data
Quinodoz, Jean-Michel.
[Solitude apprivoisée. English]
The taming of solitude: separation anxiety in psychoanalysis/Jean-Michel Quinodoz;
Foreword by Hanna Segal. – English lang. ed.
p. cm. – (New library of psychoanalysis: 20)
Includes bibliographical references and index.
1. Separation anxiety. 2. Psychoanalysis. 3. Psychotherapist and patient.
I. Title. II. Series.
RC489.S45Q5513 1993
616.89'17–dc20 93-9866
CIP

ISBN 0–415–09153–5
0–415–09154–3 (pbk)

Contents

Foreword

HANNA SEGAL

I have known Jean-Michel Quinodoz since 1978, when he was a member of a clinical postgraduate working group which I conducted in Geneva till 1984. Since then I have on several occasions discussed with him various clinical and theoretical concerns. During those years I developed a respect for Quinodoz's commitment to psychoanalysis, the seriousness of his work and his capacity for ideas. This book shows the qualities I noticed in him.

He addresses himself to the topic of separation anxiety in clinical practice. There is a vast literature on separation anxiety, starting with Freud, but very little has been written on the crucial role that separation anxiety, and the defences against it, play in the psycho-analytic process. Freud speaks of the analyst's Monday crust, but not of that of the patient. Quinodoz shows convincingly, in detailed clinical material, the various forms and varying contents of separation anxiety and the work that has to be done on defences to uncover it and enable the patient to work it through.

In the second part of the book he examines the principal existing psychoanalytic theories on separation anxiety, starting with Freud and including Klein, Fairbairn, Winnicott, Balint, Anna Freud, Spitz and Mahler. Throughout the book he makes references to a number of other writers as well.

The last part of the book is concerned with termination of a psychoanalysis, and here he introduces an original concept of his own, *portance*. He quotes the dictionary definitions of the two non-identical meanings of the word. The first is the strength of the material needed to support a structure – for instance, the foundations of a house; the second, used in physics, is the vertical force which in combination with speed gives the uplift – for instance, in a plane taking off. Quinodoz considers that a good resolution of separation anxiety results in the patient acquiring *portance*, a combination of both a firm basis in the internal world and the capacity for uplift. He describes the constellation of internal object relationships which gives the individual a *portance*. This gives the capacity not only for standing separation and alone-ness, but also a buoyancy and *un élan de vivre*.

I think *La Solitude apprivoisée* is an important book. It combines a clinical approach with a scholarly grasp of theory, and brings in new ideas which illuminate both theory and clinical practice.

PART ONE

Separation anxiety in psychoanalytic practice

Separation anxiety in transference phantasies

'Si tu veux un ami, apprivoise-moi!'   'If you want a friend, tame me!'
                                  Antoine de Saint-Exupéry, *Le Petit Prince*, p. 69

The two faces of solitude

Solitude has two faces: it may be a deadly counsellor, or, if tamed, it may become a friend of infinite worth. Can solitude be tamed? Is it possible to turn it into a genuine means of communication with oneself and with others?

In this book, I wish to show how solitude can be lived and transformed through the psychoanalytic experience, and how a sometimes hostile and desperate feeling of loneliness can gradually develop into a solitude tamed, constituting a foundation of trust for communication with oneself and with others.

This transition takes place by way of what we psychoanalysts call the working through of separation anxieties and object-loss anxieties, a process in which the psychological development of each individual and, in a similar way, the progress of the psychoanalytic relationship are manifested. Separation anxiety, where excessive, is the tragic fear of finding oneself alone and abandoned – the fount of psychical pain and the affect of mourning, as Freud showed in 1926. As loneliness, solitude may turn into a deadly abyss: '*Un seul être vous manque, et tout est dépeuplé*' ['For the want of just one being, the world is void of human life'] (A. de Lamartine, *L'Isolement*). Conversely, when tamed, separation anxiety becomes a vivifying force: the taming of solitude is a matter not of eliminating anxiety but of learning to confront it and to use it in order to place it in the service of life. Feeling alone then means becoming aware that one is oneself unique and that the other is also unique; one's relationship with oneself and others now assumes infinite worth. This is how I understand the Little Prince when he says to the roses: 'You are just the way my fox used to be. He was only a fox like a hundred thousand others. But I have made him my friend, and now he is unique in the world' (Antoine de Saint-Exupéry, *Le Petit Prince*, p. 72).

In this introductory chapter I should like to place the feeling of loneliness and separation anxiety in a psychoanalytic context. This type of anxiety is a universal fact of everyday life and is reproduced in the relationship with the person of the analyst, fundamentally moulding the development of the transference. Separation anxiety does indeed possess the essential characteristics of the transferable phenomena with which psychoanalysis is concerned. Because it tends to be reproduced like an infantile experience in the present-day relationship with the psychoanalyst, and owing to its unconscious nature, the separation anxiety that arises between the analysand and the analyst can be identified, and this allows it to be interpreted and worked through.

Separation anxiety: a universal phenomenon

Considering separation in the context of an interpersonal relationship, normal separation anxiety corresponds to an individual's painful sense of fear when an affective relationship with an important person in his[1] circle is threatened with interruption or is actually interrupted. The interruption may result from loss of the affective link (loss of love), or it may be due to the actual loss of the important person. We tend to use the word 'separation' for a temporary interruption and 'loss' if it is permanent. However, phantasies of separation tend to be confused with ones of loss, and separation is then experienced as a loss.

Separation anxiety is a universal phenomenon; indeed, it is such an intimate and familiar emotion that we almost have to make a special effort to realize that it is a concern which accompanies every instant of our everyday lives. We need only think of what we say when welcoming or parting from friends or relations: 'I am so pleased to see you again, I thought you had disappeared, I was worried that I had had no more news of you. . . . Do not leave me alone. . . . '

Through these words we express, in circumstances seemingly of the utmost triviality, a fundamental need for an affective relationship and at the same time a feeling of longing at the thought of parting from a loved one. Separation anxiety is therefore a reflection of the painful emotion – which is to a greater or lesser extent conscious – that accompanies the perception of the transience of human relations, of the existence of others and of our own existence. Yet it is at the same time

4

a structuring emotion for the ego, because the perception of the pain of our solitude makes us aware, first of all, that we exist as a single and unique being with respect to others and, secondly, that those others are different from ourselves. In this way separation anxiety constitutes the foundation of our sense of identity as well as of our knowledge of the other – that 'other' whom we psychoanalysts are accustomed to call the 'object' in order to distinguish him or her from the 'subject'.

How is separation anxiety manifested?

Separation anxiety is usually expressed in affective reactions in which we experience – and can describe – our feelings in relation to the person from whom we feel separated: for instance, the feeling of being abandoned and alone, sad or angry, frustrated or desperate. The affective reaction to separation may also take the form of any of a whole range of emotions, depending on the degree of anxiety. These reactions may be minor, such as worry or grief, or severe, involving major manifestations which may be mental (depression, delusion or suicide), functional-somatic (affecting the functions) or psychosomatic (giving rise to organ lesions). Separation anxiety is actually one of the most common proximate causes of pathological manifestations and is responsible in particular for many different forms of mental or bodily illnesses or accidents.

The capacity to contain anxiety – in particular, separation anxiety – varies from individual to individual; what is called 'normality' corresponds to a given person's capacity to cope with and work through anxiety. However, this capacity may be exceeded and anxiety may arise for both external and internal reasons, these two factors being closely connected with each other, as we shall see later. From a different point of view, reactions to separation or object-loss may be regarded as in most cases having unconscious origins and meanings, outside the realm of the subject's consciousness. We shall now consider this point.

Between the conscious and the unconscious

Let us now examine separation anxiety in terms of conscious or unconscious psychical phenomena – i.e. in accordance with Freud's first topography (1915e).

As a general rule, where separation anxiety is relatively well tolerated, the anxious subject is substantially conscious that the

5

separation concerns the relationship with a person in their circle whom they have cathected, and that their feelings – for example, sadness or abandonment – have to do with the conscious bonds of relationship with the cathected person. Every psychical reaction admittedly has a conscious and an unconscious component. However, unconscious mechanisms predominate if the anxiety is excessive: the subject then defends against the onset of anxiety by banishing it into his unconscious, either by way of defence mechanisms such as repression, displacement or other defences, or by disavowing the affects and splitting his own ego, when the anxiety is too intense, as we shall see later. These defence mechanisms against anxiety ultimately have the consequence that the subject suffering from separation no longer knows *whom* the suffering concerns, or even *what* he is feeling about the separation from or loss of the cathected object. For example, when the pain of separation is excessive, the subject may displace the feelings of sadness and abandonment and experience them in relation to someone other than the cathected person, without being aware that his sadness has been diverted from the person who is its actual source. Such displacements of feelings are often found to lie at the root of parapraxes.

These mechanisms of defence against the perception of anxiety – like the displacements or parapraxes I have just mentioned – are phenomena which substantially escape the subject's consciousness. They take place at the level which Freud (1915e) called 'unconscious', to distinguish them from phenomena perceived at a conscious level. Although it is often relatively easy for an outside observer to establish causal links between separation and the many unconscious manifestations of this type of anxiety, this is not the case for the person concerned, who is unable to see any causal connection between phenomena which escape him, because they take place outside his field of consciousness – i.e. in the unconscious. Returning to the example of displacement mentioned above, the relevant person does not himself realize that he is directing his sadness or anger towards someone who is not the real object of these feelings.

Again, with regard to separation anxiety, we can make the same observation as Freud did with a large number of mental disorders, that when a person with symptoms connected with this type of anxiety ultimately becomes conscious of their unconscious psychical origins, this consciousness may, when re-lived in the transference relationship, help to resolve the symptoms. This is one of the fundamental principles of psychoanalytic work.

We can now draw a comparison between mourning and separation anxiety. In normal mourning, the sufferer is aware of the link between their sadness, for example, and the separation from or loss of the loved person, whereas in pathological mourning this link tends to be unconscious: the person suffering from the separation or loss does not know, if not whom he has lost, at least what he has lost (Freud 1917e [1915]). It will not be possible for the subject to embark on the mourning-work whereby his symptoms may be resolved until he has been able to become aware of the unconscious links binding him to the object, so that he can consciously detach himself from it. Because psychoanalytic investigation potentially allows unconscious phenomena to be worked through, it is particularly valuable when compared with other approaches to separation anxiety.

Freud, separation and object-loss

The individual's fundamental unconscious reactions to separation and object-loss were described by Freud. Throughout his life, he enquired into the origins of this type of psychological reaction and the reasons for its diversity. What, he asked, gives rise only to pain? What tends to cause anxiety instead? What leads to pathological mourning? And, again, what is the nature of normal mourning? His answers are contained in two major contributions.

In 'Mourning and melancholia' (1917e [1915]), Freud discovers that the reason for the depressive reaction to object-loss is that the subject has partly identified with the lost object and become confused with it, as a defence against the feeling of having lost it. With 'Mourning and melancholia', Freud begins to attribute more importance to the relations between the subject and both external and internal objects, while the concept of the object, as well as that of the ego, becomes more specific. Some years later, with his second topography – i.e. a different division of the mind into ego, superego and id (complementing the first topography, in which the mind was divided into conscious, preconscious and unconscious) – Freud was to see anxiety as an affect experienced by the ego, and to modify his previous views on the origin of anxiety. Starting with *Inhibitions, Symptoms and Anxiety* (1926d), he ascribes anxiety to phantasies of fear of separation and object-loss. He regards anxiety as a state of psychical helplessness of the ego when confronted by a threat of danger – a danger which revives the state of psychical and biological helplessness experienced by the infant in the absence of its mother, a person loved and intensely desired. Freud thus makes the fear of separation into the very prototype of anxiety.

It took some time for these new views of Freud's, according to which separation and object-loss were predominant in the causation of anxiety and defence mechanisms, to gain acceptance; indeed, some psychoanalysts still dispute them. One of the main stumbling blocks in my view has to do with the difficulty of determining the part played by phantasies as compared with reality in the matter of separation and object-loss. This is a fundamental point which we shall discuss right away; it will afford us a better understanding of the impact of the psychoanalytic approach to this problem, which lies at the crossroads between reality and phantasy – i.e. between external reality and psychical reality.

Reality and the phantasy of separation and object-loss

The problem of the relations between external reality and internal or psychical reality arises in particularly acute form in separation anxiety. This is presumably due to the way this term is usually defined, because separation from or the loss of a person immediately suggests a real separation or a real loss, so that the part played by phantasies – i.e. the subject's unconscious wishes to cause the object to disappear – tends to be forgotten.

Now psychoanalysis teaches us that real experiences of separation are not to be regarded only as facts of concrete reality, but also that these events are always interpreted in terms of phantasies. Conversely, we may observe that our phantasies and our relations with the internal images of our objects have a direct influence on our relations with the real persons around us, through the constant two-way traffic of the mechanisms of projection and introjection.

The importance of phantasies as compared with reality in separation anxiety and object-loss has been rated very differently by different psychoanalysts. Some analysts' interest in studying the consequences of real separations and losses has certainly lent more currency to the idea that separation is primarily a problem of the relation with external reality and that it is outside the specific field of psychoanalysis. This has been felt to be the case with Anna Freud, Spitz and Bowlby, whose work has concentrated on separation from real persons, in particular in children, and, in the transference relationship, separation from the real person of the psychoanalyst. Anna Freud, for instance, holds that experiences of separation from the psychoanalyst during the treatment reawaken the memory of actual childhood separations, which are re-lived in the transference (Sandler *et al.* 1980).

Although Freud in 1926 was explicitly taking account of the instincts – i.e. unconscious wishes to cause the object to disappear –

and not only of reality when he ascribed a predominant role to separation in the causation of anxiety, the same charge of over-emphasizing the role of reality has been levelled at him, in particular by French psychoanalysts such as Laplanche (1980). When Freud attempts to assign different meanings to separation according to the relevant phase of development, distinguishing the separation of birth, weaning and loss of faeces in the pre-genital stages, Laplanche thus considers that Freud is exclusively seeking a first real event as the source of anxiety. In my view, in referring to a 'flattening of the Freudian doctrine' on this point (1980: 144), Laplanche goes too far in his criticism of certain ambiguities which are admittedly present in *Inhibitions, Symptoms and Anxiety*. Like many psychoanalysts today, I personally believe that Freud was seeking in this new theory of anxiety to assign different meanings to phantasies of separation and object-loss – meanings which differ according to the predominant sensations and bodily and mental experiences of infantile development and which give rise to phantasies. Even if some of Freud's formulations are tentative, for him it is ultimately need and instinct which account for the traumatic or dangerous character of separation or object-loss. This will be confirmed by the study of *Inhibitions, Symptoms and Anxiety* featuring later in this book.

For Melanie Klein, anxiety about separation and loss is primarily connected with aggressive phantasies of destruction of the object. In her view, the fear of disappearance of the object may be experienced in paranoid form – in which case the predominant anxiety is of being attacked by the bad object – or in depressive form – when the anxiety of losing the internalized good object takes precedence over the fear of attack by the bad object. Because Klein attached so much importance to the internal world and to phantasy, it may sometimes have been felt that she took little account of the influence of objects in the external world, but this is not so. Developing the earlier hypotheses of Abraham and Freud, she described in detail the instinctual and defensive conflicts which – in mania and melancholia, for example – give rise to anxieties of destruction and object-loss (relating to both internal and external objects). In my opinion, the Kleinian conception of the role of instincts and defences in phantasies of destruction of the object affords the psychoanalyst the means not only to achieve a better understanding of the complex relations between internal and external objects but also to interpret them more precisely and more appropriately in the transference relationship with the analysand.

The psychoanalytic approach to separation anxiety therefore has the merit of allowing us to gain access to and transform the conscious and unconscious psychical reactions to separation and object-loss, whether this loss has an origin in reality or is purely phantasy-based – i.e. the result of our suppressed unconscious wishes. These experiences can be re-lived in the transference relationship with the person of the analyst, thereby allowing them to be interpreted and worked through.

Separation anxiety in the analysand[2]–analyst relationship

Just as it appears in everyday interpersonal relations, so separation anxiety arises in the crucible of the relationship between the analysand and the analyst, putting its stamp on the development of the transference. The manifestations of this type of anxiety do not differ from those occurring in the relationships of ordinary life, but the analytic situation has the advantage of revealing and containing these phenomena, in the same way as it does the entire complex of transference phenomena which take place in the course of the psychoanalytic process, so that they can be interpreted.

Separation anxiety is omnipresent in psychoanalytic treatment; it is observed particularly in connection with end-of-session, weekend and holiday interruptions, or when the prospect of termination of the analysis looms. The reactions to phantasized or real discontinuities in the analytic encounter are extremely varied, as we all know from our own day-to-day clinical experience. I shall return to this point in Chapter 2 in connection with a clinical illustration. Let us say for the moment that the most characteristic and frequent reactions are affective ones such as anger, sadness or despair, acting out, momentary or relatively long-lasting regressions, or lateral transferences with displacement of affects on to one or more persons other than the person concerned; disavowal of separation anxiety is a characteristic reaction to the fear of separation and loss, in which the apparent absence of a reaction conceals excessive anxiety.

Not all analysands react to these situations in the same way. Some are capable of tolerating the absence of the analyst, whether phantasized or real, because they are able to symbolize it. These analysands can in general communicate their emotional reactions to the analyst directly, telling him without equivocation of the feelings of sadness or loneliness he is arousing in them. Other analysands, by contrast, are hypersensitive and very intolerant of the absence of the analyst, whether phantasized or real. The feeling of being abandoned for ever by the analyst may in some cases assume catastrophic proportions in these subjects and even call into question the continuation of the analysis. These analysands very often do not express their intolerance of separation directly, and we are then confronted with primitive defence mechanisms such as disavowal, splitting, projection and introjection, rather than repression. When anxiety is excessive, repression is indeed insufficient, as Freud showed (1927e, 1940a [1938]), and the ego defends against an unbearable reality, both external and internal, by splitting, with one part of the ego disavowing the reality and the other accepting it.

I for my part believe that when separation anxiety is manifested in a psychoanalytic treatment, it is essential for the analyst to detect and interpret it so that the analysand can work through it. However, a major difficulty arises here: this type of anxiety generates powerful resistances in both the analysand, owing to the predominance of narcissistic and primitive defences, and the analyst, who may become discouraged from interpreting by the analysand's repeated denials of such a transference manifestation. For all these reasons, the interpretation of separation anxiety is not a simple matter but calls for a great deal of experience on the part of the analyst, first in identifying these anxieties, which are often expressed in extremely roundabout ways, and secondly in finding the appropriate interpretation and in timing it correctly. This is the complete opposite of a stock interpretation, such as telling the analysand that if he is sad or acts in a certain way, it is perhaps because he is missing the analyst. While such an interpretation would be formally correct, its simplistic and reductive content would soon make it repetitive, and it would take no account of the huge variety of reactions to separation, whereby it becomes a pre-eminent opportunity for the analysand to become conscious of the transference.

From clinical practice to the various theories

With the unfolding of the psychoanalytic process, separation anxiety undergoes transformations which can serve as meaningful indicators of the changes occurring in the transference relationship between the analysand and the analyst.

The use of separation anxiety as a criterion of the progress of the treatment began in 1950 with the study by Rickman, who attempted to define a 'point of irreversibility' indicating that the process of personality integration had reached a level that would be stably maintained. Among the six factors adduced, Rickman regarded the analysand's response to weekends as a vitally important criterion of the transference. His work was followed by research by other analysts on the relations between separation anxiety and the psychoanalytic process, ranging from studies on the progress of the treatment as reflected in weekend phantasies or dreams to a conception of the overall psychoanalytic process from the point of view of the working through of separation anxieties (Meltzer 1967).

Although it is relatively easy for each psychoanalyst to observe these transformations – in particular, a progressive attenuation of the clinical manifestations of separation anxiety, which gradually becomes better tolerated and integrated in the Oedipal context – it proves to be much more difficult to take the step from the clinical level to theory and to account for these phenomena in a wider conceptual frame. This is borne out by a study of the historical evolution of psychoanalytic thought.

An examination of the development of the relevant psychoanalytic ideas does indeed show that separation anxiety was first considered in clinical and technical terms, and that it was only much later that these clinical facts were incorporated in theoretical conceptual frameworks. For instance, Freud himself begins by pointing out in his papers on technique that 'even short interruptions have a slightly obscuring effect on the work. We used to speak jokingly of the "Monday crust" when we began work again after the rest on Sunday' (Freud 1913c: 127). Only later in his career, when he was seventy years old, was he to include separation and object-loss in his revision of the theory of anxiety, in response to Rank's *The Trauma of Birth* (1924). Other psychoanalysts also began with clinical observation of the phenomena of separation in the treatment, without attempting to explain them theoretically. Ferenczi (1919) notes that his patients' 'Sunday neuroses' were reproduced in the analysis; this observation is confirmed by Abraham (1919: 55), who reports in his analysands 'temporary exacerbations of nervous disorders in connection with Sundays, feast-days and holidays'.

Psychoanalysts later came to understand separation anxiety more correctly as forming part of the affective dimension of the transference relationship; they embarked on an increasingly detailed study, not only of the complex nature of the affective links concerned in person-to-person relations, but also of how the ego itself is involved in and modified by the vicissitudes of object relations.

For this reason, in any study of separation anxiety, the phenomenon is always considered in the context of a psychoanalytic theory of object relations, and we shall see how these theories vary from author to author. For these reasons, there is no unitary psychoanalytic theory which embraces all the phenomena connected with this type of anxiety as observed clinically, and it will always be necessary to specify the location of separation anxiety by reference to one or other of the principal psychoanalytic theories of object relations.

Notes

1 In this book I sometimes use the masculine pronoun to refer to an analysand or analyst of either sex, for the sake of simplicity.

2 I use the word 'analysand' in this book in preference to 'patient' because the former emphasizes the active part played by the person in analysis and the latter sounds excessively medical. The term 'analysand' was originally introduced (in German) by Ferenczi (Haynal 1989: 492).

2

Separation anxiety illustrated by a clinical example

'Mais les yeux sont aveugles. Il faut chercher avec le coeur.'

'But the eyes are blind. One must seek with the heart.'

Antoine de Saint-Exupéry, *Le Petit Prince*, p. 81

The following clinical illustration is intended to demonstrate the variety of manifestations of separation anxiety during the course of the psychoanalytic process, showing how they can be interpreted, with the aim of revealing the variation in the meaning of these transference phenomena with the progress of the treatment.

The diversity of manifestations of separation anxiety

The analysand to whom I shall introduce you – let us call her Olivia – is one of those in whom the psychoanalytic process and the transference relationship are substantially dominated by separation anxiety and its transformations. Olivia had come for analysis because forming relationships with others caused her anxiety, and when she did succeed in doing so, she tended to break off the relationship she had begun. Her psychoanalytic treatment went on for several years, with four sessions per week.

From the weekend after the very first week of analysis, I was surprised at the intensity of Olivia's reaction to this initial separation; this reaction recurred subsequently, especially at end-of-session, weekend or holiday breaks, as well as upon the approach of the termination of the analysis. The manifestations of separation anxiety were at first very clamorous and spectacular, at least from my point of view, but eased off with the progress of analysis. To begin with, Olivia was unaware that there was a transference connection between these manifestations and the interruption of the regular rhythm of the sessions, even after I interpreted it to her. She subsequently gradually became conscious of the significance of her reactions, and was better able to work through them and accept interpretations about this type of anxiety without ignoring or rejecting them.

These manifestations could be of many different kinds and were extremely diverse in nature. Sometimes there were affective reactions such as fits of pure, indescribable anxiety, or outbursts of rage in which Olivia would let fly at me with direct or indirect accusations, expressed in no uncertain terms, that I was abandoning her. At other times, fits of depression or despair were the order of the day. At the beginning of the analysis, acting out was frequent and to my mind directly connected with the interruption of the sessions, although this possibility seemed hardly ever to cross her mind. She would happen to arrive late or miss one or more sessions as a break approached. Often at weekends or during holidays, Olivia would look after sick friends of either sex who were in distress, or else she would exhaust herself in activities intended to make her 'forget herself', without being able to say *what* she was forgetting and *whom* she was forgetting in this way. Interruptions sometimes constituted an occasion for Olivia to break off a relationship, or to embark on a new one. Finally, her separation anxiety also manifested itself in somatic symptoms such as headaches or stomach-aches. Olivia would also find that she was unable to sleep, or else she would sleep excessively, these sleep disorders being correlated with breaks in the sessions. I remember, too, that Olivia more than once fell ill on the first day of my absence, and had herself looked after by her family until the eve of our reunion. On that day, Olivia would come along 'cured', without herself being aware of this coincidence, although to my mind it was highly significant; for a long time it was impossible for her to imagine that all this might have any transference significance at all, but very gradually she did become conscious of it.

This enumeration gives but a sample of the infinite variety of Olivia's reactions to separations. For this reason, in interpreting such reactions, we must as far as possible take account of the transference situation of the moment, which is in a state of constant flux, and not interpret in general terms or give stock interpretations.

Of course, I cannot review all the possible interpretations of separation anxiety – first because they are infinite in number, so that each interpretation has to be created individually, and secondly because my aim is not to supply ready-made prescriptions. I shall therefore confine myself to presenting some sequences which graphically illustrate the manifestations of Olivia's separation anxiety during the course of her analysis and the way I interpreted it.

Meanings of an instance of acting out

As we have just seen, the manifestations of separation anxiety are so diverse that we are confronted every time with a new and specific situation. This applies particularly to the instances of acting out that are often correlated with discontinuities in the analytic encounter. We must therefore always ask ourselves which particular factors are involved in each individual situation.

Let us consider the example of a situation which recurred frequently in this analysis, when Olivia would suddenly take an interest in a sick person and exhaust herself in looking after someone else to the point of forgetting herself – something that would occur for the period of a weekend. The transference significance of this activity was evident from the fact that Olivia had suddenly displaced the interest hitherto concentrated on the transference relationship on to someone she had not known on the previous day. This was surely strange behaviour on the part of Olivia, to have suddenly become interested in this person, in whom she would discover feelings that resembled her own in every respect, only to lose interest in that person with equal suddenness as soon as the sessions with me resumed. On leaving one Friday, Olivia had told me very indirectly that I was neglecting her and not giving her enough attention. She had also remembered – 'by the way', she said – that her mother had used to leave her alone when she was small and that she had had to look after her brother. These associations might perhaps suggest to us that Olivia had disavowed her own psychical pain at the idea that I had left her alone for the period of the weekend separation, and that she had then displaced on to this other person her sadness as well as the unconscious wish that I should look after her during the weekend break.

I therefore had to ask myself what this displacement of cathexis by Olivia meant. Was it more than a mere momentary displacement from one person to another? I noted, too, that Olivia did not choose the person by chance, and that she seemed unconsciously to find in the relevant person the feelings which had actually been her own when we had parted for the weekend: if the feelings were depressive, the person would be depressed; if the feelings were demanding, it would be a demanding person. So the person's state of mind – according to Olivia's account – corresponded in every respect to the state of mind which she had been unable to express to me directly.

It became obvious to me that Olivia had not, by this acting out, performed a simple displacement of cathexis from me on to another person, but had effected a twofold projective identification whereby she at one and the same time defended against the anxiety of separation from me and disavowed this anxiety. On the one hand, Olivia had projected her own helplessness into the other person whom she cared for at the weekend: in looking after the other, she was in fact unconsciously looking after herself and her own pain, by projective identification with the pain of the other (narcissistically confused with Olivia). On the other hand, Olivia's acting out also represented an identification with me as an idealized carer: she would then imagine in her idealization that, heedless of any helplessness of my own, I was taking care solely of the other's helplessness (in this way she was identifying by projective identification with an omnipotent internal object – i.e. an idealized analyst lacking in sensitivity and disavowing his own helplessness). Olivia therefore no longer felt the pain of separation in her relationship with me, but instead felt doubly strong and omnipotent, in order to disavow her helplessness – either by having identified unconsciously with the person into whom she had projected her pain, or by having identified with an idealized object that was insensitive to psychical pain because omnipotent.

In this way, projective identification on to an external object combined with projective identification on to an internal object so as to disavow any suffering connected with the separation in the register of the transference. This, however, cost Olivia the loss of a part of her ego and of her good internal objects.

It was becoming urgently necessary to interpret these two forms of defence in their different facets. Initially, I would have to interpret to Olivia why she made use of the container–contained aspect of projective identification, leaving for a second stage the interpretation of the phantasy contents proper. A two-stage interpretation was called for in this case. First of all, Olivia would have to be enabled to recover her own capacity to contain anxiety. Only then, once this capacity had been re-discovered, would it become possible to draw attention to and interpret on a symbolic level the phantasy contents as presented to us by the material of her associations and dreams. For example, in the acting-out situation just described, it became possible for Olivia to grasp the fact that the acute pain of being left alone was a re-living of the times when her mother had left her by herself with her little brother, and to realize that looking after someone else had many different meanings, including an implicit reproach to me for not knowing how to look after her.

I could go on asking questions in this way; they are, after all, merely the ones each analyst puts to himself when confronted with clinical material of this kind, so as to identify the factor that will determine the choice whether to refrain from interpretation or to interpret; and if he decides to interpret, to identify the point of urgency dictated by the level of anxiety, in order to give an interpretation consistent with what is actually taking place, having regard to the context of the session and the situation of the psychoanalytic process at that particular time.

Repetition of an infantile psychical trauma

Discontinuities in the analytic encounter often awaken the memory of separations or object-losses of more or less early date, which are re-lived in the transference relationship and can then be worked through. To illustrate this aspect of separation anxiety, I should like to take as an example one of Olivia's characteristic symptoms, falling asleep, which would often occur in correlation with end-of-session or weekend breaks, particularly in the exceptional cases when these were unplanned. I had noticed from the beginning of the analysis that Olivia frequently fell asleep during the Friday session, prior to the weekend separation. On some occasions she had been overcome by an irresistible need to sleep, not only during the pre-weekend session but also throughout the weekend, and this need to sleep had evaporated the moment she had remembered that she was to come to her session, as if the mere fact of thinking of me caused the symptoms to disappear.

In the early stages of her analysis, Olivia did not realize that she had fallen asleep during the session, for how long she had been asleep, or that she had tended to fall asleep in the last session of the week – i.e. on the eve of our separation in the context of her relationship with me. Only gradually, through the material of her associations, memories and dreams, were we able to postulate that the weekend separations re-activated in her the hitherto unconscious memory of a very early separation from her mother – even earlier than the one I have already mentioned – which Olivia was reproducing with me. It turned out that before Olivia was six months old, her mother had had to entrust her to someone else for a few days. When her mother returned, Olivia had no longer been the same; she had not recognized her mother and from then on had often fallen asleep when left alone. Olivia was presumably repeating with me, as the representative of her mother in the transference, the situation of abandonment already experienced in early infancy; however, instead of expressing it in words, she was reproducing it non-verbally, acting it out in her body. Olivia was 'repeating' with me the defensive sleep of her infancy instead of 'remembering' (cf. Freud, 'Remembering, repeating and working-through' [1914g]).

This symptom of falling asleep could be regarded in general terms as the reproduction of a situation representing an infantile 'psychical trauma' that had been insufficiently worked through; on the specific level, however, we were able to observe that the phantasy content of each instance of falling asleep changed and became transformed as Olivia progressed. At first, she had thought that this reaction had nothing to do with what was happening in the relationship with me, but she gradually became aware of the connection between her falling asleep and the proximity of our separation, of the infantile content of this experience, and of the associated phantasies and affects.

Her falling asleep could have been interpreted in different ways – for instance, as a transitory regression – in which case I could have decided to allow her to live through this regression in my presence for as long as was necessary for her to emerge from it. However, I preferred a different type of interpretation, showing Olivia's falling asleep to be the result of unconscious active and aggressive defences directed both against the perception of the *separation* from me and against the perception of my *presence*. It is, after all, often the imminence of a separation or loss that causes us to perceive and appreciate the presence of a loved person. By falling asleep on the day before parting from me, Olivia therefore succeeded in disavowing the importance of the relational link with me, denying both the imminent separation and the perception of my presence. Olivia's falling asleep was also a means not only of eliminating the object perceived but also of de-activating the function of the sense organs whereby she could perceive, see, hear and come into contact with the object, as Segal (1988) has shown.

From a different point of view, Olivia's falling asleep was a form of defence with which we were already familiar: introjection of an idealized and persecuting object in a split-off part of her ego, with which Olivia partially identified. This introjection gave her the omnipotent feeling of possessing me within her and of controlling me narcissistically, so as to disavow all separation. At the same time, however, this defence reinforced the split between the idealized and the persecuting objects, as well as the splitting of affects, thus also preventing her from becoming conscious of her instincts – both libidinal and aggressive – towards me. Olivia was unable either to express them to me in words or to project them on to me in the transference. Olivia's tendency to fall asleep decreased when she eventually became capable of directly verbalizing her aggression towards me and of connecting it with her attachment to me. Instead of falling asleep, Olivia then came to trust me enough to be able to attack me directly and to criticize me for letting her go at the end of the sessions or at weekends; the same feeling had been nicely expressed by one of my analysands in the following terms: 'You are nothing but a series of absences, you are like a cheese that is all gone but for the holes. . . . '

19

Towards the working through of the Oedipal situation

On detailed consideration of Olivia's falling-asleep symptom, we also realized that, with the progress of the analysis, the significance of the separation phantasies was changing, with a gradual progression from a pre-genital to a genital level of organization, not far from the working through of the Oedipal situation.

At the beginning of the analysis, the falling-asleep symptom had been used primarily as a defence against the pain of perceiving me as different, and then separate, from herself. Later, the phantasy contents aroused by the interruptions in the regular rhythm of the sessions revealed memories of infantile abandonment situations, some earlier than others, these situations having first been repeated as such, so to speak, in the crude state. At a later stage of the analysis, the affective and phantasy contents contained within the fact of falling asleep became more explicit and more extensive, and Olivia began to express them verbally in her relationship with me, thus relegating the symptom to the background and bringing to the fore the elaboration of the affective dimension of the transference. Olivia showed herself to be more capable of tolerating frustration, anxiety and persecutory or depressive feelings. The significance of my absences for Olivia gradually changed, assuming a more sexualized tinge closer to genitality, the more I appeared as a better differentiated person having a specific sex. Separation at the beginning of the analysis had been felt primarily as an abandonment in the context of a mother–child relationship, but now gradually came to be experienced as taking place in an Oedipal register, in which first envy and then jealousy were expressed towards a couple consisting of her father and mother. I could now interpret the falling-asleep symptom differently, according to whether it seemed to me to be more an expression of Olivia's feeling of exclusion from the intimate union between her parents, or more a fulfilment of her unconscious wish to sleep with me as her father, in a context of post-Oedipal introjective identification with her mother.

This development was of course in no way linear, but consisted of a succession of advances and retreats, of forward movements and withdrawals. Nevertheless, we could discern an overall trend towards a diminution of the manifestations of separation anxiety and the defences against it, accompanied by a progressive approach to the working through of the Oedipus complex, in that, during the analyst's absence, Olivia suffered less from the absence of the object satisfying the wish than from the absence of the object that made possible the hallucination of the wish.

The link between love and hate in ambivalence

Phases in which love and hate are connected with and disconnected from each other are an essential component of separation anxiety, and it is in my view important to identify them with a view to recombining them through our interpretations. When Olivia's analysis became better established, she came to resort less to primitive defences such as splitting of the ego and of objects, projective identification and idealization, allowing a relationship dominated by love–hate ambivalence to come into being, with an increased sense of reality and of the anxiety associated with separations. Olivia was better able to cope with her affects of rage and hostility towards me and with her guilt. The discontinuities in the encounter between us began to arouse in her genuine feelings of appreciation and gratitude, despite her sadness and pain. Shortly before my holiday, Olivia had literally screamed out her hatred and despair at me in a series of stormy sessions, but one day her anger suddenly abated, and she showed by the following words that she was keenly aware of my presence and of my importance to her:

> I came along today although I was very tempted not to. Usually I think there is no point in my coming, as I cannot keep hold of you or do anything to stop you going away. At first I thought you were leaving because you didn't care about me, and then I felt I couldn't cope with your leaving. . . . I cannot bear your going away: once I can endure that, I shall no longer need to come. And then, when I arrived today, I looked into your face and I felt how important I am to you from the way you looked, and that it was genuine. I so much want to keep you when we part: when you are away, not only is the world empty but I too feel drained. Yet sometimes, such as today, I look at you and I tell myself that life is worth living.

Olivia was here expressing feelings characteristic of the depressive position, in which love and hate combine in ambivalence. We shall see later why the ambivalence of love and hate is linked to genitality.

The return of separation anxiety with the approach of the end of the analysis

With the approach of the termination of the analysis, Olivia at times relapsed into anxiety, resorting once again on a massive scale to projective identification as a defence against separation anxiety, this time connected principally with the end of the analysis. Here is an example, accompanied by my interpretation.

At a time when I was aware of rapid progress in her, I noticed an abrupt about-tack in Olivia's attitude towards me: she began to accuse me not only of neglecting her but also, worse, of using my interpretations to blame, accuse and condemn her. She added that I was losing my way, was no longer able to do my job properly and was guilty of professional errors. After a moment of doubt during which I wondered what professional errors I might have been guilty of, I succeeded in extricating myself from this persecutory atmosphere and reflected that Olivia's recent progress might perhaps be the real reason for this rekindling of anxiety, because every step forward aroused anxiety in her about the termination of the analysis, as I had already had occasion to note at other times. So I thought that, by accusing me of a professional error, Olivia might perhaps be blaming me for leading her towards a better level of differentiation which foreshadowed a final separation from me.

I interpreted this to her from different aspects, addressing myself to her as someone capable of understanding me, but all to no avail. On the contrary, Olivia became more and more scathing, literally hurling abuse at me during the sessions. The situation was becoming untenable, and I felt that I was no longer succeeding in reaching Olivia's healthy ego as she had become crazed with anxiety. Realizing that Olivia was not listening to me, I changed my tactics. I decided to put into words, as if coming directly from her, the feelings she had projected into me by projective identification: 'I am changing so much and I see my analyst so differently that I am afraid he might make a professional error. . . . '

Hardly had I finished my sentence when Olivia came to her senses. For a moment she was confused, unsure whether it was she who had spoken to me or I who had spoken for her. Olivia pulled herself together and told me that she did not know why she was hurling accusations at me, but she had been very much afraid in the last few weeks that she might not be able to continue her analysis: she had made a professional error which could have cost her her job and made it impossible for her to pay for her analysis. Olivia was thus confirming that her progress had caused her intense anxiety at the idea of terminating the analysis, and this separation anxiety had resulted in excessive recourse to projective identification – which had been reversed by the use of 'interpretation in projection', as described in detail by Danielle Quinodoz (1989).

Being oneself and tolerating solitude

At a more advanced stage of her analysis, Olivia gradually became aware of the full complexity of the feelings she was experiencing in her relationship with me. One day she explained with great subtlety what she had been feeling while resorting excessively to projective identification to combat separation anxiety, precisely at the moment when she was succeeding in detaching herself from it:

> I realized that if I lose parts of myself, it is not only *I* who lose myself but also *you* whom I lose . . . whereas if I take back a part of myself which I have deposited in you, I feel separated from you because we are no longer 'joined together', but then I am afraid of losing you.

There could be no better summing up of the transition from the impression afforded by narcissism to that conveyed by an object-relationship.

When she felt whole, Olivia had a sense of being unique and alone, different from others and from me in particular, with a new feeling of responsibility. 'The more one is oneself, the more one feels alone,' as Marcelle Spira used to say. But the pain of feeling 'alone' is very different from the anguish of feeling 'abandoned'.

Olivia realized the consequences of this new feeling and communicated the experience to me in the following terms:

> Now it is I who decide to come to the sessions; in the past I had no sense of responsibility, because I did not have to decide to come back to the sessions: I used to come back because I needed to rediscover the parts of myself I had left with you. But when I feel whole as I do now, I come back to my session because it is you I have left, and I find you here as you are, as a person who is waiting for me and to whom I am very attached.

Olivia was taming solitude. In her solitude, she no longer felt abandoned in a hostile world as she had at the beginning of the analysis, but responsible for the conduct of her life, having forged links with persons she considered valuable, in spite of their inadequacies – the analyst in particular. The analyst's absence was no longer experienced by Olivia as the presence of the hostile object, but as the absence of an important object, the precious memory of which modified her perception of the world about her, and identification with which made it possible for her to find within herself the capacity to tolerate waiting.

I have presented these different extracts not as a summary of Olivia's analysis but in order to highlight certain aspects of possible interpretations of the manifestations of separation anxiety in clinical practice. This indicates to us that discontinuities in the analytic encounter give rise to a multiplicity of transference phenomena which are classified under the general heading of separation anxiety; these circumstances afford a particularly valuable opportunity for interpretation of crucial aspects of the analysand–analyst relationship.

3

Approaches to the interpretation of separation anxiety

'Vous êtes comme était mon renard. Ce n'était qu'un renard semblable à cent mille autres. Mais j'en ai fait mon ami, et il est maintenant unique au monde.'

'You are just the way my fox used to be. He was only a fox like a hundred thousand others. But I have made him my friend, and now he is unique in the world.'

Antoine de Saint-Exupéry, *Le Petit Prince*, p. 72

Separation and differentiation

Before going any further I should like to clarify the meaning of 'separating' in psychoanalysis, in the context of separation anxiety. The word 'separation' is actually used in two different senses in psychoanalysis at present, and it is essential for them to be distinguished both theoretically and clinically.

In the first sense of the term, 'separation' means that one person parts from another with whom he has forged a relationship of trust. It may be said that the individual concerned knows *whom* he has cathected, *whom* he is missing, *who* he is himself and *what* the person who is temporarily absent is causing him to feel: loneliness, sadness, anger or pain, but also sometimes relief and freedom, these feelings not being mutually exclusive. Separation forms part of the context of a relationship in which the other person is felt to be free to come and go, free to choose his relationships or to give them up, and in which separation in space and time does not necessarily signify the breaking off of affective links with the object or loss of the love of the object, because the object, being deemed reliable, will not take advantage of the separation to abandon the subject. Interpersonal relations do not then require the constant presence of the object, even if this presence gives rise to satisfaction in the relationship and its absence to dissatisfaction. The temporary nature of the separation entails the hope of a return, even if every separation arouses fear of the ever possible eventuality of permanent real loss or a loss of love. In other words, the absence of the cathected person influences the individual's affects but does not threaten the psychical structure of their ego. In these circumstances, loss – i.e. permanent separation – gives rise to psychical pain connected with the work of mourning, but loss of the object is not accompanied by loss of ego.

Conversely, when an individual shows signs of anxiety indicating in particular that their ego feels threatened by the prospect of the danger of separation from a person felt to be important, then 'separating' takes on a completely different significance for them: the absence of the important person revives an anxiety experienced by that individual's ego when they are forced to perceive that they are not themselves that object, that the object is distinct from their ego and that they do not trust the object's intentions. The absence of the other gives rise to the painful perception of the presence of the other as non-ego, as Freud points out in connection with the infant who 'does not as yet distinguish his ego from the external world. . . . He gradually learns to do so' (1930a). In such a case, when an individual feels that 'separating' from a person unconsciously signifies a threat to the integrity of their own ego, this is because a very particular link of attachment remains between the ego and the object, one of whose characteristics is in my opinion the persistence of parts of the ego that are insufficiently differentiated from parts of the object. Anxiety appears because the separation is experienced not only as a loss of the object but also as a loss of a part of the ego itself, which in effect departs with the object in order to continue to be one with it.

'Separating' therefore has two very different meanings in psycho-analysis, depending on the level on which the separation is experienced by the individual: separation may be experienced in the context of a relationship in which one of the persons leaves the other, with the specific accompanying affective reactions, or it may be experienced as a loss of a part of the ego resulting from the feeling of having lost the object.

To denote this process in which the ego tends during the course of child development to become distinct from the object, we ought in my view to speak of 'differentiating' or 'differentiation'. This was originally suggested by Fairbairn (1941), who was one of the first analysts to draw attention to the forms of dependence of the subject on the object: he maintained that infantile dependence was based on a failure to discriminate between subject and object, whereas mature dependence involved recognition of the other as a separate, different person of a specific sex, cathected in the context of the characteristic triangular object relation of the Oedipal situation. In my view, the term 'separating' or 'separation' should be reserved for separations experienced in the context of a relationship in which one of the persons acknowledges the presence of the other cathected as an object, while 'differentiating' or 'differentiation' should be used to denote the early process of ego–object discrimination.

The concept of 'separation-individuation' introduced in the work of Mahler (Mahler *et al.* 1975) has greatly added to our knowledge of these early processes and has had a considerable impact, but the introduction of the term 'separation' in connection with the phase of ego–object differentiation gives rise to persistent misunderstandings, which have not been entirely disposed of by Mahler's clarifications. 'Separation' in her sense refers solely to an intrapsychic process and not to a real separation as investigated by Spitz or Bowlby (Pine 1979). Hanna Segal has pointed out to me that in English 'separation' is distinguished from 'separateness': 'separation' means that one person parts from another, while 'separateness' refers to the process of ego–object differentiation. I myself here use the two terms 'separating' and 'differentiating' to denote two distinct processes. (The distinction between separateness and separation cannot be made in French, while M. Valcarce and L. Grinberg tell me that the English word 'separateness' is a neologism which has been translated into Spanish as *separatividad*.)

Distinguishing for the purpose of unification

Processes of separation and of differentiation are closely bound up with each other and the two are worked through simultaneously in psychoanalytic treatment. Although these processes can be distinguished in theory and contrasted with each other for didactic reasons, and although they may be deemed to take place in succession, they are nevertheless worked through together during the psychoanalytic process, and it is very difficult to separate them in clinical practice.

The ego, after all, is in constant flux, making and re-making itself incessantly. In its constant search for identity, I agree with Spira (1985) in seeing the ego as unremittingly re-creating something new from scattered elements, by a process analogous to artistic creation. I believe, however, that within these unceasing movements of projection and introjection, of advance and retreat, a line of development can nevertheless be discerned within the relations between the ego and its objects – although this does not mean that there is a continuous upward path of progress – and that it is essential to have had certain experiences in order to be able to return to them. I see this line of development, for example, in the fact that it is essential for the process of differentiation to have become established in order for the process of separation to occur: the analysand comes progressively to perceive the presence of the analyst, gradually differentiating what belongs to the analyst from what belongs to himself, and thereby discovers their own identity and distinguishes it from that of the analyst.

With repeated separations and reunions, it is possible to work through in detail both differentiation at the level of narcissism and the encounter with the analyst at object level. One criterion of progress in analysis is the analysand's capacity to encounter the analyst as a person who gradually comes to be cathected as an object, whom he can give up at the end of the analysis while retaining the integrity of his ego, separating from him in the fullest, proper sense of the word. In this respect, too, we never complete the process of finding ourselves; nor do we ever become fully acquainted with another person. This mystery is part of the constant movement that is one of life's glories.

Separation anxiety and mourning-work

The processes of differentiation and separation are closely connected with the work of mourning, because achievement of the ability to separate from another person implies not only the capacity to perform mourning-work in terms of the relationship between two persons – one of whom accepts the separation from the other – but also the capacity to perform the work of mourning at ego level that is involved in forgoing oneness with the object from whom one is separating – one accepting differentiation from the other.

Mourning-work is implicated in the majority of psychical processes, in which it performs a clearing function both in normal development and in the resolution of psychopathology. In the first place, the work of mourning plays a key part in the development of the individual's ego: the different stages of normal development may be regarded as a succession of mourning situations connected with the changes that take place throughout life (Haynal 1977, 1985). Mourning-work is thus a crucial factor in the resolution of the Oedipus complex, which is the central organizing entity of mental life. Again, the working through of a large number of psychopathological conditions is closely connected with the capacity to perform mourning-work, an essential aspect of which is the working through of differentiation and separation anxieties. We shall be giving some examples of this.

Let us begin by examining child development in terms of the

identifications which lead to the resolution of the Oedipus complex. We can say that the individual must first differentiate and distinguish their ego from the object in order to accomplish the significant transition from narcissistic identifications to the introjective identifications characteristic of the resolution of the Oedipus complex. The latter identifications are based on acknowledgement of the distinction between subject and object, and of the difference between the sexes and generations (Fairbairn 1941). The tendency to identify with the first objects and fuse with them is the most primitive form of object-relationship – 'being' the object instead of 'having' it (Freud 1921c, 1941 [1938]). Where predominant, this tendency to identify and fuse with the not-yet-cathected object reinforces the inversion of the Oedipal situation. I have studied this aspect of identifications in female homosexual analysands (J-M. Quinodoz 1986, 1989a). Conversely, the capacity to renounce the father and mother at the time of the decline of the Oedipus complex, by way of processes of identification 'with the objects which have been renounced' (*aufgegebene Objekte*, Freud 1923b)[1] – mechanisms resembling melancholic introjection – leads to the normal processes of identification, called 'assimilative identifications' by Luquet (1964) and 'post-Oedipal introjective identifications' by Bégoin (1984). Bégoin considers excessive separation anxiety to be one of the obstacles to renunciation of narcissistic identification in favour of introjective identification; he regards this transition as being 'the main economic problem of analysis'.

The work of mourning is not only involved in normal development, as we have just seen, but is also an essential factor in the working through of object relations in many different psychopathological conditions. For instance, pathological introjections – also called 'endocryptic identifications' (Abraham and Torok 1975) – can be observed in the melancholic object relation; an essential factor in their resolution is a process of ego–object differentiation and separation. Unless worked through, these melancholic introjections have an unfortunate tendency to be transmitted from generation to generation by mechanisms of projective and introjective identification, as Faimberg (1987) has shown. Freud explained in 1917 that the phenomenon of pathological mourning characteristic of melancholia could be observed in predisposed individuals – i.e. in people who had a prior tendency to forge narcissistic relations with their objects: this tendency to confuse the ego and the object encouraged introjection of the lost object in a split-off part of the ego and identification with it. Note that from 1921 Freud was to use the term 'introjection' instead of 'identification' to describe the mechanism of melancholia.

The need to form a unity with the object and anxiety about

separating from it are also present in many other psychopathological conditions, in which they make the work of mourning difficult and even sometimes impossible, as in certain forms of perversion, psychotic states and autism. In the psychoanalytic process, the negative therapeutic reaction, for example, can likewise be seen in terms of a tendency to confuse subject and object.

The stages leading to the integration of psychical life and the discovery of the sense of identity also call for a work of mourning, which concerns not only the object but also the parts of the self which have remained attached to the object, as Grinberg (1964) pointed out; this is because every loss of the object and every change is seen by the unconscious as the loss of parts of the self which have remained bound to the object. That is why a long and painful process of mourning is necessary for the gradual recovery of the aspects proper to the ego itself which constitute identity. In my view, the work of creation is also long and painful because it involves a work of mourning directed towards the discovery of our own originality – i.e. the aspects of ourselves which make up our identity, which have remained confused with our earliest objects and from which we can never totally become differentiated.

Losses and gains

The dialectic of narcissism and object relations lies at the heart of the working through of separation anxiety.

Freud made this point in *Inhibitions, Symptoms and Anxiety* (1926d), when for the first time he distinguished two fundamental levels of anxiety: a separation anxiety which develops in the pre-genital stages of life and corresponds to a relationship between two persons, the object being primarily the mother; and a castration anxiety corresponding to a triangular relationship characteristic of the Oedipus complex. This antithesis is oversimplified and calls for some qualification. Most present-day analysts consider that the dual relationship does not exist as such and that the third person (the father) is present from the beginning, if only in the mother's phantasy. Again, concerning castration, I think it important to note that, with the introduction of his new views on the origin of anxiety, Freud distinguished between castration and separation. In order not to apply the term 'castration' to loss of the mother's breast, loss of faeces or the separation of birth, as some psychoanalysts were beginning to do, Freud from then on explicitly reserved the use of the term 'castration' for loss of the penis:

While recognizing all of these roots of the complex, I have nevertheless put forward the view that the term 'castration complex' ought to be confined to those excitations and consequences which are bound up with the loss of the *penis*.

(1909b: 8; note added in 1923)

I consider that the two contrasting entities of narcissism and object relations correspond to the two levels of anxiety distinguished by Freud: separation anxiety and castration anxiety. Considering these as alternatives, one of the aims of interpretation is to allow the analysand to become aware of what they stand to lose and to gain by the narcissistic tendency, as well as of their losses and gains in the opposite direction, that of the object. The recognition of self and object is conditional upon the working through of the various narcissistic defences directed towards two opposing aims: in the one case, non-perception and disavowal of differentiation (the narcissistic alternative), and in the other, non-discovery of the object (the object alternative).

The defences aimed at non-perception and disavowal of differentiation reinforce the tendencies towards ego–object confusion. The narcissistic alternative consists in the fascination of remaining partly united and fused with the object and of possessing it 'concretely' for this purpose in order not to lose it. Concrete does not mean real: when the ego is not yet sufficiently differentiated from the object, a part of the ego identifies narcissistically with the object, and the early symbols are not experienced by the ego as symbols or substitutes but as the original object itself; this gives rise to the formation of 'symbolic equations' (Segal 1957). The concept of absence hardly exists, any more than those of space and time. This explains why many analysands react to separations by seeking concrete substitutive relations with objects, into whom they project parts of their ego or of their internal objects and identify with them; these projections are made either into external objects (acting out) or into internal objects or parts of the body taken as objects (depression, hypochondria or somatizations). Any difference between the ego and the object perceived within these transference projections and introjections – which we refer to as emergence from primary narcissism, breakage of the symbiotic link, or loss of fusion, as we shall see below – is then experienced with anxiety as a total loss, as the subject cannot imagine any form of relationship other than concrete possession of the object. 'All the same, I am not going to give up the substance for the shadow,' I was told by an analysand who was filled with anxiety at the inescapable perception of having to allow the object to go.

31

Other defences are erected against discovery of the object. The object alternative involves the relationship of a subject who acknowledges the object and trusts it. Although the object is known, it retains an element of mystery because the subject has relinquished its concrete possession. Likewise, the subject is prepared no longer to form a unity with the other and to differentiate from him; he tolerates the unfathomable and enigmatic character of the object because the relations are situated on a symbolic psychical level which confers an internal reality upon the object. When abandoning a narcissistic relationship in favour of an object-based relationship, the analysand first feels what he will be losing in terms of the concrete object: it is difficult for an analysand who has established relations of possession and omnipotent control with the object to imagine, before actually having experienced it, what he will gain in terms of trust and continuity in the symbolic presence of the internalized object (Segal 1957), in terms of the capacity to communicate with a person acknowledged to be different, in terms of sexually desiring the object acknowledged as heterosexual, or in affective terms of loving the object. For it is only possible to love an object genuinely if the subject has renounced its possession and is prepared to grant it its liberty.

To sum up, an object can be known only to the extent that the subject has succeeded in differentiating from it, and it is impossible truly to separate from the object without excessive anxiety unless the subject has genuinely encountered that object. This process lies at the very heart of the working through of separation anxiety and must be interpreted in all its many and constantly changing aspects.

At the junction between narcissistic relations and object relations

Clinical experience shows that these two levels of relationship, object-orientated and narcissistic, have their counterparts in two distinct levels of separation-anxiety reactions by analysands. Analysands on an object-relations level generally react with moderation to end-of-session, weekend and holiday breaks; the relevant manifestations are close to consciousness. Where these manifestations are repressed and the analyst interprets them in the context of the transference, these analysands realize without too much resistance that their reactions to the separation form part of the context of the relationship with the analyst, and they accept it. Conversely, analysands whose relationship level is narcissistic react frequently and with a great deal of anxiety to discontinuities in the analysand–analyst encounter, while usually remaining unconscious of the link between their manifestations of anxiety and the vicissitudes of the transference relationship. They often fail to see that the miscellaneous troubles that may arise are connected with a separation which they trivialize or of whose importance to them they are totally unaware. Not only does the separation cause them to resort to defence mechanisms which adversely affect their ego – such as disavowal, splitting, projection or introjection – but the existence of the object itself tends to go unrecognized by these analysands. In this situation it is essential first of all to restore the integrity of the ego through our interpretations, before giving interpretations addressed by one person to another. Only when the analysand has, so to speak, been brought back into the session will they be able to recover their identity and experience what they are really feeling 'here and now', thus enabling them to relate their reactions to the separation in the context of the transference. I shall illustrate this later by a clinical example.

In the case of the analysands on the object–relations level to whom I referred first, separation anxiety belongs within an object-relationship between persons who are different from each other, who meet and separate; with analysands on the level of narcissistic relations, however, separation anxiety tends to be experienced primarily as a loss of ego, because the need to stay united with the object has had damaging consequences for the ego, including a lack of differentiation between ego and object.

One of the central problems of the psychoanalytic process is how to promote in the analysand the transition from one level of psychical functioning to another – i.e. from a narcissistic level of relationship, which is that of analysands who react strongly to separations and fail to apprehend the link relating them to the analyst, to the object–relations level of analysands who experience the separation in the context of an interpersonal relationship and who acknowledge the link with the analyst. Whichever object-relations theory is taken as one's basis, the working through of separation anxiety is a turning point and a pivotal stage in the psychoanalytic process. The various characteristics of these transformations have been described from different standpoints and examined in terms of the development of the psychoanalytic process itself, evaluation of the termination of the analysis, or their effects on phantasy contents – for instance, in Monday dreams (Grinberg 1981). I myself have been most impressed by the appearance of the sense of 'buoyancy' which is progressively internalized by the analysand as they gradually come to see that they will be able to do without the analyst and to 'fly with their own wings'. I shall return to this point in my conclusion.

Separation anxiety and narcissistic disorders

So far I have deliberately dealt with the problems of separation anxiety in psychoanalytic treatment in clinical terms and then discussed them generally, without explicit reference to precise psychoanalytic theories. The time has now come to examine these problems in the light of different psychoanalytic theories, and this will be the subject of Part Two of this book.

Although the clinical facts which have constituted our starting point can be observed and described in overall terms so that they can be understood by all psychoanalysts, the same clinical facts are perceived and interpreted very differently by each psychoanalyst according to his or her own theoretical vantage point. We find more than ever that the analyst's personal psychoanalytic theories directly affect their counter-transference attitude and, in the case with which we are concerned, their way of interpreting separation anxiety when it arises in their relationship with their analysand, or of refraining from interpreting it. As we shall now see, these technical choices are based on different theoretical positions.

To illustrate my thesis, let us take the example of the problem of the different conceptions of narcissism when applied to separation anxiety, considering the pivotal role of this type of anxiety in the transition from narcissism to object relations. We find that psychoanalysts have two fundamentally contrasting conceptions of narcissism, according to whether the object is or is not held to be perceived from birth, and that these conceptions each have very different consequences for the technique of interpretation.

If the theory of primary narcissism is accepted, the ego is not at first differentiated from the object; in this case primary narcissism is, at it were, a natural state which the individual gradually grows out of during the course of their infantile development. This is the position adopted by Freud in connection with the oceanic feeling (1930a). The same position is embraced by Anna Freud, Fairbairn, Mahler, Kohut, Grunberger and Winnicott, as well as many other authors. For these analysts, once the child begins to perceive the difference between the ego and the object, he emerges stage by stage from a state of primary narcissism. This process is considered to be a fundamental phase of libidinal development, in which separation anxiety plays a central part. In the analytic situation, the analysand is deemed to regress to the level of the infantile stages of development on which he had remained fixated, so that the natural processes of maturation can be resumed.

Conversely, for Melanie Klein and the analysts who followed her, the ego and the object are perceived from birth and the phase of primary narcissism does not exist. However, ego-object fusion is not absent from the Kleinian view, and the notion of narcissism reappears with the introduction of the concept of projective identification (Klein 1946). This concept allows at one and the same time for an object-relationship (since the subject needs an object in order to project) and a confusion of identity between subject and object (Segal 1979). Post-Kleinian psychoanalysts such as Rosenfeld, Segal, Bion and Meltzer subsequently developed the consequences of the involvement of projective identification and envy in narcissistic structures, applying them to transference phenomena and also to the course of the psychoanalytic process itself.

In this way, by very different routes from those of the analysts who believe in the existence of primary narcissism, the analysts mentioned above, while retaining a conceptual framework modelled on that of Klein, in turn came to recognize the importance of narcissistic phenomena in object relations; hence the importance of the working through of separation anxiety in the psychoanalytic process.

Other approaches lie between these two antithetical conceptions of narcissism, such as those of Kernberg (1984), who emphasizes the part played by aggression in narcissistic disorders of the personality, or Green (1983), who contrasts a narcissism of life with a narcissism of death, or negative narcissism.

For all the diversity of the psychoanalytic views on narcissistic phenomena which attempt to account for the problems posed by differentiation and separation, I must emphasize that, besides the divergences and opposing convictions, recent research also shows some convergences. For this reason, I consider that the dilemma of whether or not to accept the postulate of primary narcissism is currently receding into the background. I personally believe that an object-relationship exists from birth and even before birth, but what matters most to us as analysts is to be able to conceptualize clearly what we observe in the course of our day-to-day clinical practice, so that we can interpret it precisely.

Note

1 Rendered in English (and French) as 'abandoned' objects. I prefer to translate these words as 'objects which have been renounced', as this conveys more faithfully Freud's contrast, which is clear in German, between introjection of the *lost* (*verloren*) object and identification with the father and mother, objects *which have been given up* (*aufgegeben*);

the latter term emphasizes the active renunciation proper to the normal work of mourning as compared with pathological mourning, in which the object is stated to be 'lost' (*GW* 1923b, 13: 257–9). Albrecht Kuchenbuch has pointed out to me that the word *aufgegeben* was formerly used in Austria in the sense of 'closed down' or 'left derelict or abandoned', as applied, for example, to a house or factory.

PART TWO

The place of separation anxiety in psychoanalytic theories

While hoping that this image is not too relevant to the analyst behind his couch, let us acknowledge that, in every field of experimental science, the exponential growth of the mass of information is liable to be accompanied by a relative ignorance increasing at the same rate.

Michel Gressot, 1963 [1979]

4

Freud, separation anxiety and object-loss

Freud's principal theoretical contributions on this subject are contained in two works, 'Mourning and melancholia' and *Inhibitions, Symptoms and Anxiety*. In 'Mourning and melancholia', which was published in 1917, Freud describes the fundamental mechanism of defence against object-loss, showing how depression originates from introjection of the lost object in a split-off part of the ego. A few years later, in 1926, in *Inhibitions, Symptoms and Anxiety*, he attributed anxiety to the fear of separation and object-loss; this constituted a radical revision of his earlier views on the origin of anxiety. These two essential pillars of Freud's *oeuvre* cannot possibly be understood in isolation, and we shall also have to take account of other important texts which foreshadow, illuminate or complement them.

Although Freud put forward fundamental hypotheses about the psychoanalytic dynamics of the individual's relation to separation and the loss of a loved person, his works are found to contain few if any explicit clinical references to separation in the register of the transference. In his principal contributions on the subject, Freud essentially bases his views on general psychopathology and observations from normal life, without referring explicitly to analytic experience with his patients: his successive models of anxiety are, for example, the child who is afraid of the dark in 1905, the child playing with the reel in 1920, and the infant who is afraid of losing his mother in 1926. However, throughout his writings and his correspondence, Freud showed himself to be particularly sensitive to the feelings of longing, loneliness and mourning which he himself experienced or observed in other people in connection with separation and the loss of loved persons.

1 Separation and object–loss in Freud's early writings

Infantile dependence and helplessness

Freud's earliest writings already contain broad indications of the importance he attributes to early object relations, which are shown to be essential to the infant's emergence from the state of helplessness and biological and psychological dependence that characterizes the beginning of his existence.

The first references to the problem of separation anxiety in Freud's work may be deemed to occur in his letters to Fliess – in particular, in Manuscript E, on the origins of anxiety – and in 'A project for a scientific psychology' (1950a [1895]). There are several mentions here of the human being's need, from the beginning of life, to find among those around him a person (generally the mother) who will allow him to discharge the tension arising from his internal physical and mental needs. He calls this meeting between the need for discharge and the person who satisfies it 'the experience of satisfaction'. If the necessary specific action – for instance, feeding – by the 'helpful person' does not allow this process of satisfaction to take place, there follow disturbances in the development of the physical and mental functions of the infant due to his immaturity and states of helplessness (*Hilflosigkeit*). Freud uses another concept, that of the 'communication' ('mutual understanding' might be a better translation of Freud's word *Übereinstimmung*) which arises between the infant and his mother (1950a [1895]: 318), to set down the earliest outlines of a psychoanalytic conception of the part played by the early mother–child relationship, a conception that was later to be developed further in Winnicott's (1955) theory of holding and in the container–contained notion of Bion (1962).

Freud also considered that the object-loss which occurs in the experience of satisfaction – both real and hallucinatory – also constitutes the eventual foundation of the appearance of the wish and the subsequent quest for objects: it is in the absence of the object of satisfaction that the image of the satisfying object will be re-cathected as a symbolic representation (hallucinatory fulfilment of the wish). Later, when the individual begins to look for new objects, he seeks in Freud's view not only to find an object, but to *re-find* the original lost object, which had in the past afforded a real satisfaction ('Negation', 1925h).

Contemporaneously with the letters to Fliess, Freud notes that the object is first perceived by the ego on account of the pain caused by its perception: 'In the first place there are objects – perceptions – that make one *scream*, because they arouse pain' ('Project', 1950a [1895]: 366). Later, in 'Instincts and their vicissitudes' (1915c), Freud was to link the appearance of hate with psychical pain, associated with the perception of the different aspects of the object, which would be deemed 'loved' if a source of pleasure and detested and hated if a source of unpleasure. Freud in this way accounts for the appearance of hate towards the object in painful, traumatic situations which are experienced as a threat to the individual's psychical life and survival; these are the feelings that lie at the root of the hostility and negative transference which play such an important part in the interpretation of separation anxiety.

Fear of separation as the source of anxiety in the child

Freud had in 1905 already directly linked the onset of anxiety in children with the feeling of the absence of a loved person: 'Anxiety in children is originally nothing other than an expression of the fact that they are feeling the loss of the person they love' (1905d: 224). Freud bases his view on the observation of a three-year-old boy who is afraid of the dark, and concludes that 'what he was afraid of was not the dark, but the absence of someone he loved; and he could feel sure of being soothed as soon as he had evidence of that person's presence' (p. 224, footnote). Although Freud explicitly attributes this child's anxiety to the absence of the loved person, he nevertheless remains faithful in his theoretical explanation to the idea that anxiety stems from the direct transformation of unsatisfied libido. It was not until 1926 that he returned once and for all to the notion that the origin of anxiety lay in the fear of separation and object-loss – not only in children but also in adults.

Similar considerations apply to Freud's subsequent reflections (1920g) on the child playing with the reel in order to reproduce the disappearance and reappearance of his absent mother. This description has been the subject of a large number of commentaries in the psychoanalytic literature. At this point I should merely like to draw attention to a note on it by Freud, concerning this child's identification with his mother and describing how he played in front of a mirror at disappearing and reappearing. This is the characteristic defence of identification with the lost object, as described by him in 1917, which can also be regarded as an 'identification with the frustrating object' (Spitz 1957) or as a means of transforming passivity into activity (Valcarce-Avello 1987).

The question of primary narcissism

At the beginning of the infant's or child's life, is there or is there not a phase in which he cannot yet differentiate himself from others (narcissistic phase), and can the beginnings of the perception of others as different from oneself (object phase) be situated at a subsequent point in the child's development?

Freud re-interpreted the concept of narcissism several times during the course of his career. He first used the term 'narcissism' to describe a relationship in which a person takes his own body as a sexual object ('On narcissism: an introduction', 1914c). Later, after the introduction of the second topography, Freud was to contrast a primary narcissistic state without objects, on the one hand, with object relations, on the other. He calls this primitive state 'primary narcissism' and characterizes it as an early phase of development which lasts for some considerable time, in which the ego and objects are indistinguishable from each other and whose prototype is intra-uterine life (1916–17: 417). He retains the idea of a narcissism through identification with objects, which he calls 'secondary narcissism'.

However, Freud points out that he has never had any clinical material that demonstrates primary narcissism, and that his ideas are based on the observation of primitive peoples and on theoretical considerations. As already stated in the previous chapter, the question of the existence or otherwise of a primary narcissistic phase remains contentious, and continues to influence the principal psychoanalytic theories of object relations.

2 'Mourning and melancholia' (1917e [1915])

Introjection of the lost object

In 'Mourning and melancholia', which was written in 1915 at the same time as the 'Metapsychological supplement to the theory of dreams' but not published until 1917, Freud enquires into the individual's reactions to a real loss or a disappointment caused by a loved person, or the loss of an ideal: why do some people react with an affect of mourning which is eventually overcome, while others succumb to a *depressive* state (known at the time as 'melancholia' [Strachey 1957; Laplanche 1980])?

Freud notes that, unlike normal mourning, which takes place mainly at conscious level, pathological mourning proceeds unconsciously. He draws attention to the melancholic's inhibition, which he ascribes to a loss of ego resulting from the loss of object. Melancholia is also accompanied by self-accusations which may extend even to a delusional expectation of punishment.

With his intuition that the melancholic's self-accusations are really directed at someone else – the important person in his immediate environment 'who has occasioned the patient's emotional disorder' (p. 251) – Freud discovers the key to the mechanism of melancholia. This turning back of reproaches on to the subject himself is made possible by the fact that the lost object responsible for the disappointment is set up again in the ego, which splits into two, one part containing the phantasy of the lost object and the other becoming the critical agency:

> Thus the shadow of the object fell upon the ego, and the latter could henceforth be judged by a special agency, as though it were an object, the forsaken object. In this way an object-loss was transformed into an ego-loss and the conflict between ego and the loved person into a cleavage (*Zwiespalt*) between the critical activity of the ego and the ego as altered by identification.
>
> (1917e [1915]: 249)

This mechanism of introjection of the lost object and splitting of the ego as a defence against object-loss is subject to a number of conditions which Freud describes and which can be summarized as follows: (1) in order for object-choice to regress to narcissistic identification, the object-cathexis must be weak and must previously have been narcissistically based; and (2) in order for it to be possible for the lost object to be introjected, the libido must regress to the oral or cannibalistic phase, in which, by virtue of ambivalence, love for the object is transformed into identification and hate is turned back upon this substitutive object. In this way the sadistic tendencies towards an object are turned back on the subject himself. However, Freud points out that the sadism directed against the subject himself at the same time remains addressed unconsciously to the relevant person in his immediate environment:

> The patients usually still succeed, by the circuitous path of self-punishment, in taking revenge on the original object and in tormenting their loved one through their illness, having resorted to it in order to avoid the need to express their hostility to him openly.
>
> (1917e [1915]: 251)

It is this turning back of sadism against oneself that explains why melancholics commit suicide. As for mania, Freud finds that it is an attempt to come to terms with the same complex as melancholia, to which the ego has succumbed in melancholia, whereas in mania it has mastered it or pushed it aside (p. 254).

Ambiguities in Freud

Freud's intuition that, when a depressive says 'I hate myself', he really means 'I hate you', this statement being filled with unconscious hatred for the loved object, was a stroke of genius. However, this fundamental clinical intuition has in my opinion not been fully understood, and psychoanalysts certainly still take insufficient advantage of it in the practice of transference interpretation.

This is presumably due to certain ambiguities in Freud's later formulations, as a number of authors have pointed out. When we read his later writings, we do indeed find that, while some formulations are unequivocal – for example when he situates identification with the lost object in a split-off part of the ego which is set against the other part – other formulations, conversely, are ambiguous. For instance, it is legitimate to enquire as to the part of the ego in which Freud locates the subject-ego ('I'). Similarly, in what part of the ego does he place the 'critical ego', the 'critical agency' or, later, the 'ego ideal' and the 'superego'?

The answers to these questions are crucial, because our approach to the reciprocal relations between the ego and objects will determine how we shall interpret projection and introjection of the lost object when they occur in the transference during the treatment; I shall give an example of this later.

Many authors have noted these imprecisions in Freud. For example, Laplanche asks: 'Who persecutes whom in the depressive's topography?' (1980: 329), and he wonders 'What is the locus of the discourse?' and 'Where do the words of the depressed subject come from?' In his view, it is preferable not to try too hard to localize the subject-ego, in order to avoid 'the fascination that would have us locate the subject somewhere *once and for all*' or accommodate him in an agency. It would be better to be more pragmatic by enquiring instead 'What is the provenance of the discourse?' (. . .), where is it speaking from? (1980: 331). Meltzer (1978) draws attention to the same hesitation in Freud:

> It seems that Freud himself becomes very mixed-up, being unsure whether it is the ego accusing or, the ego-ideal turning against the ego. However, the relevant point is that he has come to realize that there is a question: 'Who is in pain?' – is it the ego or its object that

is in pain; and 'Who is the one that is being reviled?'

(1978: 85)

But it seems to me that if Freud's contributions are read attentively, these ambiguities can be resolved, and the analyst will then have everything he needs in order to identify the specific conflict of the melancholic in the transference relationship, so that it can be interpreted and worked through.

It is the subject-ego that criticizes the object and not the other way round

If we examine one after another the formulations used by Freud in 1917e [1915], 1921c and 1923b to describe the melancholic's intra-psychic conflict, we find that he consistently distinguishes two parts of the ego separated by splitting and set against each other: one consistently corresponds to the subject-ego ('I'), while the other consistently corresponds to the part of the ego identified with the introjected lost object. The former directs its 'criticism' against the latter, which is confused with the object.

This is already evident in 'Mourning and melancholia' (1917e [1915]): 'We see how in him one part of the ego sets itself over against the other, judges it critically, and, as it were, takes it as its object' (p. 247). Later in the same paper: 'the conflict between the ego and the loved person [is transformed] into a cleavage between the critical activity of the ego and the ego as altered by identification' (p. 249). Or again: 'the hate comes into operation on this substitutive object, abusing it, debasing it, making it suffer and deriving sadistic satisfaction from its suffering' (p. 251). The formulation in 1921c is similar: in melancholia, the reproaches 'represent the ego's revenge upon it [the object]' (p. 109), or 'one of [the pieces of the ego] rages against the second. This second piece is the one which has been altered by introjection and which contains the lost object' (p. 109).

Etchegoyen confirms my reading of Freud in his categorical statement that, in 'Mourning and melancholia', 'the critical ego belongs to the subject, *not* to the incorporated object'. In his view, this is a 'point which Freud himself does not perceive and which is taken into scant account by his followers. To my mind, the ambiguity is a latent encumbrance in many technical discussions' (1985: 3).

Even if this opposition between the part of the subject-ego and the part containing the lost object were all that was involved in the melancholic conflict, the problem would still not be simple. What makes the whole picture more complicated, however, is that the

45

subject-ego of the melancholic is not a subject-ego performing its normal protective function – i.e. that of the 'conscience, a critical agency within the ego, which even in normal times takes up a critical attitude towards the ego' (1921c: 109) – but instead an ego which criticizes 'so relentlessly and so unjustifiably' and has lost its protective function. This extremely severe agency which develops in the ego detaches itself, according to Freud, *from the subject-ego* to form what he first called the 'ego-ideal' (1921c) and later the 'super-ego' (1923b). In melancholia, 'the excessively strong super-ego which has obtained a hold upon consciousness' now rages against the ego with merciless violence (1923b: 53).

These are no idle questions, but are of crucial importance to the psychoanalyst who wishes to apply Freud's intuitions to the technique of interpretation. For the psychoanalyst needs to know *who* is the subject-ego and *who* is the object, because, unless he knows who is doing what to whom, he may be liable to confusions or to refrain from interpreting this type of conflict when it arises in the transference relationship.

In my experience, a positive response by my analysands to interpretations concerning the introjection of the analyst-object treated as the lost object – to which the subject is attached and against whom he directs his hatred by turning it back upon himself – tellingly confirms that in the melancholic reaction it is indeed the subject-ego that hates the introjected object and not the other way round. Later on I shall give two clinical examples of this common transference phenomenon and my interpretation of it.

Where does the sadism of the superego come from?

It is also difficult to determine which identifications are specifically involved in the constitution of the superego, the ego-ideal, the ideal ego and even the ego, as Laplanche and Pontalis (1967: 437) have pointed out. It is therefore not easy to pinpoint the identifications concerned in the melancholic's intrapsychic conflict. Freud was to turn the critical ego into the superego in the second topography (*The Ego and the Id*, 1923b), declaring the sadism of the superego in the melancholic to be 'a pure culture of the death instinct' which 'often enough succeeds in driving the ego into death, if the latter does not fend off its tyrant in time by the change round into mania' (p. 53).

By 1930, Freud was seeing the sadism of the melancholic superego in a different way, which does not invalidate his earlier views: he expresses his agreement with Melanie Klein that the superego's hate for the ego is nothing other than the result of the projection of the ego's hatred for the object, ascribed to the superego and turned back on the subject-ego. Melanie Klein considers that the severity of the superego as observed in children bears no relation to the severity of the parents: what is internalized by the child is an image of parents on to whom the child has projected his own destructive instincts. Freud adopts this view with an explicit reference to Melanie Klein and other English authors: 'the original severity of the super-ego does not – or does not so much – represent the severity which one has experienced from it [the object], or which one attributes to it; it represents rather one's own aggressiveness towards it' (*Civilization and its Discontents*, 1930a: 129–30).

This last point is of vital importance to technique, as the analyst may interpret the analysand's self-destructiveness towards himself as the result of the projection of his aggression against the analyst, turned back on the analysand's ego which is confused with the introjected analyst-object. In accordance with Freud's intuition, the conflict between the ego and the object (in this case, the analyst) has thus been transformed into an intrapsychic conflict between two parts of the ego, in which the subject-ego attacks the introjected object and directs the aggression aimed at the object against himself.

Splitting of the ego and disavowal of reality as defences against object-loss

The concept of splitting of the ego was introduced in 'Mourning and melancholia' as a specific defence mechanism against object-loss following introjection of the lost object. The conflict between ego and external object is transformed into a conflict between two parts of the ego, which affects the very structure of the ego: 'In this way an object-loss was transformed into an ego-loss and the conflict between the ego and the loved person into a cleavage (*Zwiespalt*; *GW* 1917e, 10: 435) between the critical activity of the ego and the ego as altered by identification' (p. 249). (The French translation of this passage uses the word *scission*, which fails to convey the idea of splitting inherent in the German word *Zwiespalt*, which includes the root *Spalt*, itself closely related to *Spaltung* [splitting]. To preserve the psychoanalytic concept of splitting, *Zwiespalt* should in my view be translated literally so as to convey the notion of 'splitting into two'.[1] The idea of splitting is in fact explicit elsewhere in 'Mourning and melancholia': 'the critical agency which is here split off from the ego' [p. 247].)

The notion of splitting of the ego, as introduced in 'Mourning and melancholia' in relation to object-loss, was subsequently complemented by that of the disavowal of reality. Freud initially presents disavowal of reality as a defence mechanism specific to psychosis. Later, however, he differentiates this concept by introducing the idea of a partial disavowal of reality, affecting only a part of the ego – corresponding to the psychotic part – while the other part of the ego retains its relation with reality.

The concept of the disavowal of reality as a defence against object- loss actually appears in 1924, when Freud distinguishes repression from the disavowal of reality, the latter being regarded as a specific defence mechanism of psychosis. Freud gives the example of a young woman who was in love with her brother-in-law and who, standing beside her sister's death-bed, repressed the feeling she had: 'the psychotic reaction [of the young woman] would have been a disavowal of the fact of her sister's death' ('The loss of reality in neurosis and psychosis', 1924b [1923]: 184).

In 'Fetishism' (1927e), Freud notes that the disavowal of reality may be only partial, affecting only the part of the ego for which the loss of the object is disavowed in reality. He returns to his previous clear-cut opposition of neurosis and psychosis, recognizing henceforth that a splitting of the ego may exist in one and the same individual, with one part of the ego disavowing reality while the other accepts it. He gives as an example the analysis of two young men who had 'scotomized' their father's death in their childhood, without on that account becoming psychotic. According to Freud, this scotomization is based on disavowal of the reality of the father's death, at least as far as a part of the ego is concerned. The young men's egos were divided into two currents by 'splitting':

> it was only one current in their mental life that had not recognized their father's death; there was another current which took full account of that fact. The attitude which fitted in with the wish and the attitude which fitted in with reality existed side by side.
>
> (1927e: 156)

Starting with 'Mourning and melancholia', Freud thus seems to have gradually arrived at the idea that the ego defends itself against object-loss by splitting: one part of the ego identifies with the lost object while denying the reality of the loss, while the other part of the ego acknowledges the reality of the loss. He was to give more detailed accounts of this notion of the splitting of the ego into two parts in *An Outline of Psycho-analysis* (1940a [1938]) and in 'Splitting of the ego in the defensive process' (1940e [1938]). Bion (1957) was to develop these ideas in a new way through his distinction between the psychotic and non-psychotic parts of the personality, a concept which lends itself particularly well to describing the phenomena of splitting in the transference observed in clinical practice in pathological mourning.

A transference example of introjection of the lost object and of the turning back of hate against oneself

On the basis of two short clinical examples, I should like to illustrate how the lost object – the analyst – is introjected in the transference when the love–hate ambivalence that often confronts us in connection with between-session breaks, weekends or holidays is re-activated. The object of interpretation here is to prevent these defence mechanisms, which are characteristic of depressive reactions, from becoming permanently established. Another aim is to bring into consciousness the unconscious attachment to the analyst – replaced by an introjection, with confusion between analysand and analyst – and the turning back on the subject himself of the hate directed towards the object instead of being projected in the transference.

The first example concerns a slightly depressive and ambivalent patient whose reactions to weekend breaks had several times surprised me. For instance, one Friday, before a weekend separation, I noticed that he was fully engaged in the process of working through, his mood cheerful and active; but when he came along to his Monday session after the weekend interruption, he was downcast, uncommunicative and discontented, and seemed to have come along reluctantly. A radical change had taken place in his relationship with me: he seemed to have lost all interest in me and to ignore my presence; he showed no interest in what he had worked through during the previous week, and even less in what he was feeling at that moment. I did not understand what was happening, and wondered whether something serious had happened in his life, whether he had done something stupid which he did not dare to tell me about; I felt worried. His only words, uttered with an air of gloom, were as follows: '*I am a cipher, I cannot do anything, I am worthless.*'

I did not immediately realize that by accusing himself, he was in fact accusing me. As a result of the ensuing associations about the forthcoming holidays, I was able to interpret to him that by seemingly telling himself, 'I am a cipher, I cannot do anything', he was in fact implicitly addressing me, telling me that as an analyst I was a cipher who could not do anything. I added that, instead of expressing his anger towards me in words for having left him alone at such an important moment, he was saying nothing, but instead turning himself into a living reproach, impressing on me that as an analyst I was a cipher who could do nothing.

My patient's reaction to my interpretation was immediate: no sooner had I finished my sentence than all his vitality and strength returned; his depression seemed to have vanished into thin air as if by magic, and I heard him tell me in no uncertain terms how angry he had in fact been with me, without realizing it until now. On the one hand, I believe that my interpretation had not only brought his attachment to and hatred of me into consciousness but had also drawn attention to how he was turning back on himself the aggression intended for me – directed towards me as confused with himself in a part of his ego (introjection of the lost object). Again, I believe that this patient was able to respond quickly to my interpretation and criticize me overtly because he was not afraid of losing me by expressing his aggression towards me. This reaction differed from that of patients who do not dare to express their hate for the analyst other than unconsciously, because, as long as hate is not sufficiently linked in their minds to the libidinal tendency towards the object – the analyst in the transference – in the sense of the fusion of instincts (Freud 1920g, 1923b), they imagine that their hate for the analyst has the effect of destroying the object. On another level, my analysand had felt drained and impoverished during the weekend, but recovered his resources with the interpretation.

My second example relates to a depressive, obsessional patient who reacted to a transference situation of object-loss during the analysis – the approach of holidays – by a tendency to sabotage himself; this was the unconscious expression of rage against me in the transference, turned back against himself in a self-destructive sadistic and masochistic form. This man had been abandoned on more than one occasion in his early life and had suffered from it; he appeared to be in a shell and was distrustful of others. However, his relations with me and with those around him had slowly improved during the analysis; he had secured a professional position more in keeping with his abilities, and his tendency to make the men and women around him ill-treat him had declined. There came a point when he had an inexplicable relapse, which was so severe that he could no longer work properly, and I was afraid that he might lose his job. I felt that I did not now have the same contact with him as before; he did not talk to me about what he was feeling but only about his work, in which, for all his efforts, his difficulties were increasing, and his boss was threatening more and more overtly to dismiss him. '*I am flogging myself to death and I shall get myself thrown out,*' he repeated to me.

This form of words reminded me that the summer holidays were not far off, and I thought that, by trying to get himself thrown out by his boss, he was unconsciously attempting to throw me out, because, if he had no job, he could no longer finance his analysis. He was thus attacking himself by sabotaging his work, but he was also attacking me. When I interpreted to him that the hate directed against himself was unconsciously meant for me, he was able, not without difficulty, to halt the process of self-destruction, to deflect the hate turned back against himself and to direct it back towards the object; this was made possible by the linking of love and hate in my interpretation.

This type of interpretation is based on the melancholic's intrapsychic conflict between love and hate as described by Freud (1917e [1915]), in which love has become dissociated from hate: the love-cathexis has taken refuge in narcissistic identification, and 'the hate comes into operation on this substitutive object' (p. 251). Freud adds that the unconscious sadism turned back on the subject's own person following introjection *at the same time remains directed against the relevant person in his immediate environment* (p. 251). This point is of vital importance to the interpretation, as Freud thereby emphasizes that the libidinal and aggressive instinctual current is always bidirectional, directed at one and the same time against an introjected object 'inside' and a previously cathected external object 'outside' which corresponds to the former. When Abraham showed in 1924 that the ego can succeed in emerging from ambivalence only by owning the hostility towards the object, he helped to make it possible for the first time for the depressive patient to be made aware of his sadism and his unconscious oral attachment to the object: Abraham considered that *the object is lost because sadism wants to destroy it*, and not because of a collateral, chance effect of libidinal incorporation, as Etchegoyen (1985) has discerningly pointed out.

3 Inhibitions, Symptoms and Anxiety (1926d)

Separation anxiety as encountered in clinical psychoanalysis is described by Freud in 1926 in *Inhibitions, Symptoms and Anxiety*, in which he puts forward fresh hypotheses about the origins of anxiety and abandons the old ones. From now on, he regards anxiety as an affect experienced by the ego in response to a danger which ultimately always has the significance of fear of separation and object-loss. He also casts new light on the problem of defences, distinguishing them from repression, and postulates that the ego forms symptoms and erects defences primarily in order to avoid perceiving anxiety, which stands for the fear of separation and object-loss.

This new theory of anxiety replaced the one to which Freud had remained faithful for over thirty years, to the effect that anxiety stemmed directly from unsatisfied libido which turned into anxiety, with which it was related 'in the same kind of way as vinegar is to wine' (Freud 1905d: 224, note added in 1920). Until 1926, Freud had indeed deemed the mechanism of the onset of anxiety to be a purely physical phenomenon, in which excess stimulation (or libido) found a channel in which it could discharge by becoming transformed directly into anxiety. If repression was the cause of the accumulation of stimulation in the neuroses, it was in his view unnecessary to invoke a psychological factor to explain the transformation of libido into anxiety. From 1926 on, Freud once and for all abandons his former explanation, henceforth considering that anxiety has a twofold origin: 'one as a direct consequence of the traumatic moment and the other as a signal threatening a repetition of such a moment' (1933a: 95).

Inhibitions, Symptoms and Anxiety makes no easy reading, as Freud deals with a large number of subjects and, as Strachey (1959) points out, experiences unwonted difficulty in conferring unity on this work. Furthermore, he tackles the same subjects again and again, in very similar terms, and it is only at the end of the book, in the Addenda, that the most fundamental formulations are to be found. Lecture XXXII of the *New Introductory Lectures on Psycho-analysis* (1933a) contains a recapitulation of Freud's 1926 hypotheses about the origins of anxiety, expressed this time with greater clarity and conciseness.

After reviewing the background to Freud's publication of *Inhibitions, Symptoms and Anxiety*, I shall offer a key to its understanding, based on my own reading of it, summarized in broad outline for the sake of brevity.

Freud and Rank's The Trauma of Birth

Freud issued his revision of his theory of anxiety in response to the publication of *The Trauma of Birth* by Rank (1924), who had also attempted to account for the separation anxiety observed in his analysands. For Rank, all attacks of anxiety could be regarded as attempts to 'abreact' the first trauma, that of birth. He explained all neuroses on the basis of this initial anxiety, reductively and with gross oversimplification; he proposed a modification of psychoanalytic technique intended to overcome the trauma of birth, relegating to the background the part played by the Oedipus complex in neurotic conflicts.

Freud's attitude to Rank's theories fluctuated; at first he seemed to support them, having himself been the first to assert that birth was the first experience of anxiety in a child (1900a) or 'the first great anxiety-state' (1923b). Later, spurred by his critique of Rank's views, he presented the result of his own reflections in *Inhibitions, Symptoms and Anxiety*. One of Freud's principal objections to Rank was that the latter placed too much emphasis on birth as an external danger and not enough on the immaturity and weakness of the individual (1926d: 151). Freud also took the view that birth was a purely biological phenomenon and not a psychological one, and that the infant was unable to experience the type of anxiety postulated by Rank because it did not yet perceive an object. Nowadays, we believe that the neonate and the infant do have a perception of the mother, albeit partial, but very early, from birth and even before. Many psychoanalysts now include birth among the factors making up unconscious phantasies.

Anxiety as a reaction of the ego to the danger of object-loss

Freud's central new thesis about anxiety is based on his distinction between the 'traumatic situation' which swamps the ego and triggers *automatic anxiety* and the 'danger situation', which may be foreseen by the ego and triggers the *signal of anxiety* when the individual has become capable of fending off the danger (1926d; Addendum B: 164–8).

The proximate cause of automatic anxiety is the onset of a traumatic situation, and the traumatic situation *par excellence* is represented by the biological and psychical helplessness (*Hilflosigkeit*) of the immature ego, which is unable to cope with and master the accumulation of stimulation, whether of external or internal origin. Freud later (1933a) put it in these terms: 'What is feared, what is the object of the anxiety, is invariably the emergence of a traumatic moment, which cannot be dealt with by the normal rules of the pleasure principle' (p. 94). The concept of a traumatic situation is in the direct line of descent from his first writings on the origins of anxiety, seen as the accumulation of a state of tension which cannot achieve discharge, but from now on the emphasis is placed on the weakness of the individual's ego.

During the course of development, when the ego has acquired the capacity to abandon passivity for activity, it can recognize the danger and forestall it by the signal of anxiety: 'Anxiety is the original reaction to helplessness in the trauma and is reproduced later on in the danger-situation as a signal for help' (pp. 166-7). This first displacement of the anxiety reaction allows a transition from the situation of helplessness to the expectation of that situation (the situation of danger): 'after that come the later displacements, from the danger to the determinant of the danger – loss of the object and the modifications of that loss' (p. 167). After all, whereas the traumatic situation or the danger situation from which the anxiety stems varies with age, all such situations have in common the fact that they stand for a separation from or loss of a loved object or the loss of that object's love, according to Freud.

To reach this conclusion, he too starts from the onset of anxiety in the child and deductions on the generation of anxiety in neurotics. Anxiety in a child can be reduced to a single condition, the absence of someone who is loved (and longed for) or of a substitute for that person (p. 136). Again, in re-examining the part played by the formation of symptoms and defences in the onset of anxiety in neurotics, Freud comes to an identical conclusion: he considers that, beyond the danger of castration in neurosis and the danger of death in traumatic neurosis, the real dangers which give rise to neurosis are loss and separation (p. 130). For him, the danger situation to which the ego reacts in traumatic neurosis is not the fear of death – because nothing resembling death has ever been experienced, or if it has, 'it has left no observable traces behind' in the mind (p. 130) – but abandonment by the protecting superego. The castration anxiety which plays such an important role in the aetiology of the neuroses has been preceded by other, prior, experiences having the effect that 'the ego has been prepared to expect castration by having undergone constantly repeated object-losses', such as separation from the intestinal contents or loss of the mother's breast at the time of weaning (p. 130).

The dangers vary according to the time of life

The dangers which can produce a traumatic situation vary, according to Freud, from one period of life to another, and a characteristic common to all of them is that they involve separation or the loss of a loved object, or a loss of love on the part of the object. This loss or separation may lead in various ways to an accumulation of unsatisfied desires and so to a situation of helplessness (Strachey 1959: 81). Freud specifies the dangers in chronological order: birth, loss of the mother as an object, loss of the penis, loss of the love of the object, and loss of the love of the superego.

(a) THE DANGER OF BIRTH

For Freud, the process of birth is the first 'danger' situation, and the economic upheaval to which it gives rise becomes the prototype of the anxiety situation (pp. 150-1). The situation experienced by the new-born baby and the infant in arms as a danger is that of non-satisfaction, of 'a *growing tension due to need*, against which it is helpless' (Freud's emphasis, p. 137). In the situation of non-satisfaction, 'amounts of stimulation rise to an unpleasurable height without its being possible for them to be mastered psychically or discharged', and this economic disturbance constitutes in his view 'the real essence of the "danger"' (p. 137). At this stage, the anxiety would be solely the result of a state of helplessness and there would be no need to invoke the separation from the mother – whether separation from the mother's body or psychological separation – because, in Freud's opinion, neither the neonate nor the infant at the beginning of life knows the maternal object. All that is perceived is the danger of helplessness, and the anxiety arising in reaction to this danger leads to the muscular and vocal discharge of calling the mother. 'It is unnecessary to suppose that the child carries anything more with it from the time of its birth than this way of indicating the presence of danger' (p. 137).

So the first anxiety described by Freud appears to correspond to a fear of annihilation and not to the fear of separation proper. Freud sees it as the result of the immaturity and weakness of the new-born baby and the infant in arms, and he was later to return to the idea that in a similar way the ego makes use of anxiety 'as a signal to give a warning of dangers that threaten its integrity' (1940a [1938]: 199). Freud's view that the first danger consists in 'the growing tension due to need' and the accumulation of amounts of stimulation which rise to 'an unpleasurable height without its being possible for them to be mastered psychically or discharged' (p. 137) seems to come close to Melanie Klein's position, that the first anxiety is the ego's fear of being annihilated by the death instinct. However, Freud does not connect the helplessness of the new-born baby with the death instinct. The emphasis placed on the danger of annihilation, and the threat of overwhelming of the ego, is important because it means that the most regressive and psychotic reaction to separation probably arises because the fear of separation is equivalent to a fear of annihilation.

Freud considers that the danger situation is displaced only at a later stage in child development from helplessness to the fear of separation and object-loss, when the infant is capable of perceiving its mother as an object:

> When the infant has found out by experience that an external, perceptible object can put an end to the dangerous situation which is reminiscent of birth, the content of the danger it fears is displaced from the economic situation on to the condition which determined that situation, viz., the loss of object. It is the absence of the mother that is now the danger; and as soon as that danger arises the infant gives the signal of anxiety, before the dreaded economic situation has set in.
>
> (1940a [1938]: 137–8)

(b) LOSS OF THE MOTHER AS AN OBJECT

According to Freud, then, the loss of the mother as an object occurs at a later date. 'Since then repeated situations of satisfaction have created an object out of the mother; and this object, whenever the infant feels a need, receives an intense cathexis which might be described as a "longing" one' (p. 170). When the infant begins to perceive the presence of its mother, 'it cannot as yet distinguish between temporary absence and permanent loss. As soon as it loses sight of its mother it behaves as if it were never going to see her again' (p. 169).

Freud describes the successive anxieties which appear in relation to the danger of loss of the maternal object, and how the child gradually moves on from the fear of losing the object to the fear of losing the love of the object (pp. 169–70).

(c) ANXIETY ABOUT CASTRATION SEEN AS A DANGER OF OBJECT-LOSS

The next danger is the fear of castration, which arises during the phallic stage. Freud tells us that castration anxiety 'is also a fear of separation and is thus attached to the same determinant', but that the helplessness is due to a 'specific need', genital libido (p. 139).

(d) THE DANGER OF LOSS OF THE LOVE OF THE SUPEREGO

As its development proceeds, the child, who initially ascribed castration anxiety to an introjected parental agency, gradually comes to attribute it to a more impersonal agency, and the danger itself becomes less defined: 'Castration anxiety develops into moral anxiety'; the ego now deems the fear of loss of the superego's love to be a danger and responds to it with a signal of anxiety. Freud adds: 'The final transformation which the fear of the super-ego undergoes is, it seems to me, the fear of death (or fear for life), which is a fear of the super-ego projected on to the powers of destiny' (p. 140).

Freud, of course, emphasizes the genetic link between these different dangers which succeed each other during the course of development (p. 162). In normal development, each stage has its appropriate determinant of anxiety (p. 146), and earlier danger situations tend to be set aside. However, Freud points out that all these danger situations can persist side by side in one and the same individual and come into operation simultaneously. It seems to me that, in writing *Inhibitions, Symptoms and Anxiety*, Freud must have been influenced by the work of Abraham (1924) on the stages of libidinal development, as Freud is seen to adopt a similar approach in describing the successive stages in perception of the object, reactions to its disappearance, the development of the phantasy contents of separation and loss according to the particular time of life, and also the ego's capacity to cope with anxiety.

To sum up, in introducing different levels of anxiety during the course of infant development, Freud's 1926 contribution is surely important in throwing light on the relations between the two principal types of anxiety encountered in the clinical practice of psychoanalysis: *separation anxiety*, which is characteristic of the pre-genital stages and has to do with a bipersonal or dual relationship, and *castration anxiety*, which is characteristic of the Oedipus complex and connected with a three-person or triangular relationship. We do indeed find in our clinical practice that the working through of separation anxiety at pre-genital level gradually brings the analysand to confront the working through of the genital anxieties proper to the Oedipus complex.

Repetition, remembering and expectation of the traumatic situation

Freud considers that the ego not only produces symptoms and defences with a view to avoiding the onset of anxiety and in order to bind it, but that the ego, once it has grown stronger, also proves capable of anticipating the trauma, expecting it and reproducing it in attenuated form in order to work through it. Repeated experiences of satisfaction also modify anxiety, and the following passage cannot but remind one of the alternation of separations and reunions in analysis:

> Repeated consoling experiences . . . are necessary before it [the infant] learns that her [the mother's] disappearance is usually followed by her re-appearance. Its mother encourages this piece of knowledge which is so vital to it by playing the familiar game of hiding her face from it with her hands and then, to its joy, uncovering it again. In these circumstances it can, as it were, feel longing unaccompanied by despair.
>
> (1926d: 169–70)

The relationship between external and internal danger

By stressing the fundamental role of the danger of separation and object-loss, as well as that of the danger of castration, in the generation of anxiety in neurosis, is Freud not placing too much emphasis on the external danger at the expense of the internal danger in the appearance of anxiety? He himself answers this objection:

> One objection to it [this comparison] is that loss of an object (or loss of love on the part of the object) and the threat of castration are just as much dangers coming from outside as, let us say, a ferocious animal would be; they are not instinctual dangers. Nevertheless, the two cases are not the same. A wolf would probably attack us irrespectively of our behaviour towards it; but the loved person would not cease to love us nor should we be threatened with castration if we did not entertain certain feelings and intentions within us. Thus such instinctual impulses are determinants of external dangers and so become dangerous in themselves; and we can now proceed against the external danger by taking measures against the internal ones.
>
> (1926d: 145)

However, the converse is also true, and Freud adds that 'an instinctual demand often only becomes an (internal) danger because its satisfaction would bring on an external danger – that is, because the internal danger represents an external one' (pp. 167-8). It is ultimately the need (instinct) which accounts for the traumatic – or, conversely, dangerous – character of the situation of object-loss, in Freud's view (p. 170).

Unlike Laplanche (1980), who considers the importance attached by Freud to the 'real' from 1926 to be 'horrible', I believe that Freud's new position validly answers the questions raised in clinical practice by the interaction between reality and phantasy.

The affects of anxiety, pain and mourning

Freud concludes his book by enquiring when separation from the object gives rise to anxiety, when it gives rise to mourning and when it gives rise to pain only (1926d: 169). Pain appears once the object is known and provided that the subject needs the object ('longing' cathexis): according to Freud, 'pain is thus the actual reaction to loss of object, while anxiety is the reaction to the danger which that loss entails and, by a further displacement, a reaction to the danger of the loss of object itself' (p. 170). As for the affect of (normal) mourning, he explains this as another affective reaction to object-loss 'under the influence of reality-testing; for the latter function demands categorically from the bereaved person that he should separate himself from the object, since it no longer exists' (p. 172).

Splitting of the ego, Freud's third theory of anxiety

It is, properly speaking, not true that only two theories of anxiety are to be found in Freud; there is also a third, which appears later in his work, but it is not normally considered to be such. We are familiar with his first theory, according to which anxiety results from the direct transformation of unsatisfied libido, and I have just mentioned the second, which states that anxiety stems from the ego's perception of danger, a danger having the significance of separation or object-loss. It seems to me that Freud is putting forward a third theory of anxiety when he posits in 1938 that *anxiety appears when the ego feels threatened in its integrity*. He writes in *An Outline of Psycho-analysis* (1940a [1938]): '[The ego] makes use of the sensations of anxiety as a signal to give a warning of dangers that threaten its integrity' (p. 199). In other words, it is now not only the subject who, when faced with the danger, experiences a fear equivalent to loss of his mother's protection: this time it is the ego which reacts to the danger with the fear of losing its own integrity. This intuition of Freud's is inserted in a passage in which he returns once again to the problems of the ego's response to danger, whether of external or internal origin, and in this last formulation he adds that the ego tends to react to an intolerable reality (both external and internal) by splitting, with one part of the ego acknowledging the reality and the other part disavowing it.

In my view, Freud's second theory of anxiety, as presented in *Inhibitions, Symptoms and Anxiety*, is in no way inconsistent with the third, which I have just mentioned, concerning disavowal and splitting of the ego. On the contrary, this third theory of anxiety not only complements the hypotheses of 1926 but also supplies a connection between the hypotheses of *Inhibitions, Symptoms and Anxiety* and those put forward in 'Mourning and melancholia'. After all, the anxiety that is the subject of the 1926 contribution may be regarded as the anxiety experienced by the whole ego for a whole person – i.e. the fear experienced by the subject of separation from a person acknowledged to be important – whereas in 1938 it is a matter of an ego that is resorting to disavowal and splitting in response to the danger threatening its own integrity. This latter case reminds us of the splitting of the ego already described in 1917 in the introjection of the lost object, as a defence against object-loss, and the splitting of the ego described in 1927 in fetishism. However, Freud adds something in 1938, in *An Outline of Psycho-analysis* (1940a [1938]), by attributing anxiety to the ego's fear of losing its own integrity. As stated above, this would mean that the most psychotic reaction to separation would be the fear of annihilation – i.e. the ego's fear of losing its integrity.

The influence of Inhibitions, Symptoms and Anxiety

The views expressed by Freud in *Inhibitions, Symptoms and Anxiety* in 1926 were partly accepted, partly rejected and partly ignored (Kris 1956; Bowlby 1973). Some of Freud's contributions underwent substantial development and gave rise to the psychoanalytic movement represented by ego psychology. Other aspects were disputed. Thus, for example, Bowlby's (1973) hypothesis about the nature of the child–mother link is based solely on a biological theory of instinctive attachment behaviour, whereas Freud refers to 'needs' and 'instincts' ('*Triebe*'). In the view of Laplanche (1980), on the other hand, Freud appears to be abandoning the instinctual basis in seeking to modify his earlier views on the origins of anxiety from 1926. The connection between anxiety and separation, for its part, has practically disappeared from the work of Anna Freud on the ego and the mechanisms of defence (1936); at any rate, she fails to attribute the same importance to it as Freud had done. The analysts who follow Melanie Klein attribute great importance to the interpretation of separation anxiety in clinical practice and agree in this respect with Freud's views, but anxiety for them is a direct response to the work of the death instinct. Generally speaking, it is certainly the case that the contents of *Inhibitions, Symptoms and Anxiety* have been seen by many primarily as a theoretical speculation; I personally, however, believe that they are an elaboration of clinical phenomena observable routinely in the course of analytic treatment, by which Freud could not fail to have been intrigued.

Note

1 The English translation 'cleavage' does convey this idea.

5

The views of Melanie Klein and her school on separation anxiety and object-loss

Separation anxiety phenomena are very important in the theory and practice of Melanie Klein and her school. The work of Klein is, as we know, a continuation of the early psychoanalytic research begun in 1911 by Abraham on depression and manic–depressive states. Abraham's research had preceded Freud's and had occasioned the latter's writing of 'Mourning and melancholia' (1917e [1915]).

Drawing on her own experience of analysing very young children and also using her self-analysis of her own bereavements, Melanie Klein discovered the early roots of depression in infancy, and ascribed to mourning a central role not only in psychopathology but also in normal development.

We shall give a brief account of the place of separation anxiety and object-loss in Klein in the light of the fundamental concepts contributed by her, such as the early Oedipus complex and the paranoid–schizoid and depressive positions, in relation to anxiety, projective identification and envy. We shall then discuss the contributions of the principal members of her school – in particular, Rosenfeld, Segal, Bion and Meltzer.

1 Separation anxiety and object-loss in Melanie Klein

In Melanie Klein, separation anxiety and object-loss must be seen in the context of her conception of object relations and her own theory of anxiety.

In her view, the situation at the beginning of life is not one of non-differentiation between ego and object as it was for Freud (primary narcissism); Melanie Klein believed that the perception of the ego and of the object exist from birth, anxiety being a direct response to the internal work of the death instinct. She considers that this anxiety takes two forms: a persecutory anxiety which belongs to the paranoid-schizoid position, and a depressive anxiety which is proper to the depressive position. As Segal (1979) points out:

> The fundamental anxiety about the loss of the object postulated by Freud could, according to her, be experienced in either way, or, of course, in any combination of the two: it can be experienced in a paranoid way, as the object turning back and attacking, or in a depressive way – that is, the object remains good and the anxiety concerns losing the good rather than being attacked by the bad.
>
> (1979: 131)

I do not wish here to go into the conception of early object relations used by Klein as a basis for her description of the paranoid-schizoid position and the depressive position during the course of infant development, but should like to consider briefly how anxieties about separation and object-loss fit into the context of these two fundamental types of anxiety which she describes.

Separation and object-loss in the paranoid-schizoid position and the depressive position

The first infantile anxiety described by Klein is the fear of being annihilated by the death instinct. This instinct must therefore be projected outside; this primordial projection later gives rise to the phantasy of the bad object which threatens the ego from without. Hatred is then directed towards this external bad object, but it is impossible to project the totality of the death instinct, and a part of it always remains inside. Again, owing to the simultaneous projection and introjection, the persecuting object becomes threatening within, alongside the protective good object which has been introjected. The fear of annihilation described by Klein as the first anxiety, as stated above, is not dissimilar to the first situation of danger to the ego described by Freud in 1926 – i.e. the fear of being overwhelmed by excessive stimulation which cannot be mastered.

At the stage of the paranoid-schizoid position, the predominant anxiety is that the persecutor might destroy at one and the same time the ego (self) and the idealized object. In order to protect itself from this anxiety, the ego therefore resorts to schizoid mechanisms such as reinforcement of the split between the idealized object and the bad object, as well as the excessive idealization and omnipotent disavowal used as defences against persecutory fears. Segal points out that at that primitive stage of development there is no experience of absence – the lack of a good object is felt as an attack by bad objects. (. . .) Frustration is felt as a persecution. Good experiences merge with and reinforce the phantasy of an ideal object.

(1979: 116)

The anxieties of the depressive position arise out of ambivalence: the infant fears in particular that his hate and destructive instincts might annihilate the object which he loves and on which he is totally dependent. The discovery of his dependence on the object – which he perceives as autonomous and capable of going away – intensifies his need to possess the object, to keep it inside him and, if possible, to protect it from his own destructiveness. Since the depressive position begins during the oral phase of development, in which loving is the same as devouring, the omnipotence of the mechanisms of introjection leads to the fear that the instincts might annihilate not only the external good object but also the introjected good object, transforming the internal world into chaos.

If the infant is better integrated, he can remember the love for the good object and preserve it when he hates it. The mother is loved and the infant can identify with her; her loss is then experienced cruelly and a new range of feelings appear. As Klein puts it in 'A contribution to the psychogenesis of manic–depressive states' (1935):

Through this step the ego arrives at a new position, which forms the foundation of the situation called the loss of the loved object. Not until the object is loved *as a whole* can its loss be felt as a whole.

(1935: 284)

In such a situation, the infant experiences not only feelings of loss, sadness and longing for the good object which is felt to be lost, but also a sense of guilt stemming from the danger threatening the internal object, felt to be due to his own instincts and phantasies. The infant is then exposed to 'depressive despair', as Segal (1964) puts it:

He remembers that he has loved, and indeed still loves his mother, but feels that he has devoured or destroyed her so that she is no longer available in the external world. Furthermore, he has also destroyed her as an internal object, which is now felt to be in bits.

(1964: 70)

There is a constant fluctuation between persecutory anxiety, when the hate is stronger, and depressive anxiety, when love predominates over hate (Klein 1940).

The aim of the working through of the depressive position is the

63

installation within the infant's ego of a whole internal object that is sufficiently stable. If this process fails, the child is liable to suffer from mental disorders of the paranoid or manic-depressive type. The depressive position for this reason constitutes the vital boundary between the point of fixation of the psychoses and the neuroses.

Klein first described the paranoid-schizoid position as preceding the depressive position in the course of development, but later seems to have revised her views, considering that the depressive position could be present from the outset. Nowadays, of course, the concept of 'position' is taken to refer more to instantaneous states of organization of the ego, subject to constant fluctuation, than to an organization having a fixed sequential chronology during the phases of infant development.

The manic defence

In her 1935 paper referred to above, Klein describes new defences against the fear of separation and object-loss, which she calls manic defences, the characteristic feature of which is the tendency to disavow the psychical reality of depressive pain. These defences become established during the course of the depressive position. The object is controlled omnipotently in a triumphant and contemptuous manner, so that loss of the object gives rise neither to pain nor to guilt. Either alternately or simultaneously, the subject may flee towards the idealized internal object, or disavow any feeling of destruction and loss. These defences are a part of normal development, but if they are excessive and persist for too long, they prevent the development of a relationship with a good whole object and the working through of the depressive position (Segal 1979: 81).

The manic defence is one of the principal defences against separation anxiety caused by interruptions of the analytic encounter, constituting the nucleus of a large number of reactions aimed at disavowing the depressive pain of the loss, such as, in particular, acting out, which can be regarded as a flight to idealized external objects.

External reality and psychical reality

For Klein, external reality and internal or psychical reality are constantly interrelated, and experiences of separation or loss involving real objects influence the psychical experiences, but always indirectly, by way of the phantasy relations with internal objects. In her view, frustrations or threats to the satisfaction of the child's needs are always experienced as stemming from the object, which thereby becomes a persecutor, and this external persecutor is immediately internalized as an internal persecutor, the internalized bad object.

Conversely, however, positive experiences with reality favourably influence relations with the internalized objects. The mourning processes associated with the depressive position are thus influenced by the positive experiences the child has had with real objects. Reality testing allows the child to overcome its anxieties, for example, and to observe that its phantasies of destruction have not come true. Later, when Klein developed her ideas on the part played by guilt and reparation in psychical development, she was to show how restorative wishes and phantasies allow a good internal object to be established. In this process, the reality of the mother's reappearance is essential to the child, as Segal (1979) points out:

> Her reappearance reassures him about the strength and resilience of his objects and over and above that, it lessens his belief in the omnipotence of his hostility and increases his trust in his own love and reparative powers. The non-appearance of his mother or the lack of her love can leave him at the mercy of his depressive and persecutory fears.
>
> (1979: 82)

In children or adults who suffer from depression and feel threatened in regard to the possession of good internal objects, the fear of losing the internalized 'good' object becomes a source of perpetual anxiety at the possibility of the death of the real mother, and conversely every experience that calls to mind the possibility of loss of the real loved object arouses the fear of also losing the internalized object.

In his survey of Klein's views on the position of separation anxiety and object-loss in children, Manzano (1989) points out that, in addition to the external and internal sources of anxiety in the child, Klein mentions two other external sources of anxiety, to which little attention is customarily paid. One is the fear that the loss of the mother might at the same time constitute the loss of a 'first line of defence', as the mother represents for the child a possibility of containing his anxieties

> in particular by allowing him to project and displace on to her 'the parts of the self' and the bad objects, and thereby to contrast them with reality in order to be able subsequently to reintroject them in modified form.
>
> (1989: 251)

Similarly, Manzano stresses the function of the mother as a 'presence-of-the-mother' object, as Klein puts it – the 'fifth object' in addition to the four others described by her, according to Baranger (1980). This 'presence-of-the-mother' object has immediate references to the real and to perception, and 'for this reason it is of particular interest to us when we consider the separation reactions to which the physical presence of the mother gives rise' (1980: 250).

Separation and loss in infantile development

During the course of development, each child experiences situations of separation or loss which to him represent a threat, and from this point of view every stage of development entails a loss. For Klein, the first and most important losses are birth and weaning. Weaning is the prototype of all subsequent losses; in particular, the loss of the idealized breast which it represents gives rise to a mourning reaction, accompanied by sadness and longing, making it an essential component of the depressive position.

As the child's development proceeds, these losses are experienced less and less on the persecutory level (loss-of-ego anxiety and fear of being attacked by the bad object) and increasingly in depressive terms (fear of losing the internalized good object). Whenever there is a loss during the course of the subject's life, depressive feelings are re-activated. Segal (1979) summarizes these stages of life as follows:

> In toilet training there is the need to renounce an idealized internal stool; achievements in walking and talking also involve acknow-ledgements of separateness and separation; in adolescence infantile dependence has to be given up; in adulthood one has to face the loss of one's parents and parental figures, and gradually the loss of one's youth. At every step the battle must be waged anew between, on the one hand, regression from the depressive pain to the paranoid-schizoid mode of functioning or, on the other, working through of the depressive pain in a way leading to further growth and development. In that sense one could say that the depressive position is never entirely worked through: the working through of the depressive position would result in something like the perfectly mature individual. But the degree to which the depression has been worked through and internal good objects securely established within the ego determines the maturity and stability.
>
> (1979: 135–6)

I shall have more to say about the concept of integration in Chapter 12, in connection with Klein's paper 'On the sense of loneliness' (1963).

Interpretation in the analytic situation

In the analytic situation, Klein sees the reactions to separations as re-awakening paranoid and depressive anxieties. She and the analysts who follow her attribute great importance to detailed and precise analysis of the phantasies and instinctual and defensive movements in the transference which arise whenever there is a break in the analytic encounter.

In both children and adults, for example, Klein interprets the fear of abandonment during interruptions in very different ways, depending on the transference context and the predominant feeling: the analysand may perhaps feel that the object is abandoning him because of the unconscious aggressive phantasies directed towards it, in which case he feels as though he were delivered up to the bad object (paranoid anxieties); or else he may feel afraid of losing the security afforded by the internalized good object (depressive anxieties). The specific defensive modes are then analysed – in particular, manic defences, for example – as well as how projective identification is used in the here and now against the fear of being separate or of losing the object.

Narcissism, projective identification and envy

Klein later introduced some new ideas, adding to our understanding of object relations by developing the original concepts of paranoid-schizoid and depressive anxieties. In particular, she introduced the concepts of projective identification and envy, which throw new light on the function of narcissism as a defence against perception of the object as separate and different.

The implications of narcissism as a defence against paranoid anxiety, depressive anxiety and envy and its transformations have been described principally by the post-Kleinian psychoanalysts – in particular, Rosenfeld, Segal, Bion and Meltzer. Although Klein had little to say about narcissism, the concept is nevertheless present in her writings, as Segal and Bell have shown in a study of the theory of narcissism in Freud and Klein (1991). In the description of projective identification given in 'Notes on some schizoid mechanisms' (1946), for instance, Klein explicitly states that, when the relationship with another person is based on the projection into that person of the 'good' or 'bad' parts of the subject, it 'is of a narcissistic nature, because in this case as well the object strongly represents one part of the self' (p. 13). Klein is also referring implicitly to narcissism in *Envy and Gratitude* (1957), when she shows how projective identification is a means of achieving the aims of envy while at the same time being a defence against envy. This is the case, for example, when the envious subject introduces himself into an object and takes possession of its qualities. However, in making this comparison, she does not refer explicitly to narcissism, although the idea that there must be an intimate relationship between narcissism and envy is inherent in this work, as Segal (1983) pointed out.

In summarizing the successive contributions of Klein and applying them to clinical practice and the development of the transference, we observe a constant alternation during the psychoanalytic process: we see first of all how separation initially mobilizes omnipotent projective identification with the object, in order not to perceive the object as separate. Next, perception of the object as different and having a specific sex mobilizes envy, which will gradually turn into jealousy in regard to the primal scene. At this point feeling separate assumes another meaning: the mother is no longer experienced as belonging solely to the child but as forming a couple with the father, and this eventually gives rise to a feeling of exclusion from the parents' sexuality, accompanied by a wish to identify with them in the context of the Oedipus complex.

2 Rosenfeld: projective identification and narcissistic structure

On the basis of the work of Klein on early object relations, Herbert Rosenfeld examines the role of omnipotence, introjective and projective identification and envy as defences against acknowledging separation between the ego and the object. He thus defines a narcissistic structure of the personality, as observed in psychoanalysis, and distinguishes two types of narcissism: libidinal narcissism and destructive narcissism.

Projective identification and envy as sources of confusion between the ego and the object

In connection with the first case of psychosis treated by a purely psychoanalytic technique, Rosenfeld had shown in 1947 how a female analysand used projective identification to defend against anxieties – in particular, anxieties about holiday-break separation and the idea of the termination of the analysis. He had attributed her moments of depersonalization to phantasies of forcibly introducing herself into the analyst in order to secure everything she wanted, but at the cost of losing herself there and feeling dead or disintegrated.

In 1964, Rosenfeld developed his views on narcissism in his paper 'On the psychopathology of narcissism: a clinical approach'. This contribution marks a turning point in the psychoanalytic conception of narcissism; in it he examines the nature of object relations in narcissistic patients and the associated defence mechanisms. Rosenfeld considers that the clinical phenomena described by Freud as experiences of primary narcissism – i.e. in which there is no object – should in fact be regarded as object relations of a primitive type. In his view, narcissism is based on omnipotence and on self-idealization, obtained by introjective and projective identification with the idealized object. Klein had described identification with the idealized breast by introjection and projection as a narcissistic 'state' (1946), but Rosenfeld now turns it into a *structure* which has become organized. This identification with the idealized object has the ultimate effect of disavowing the difference or the boundary between self and object; for this reason, according to Rosenfeld, 'in narcissistic object relations defences against any recognition of separateness between self and object play a predominant part' (p. 171). He also assigns an essential function to envy in narcissistic phenomena. He holds that envy contributes to the reinforcement of narcissistic object relations in two ways: first, omnipotent possession of the idealized breast represents a fulfilment of the objectives of envy, because 'when the infant omnipotently possesses the mother's breast, the breast cannot frustrate him or arouse his envy' (p. 171); and secondly, identification with the idealized object affords protection against the appearance of the feeling of envy. During the analysis, when this narcissistic relationship begins to be worked through and the consciousness of separation appears, recognition of the object gives rise to envy when the 'goodness' of the object is perceived. Perception of the object as separate may then lead to a return to narcissism by means of projective identification, in order to possess anew the envied object and to avoid feeling envy of and dependence on the object. The alternation between narcissistic positions and ones in which the object is recognized can be analysed in detail in the transference relationship.

Libidinal narcissism and destructive narcissism

Continuing his research on narcissistic states, Rosenfeld introduces a distinction between what he calls libidinal narcissism and destructive narcissism, in a paper entitled 'A clinical approach to the psychoanalytic theory of the life and death instincts: an investigation into the aggressive aspects of narcissism' (1971). He emphasizes that when the narcissistic position towards the object is abandoned, aggression against the object becomes inevitable, and the persistence of narcissism is due to the strength of the envious destructive instincts. In most patients the libidinal and destructive aspects of narcissism exist side by side, and the violence of the destructive instincts varies. The difference between these two forms of narcissism depends in his view on the degree of predominance of the death instinct over the life instinct.

In libidinal narcissism, the self-overestimation is based on introjective and projective identifications with idealized objects, so that the narcissistic subject feels that everything of value in external objects is a part of himself. As long as the external object is experienced as forming part of himself, the patient does not perceive the object, but as soon as the external object is recognized, its perception generates hate and contempt: 'Destructiveness becomes apparent as soon as the omnipotent self-idealization is threatened by contact with an object which is perceived as separate from the self' (p. 173). The patient feels humiliated as soon as he notices that the external object has qualities. However, when the resentment can be analysed, the envy is experienced consciously, and 'it is then that he becomes aware of the analyst as a valuable external person' (p. 173).

When the destructive aspects are preponderant, the envy is more violent and takes the form of a wish to destroy the analyst, because he or she represents the object that is the true source of what is alive and good. At the same time, violent self-destructive instincts make their appearance, and the narcissistic patient imagines himself to be self-sufficient, thinks he has given life to himself and has no need of parents, that he can feed himself all by himself and that he need not depend on anybody. When confronted with the reality of their dependence on the analyst, some patients would rather not exist, preferring to destroy the progress of the analysis or to spoil their professional success or personal relations. In some patients the wish to die is idealized as a solution to all problems; this is a pure and unadulterated expression of the death instinct as an isolate.

In both libidinal and destructive narcissism, what is attacked and hated are the positive libidinal object relations – i.e. the need to establish 'good' relations and the wish to accept someone else's help.

These narcissistic patients experience the need for help and love as an intolerable humiliation, and when the analyst makes them aware of the necessity of depending on others, they experience this as an enslavement which jeopardizes their superiority. The destructive and envious parts may do their work in silence and hide behind the seeming indifference of narcissistic subjects towards the objects of the external world. Sometimes this destructiveness is manifest and clamorous, and the split may be so extensive that almost the whole of the personality is identified with the omnipotent destructive part, while the libidinal part of the self is projected on to the analyst, who is then attacked. However, this attack on the analyst is also an attack on the libidinal aspects of the patient himself, projectively identified with the analyst. Rosenfeld considers that this extreme split is a result of the disjunction between the life instinct and the death instinct.

Whatever the strength of the destructive instincts, it is therefore clinically essential to find a way of gaining access to the dependent libidinal part, so as to weaken the influence of hate and envy and thereby allow the patient to establish good object relations. 'When the problem is worked through in the transference and some libidinal part of the patient is experienced as coming alive, concern for the analyst, standing for the mother, appears which mitigates the destructive impulses and lessens the dangerous defusion' (p. 173).

Rosenfeld's research paved the way for a detailed exploration of the early object relations at the root of the narcissistic structure of many analysands, and made it possible to find out why, for example, some can never tolerate separation, appearing indifferent to the analyst's absences because they do not accept the presence of the object, their unconscious wish being to be held, fed and satisfied throughout their lives.

3 Segal: narcissism, ego–object differentiation and symbolization

Hanna Segal's clinical and theoretical contributions to our problem concern, on the one hand, the question of narcissism and its relations with envy and the death instinct and, on the other, the role of differentiation between the ego and the object in symbol formation.

Narcissism as an expression of the death instinct

Hanna Segal's views on narcissism are similar to those of Rosenfeld, but differ on one point: the latter's distinction between libidinal and destructive narcissism. For Segal, every instance of persistent pathological narcissism is based fundamentally on the death instinct and on envy. Although libidinal components are inevitably involved in the fusion of instincts, this persistence of narcissism always remains under the sway of the death instinct (Segal 1983).

Segal believes that the concept of the life and death instincts can help to solve the problem of Freud's hypothesis of primary narcissism. She compares the Freudian and Kleinian conceptions on this subject: according to Freud, in primary narcissism the child experiences itself as the source of all satisfactions, so that the subsequent discovery of the object gives rise to hate, whereas in Klein's view it is envy that arises when the object is discovered. In the Freudian model of primary narcissism, the goodness of the external object is discovered relatively late and leads to narcissistic rage; the hatred of the object stems from the rejection of the external world, and it is the narcissistic ego that is the rejecting agency (Freud 1915d). If Klein's view that the capacity to recognize the external object is present from birth is accepted, then narcissistic rage is an expression of envy. Segal concludes that narcissism can then be deemed a defence against envy and can be connected more with the action of the death instinct and of envy than with the operation of the libidinal instincts (Segal 1983). She considers that the life instinct includes love for oneself and love for the objects which give life. The relationship with the idealized object, which is the first expression of the life instinct, does not give rise to a persistent narcissism, but is a temporary state, which Klein intuitively qualified as 'narcissistic'. This relationship develops towards an internal object which is 'good' rather than idealized, and lies at the root of self-love and the love of both internal and external objects. The death instinct and envy, on the other hand, give rise to destructive and self-destructive object relations and internal structures.

In her contribution to the 1984 EPF Symposium on the death instinct, 'On the clinical usefulness of the concept of the death instinct', Segal (1987) further explored the idealization of death in narcissistic patients. In some of these patients, the idealization of narcissism takes the form of an idealization of death and a hatred of life. Death delusionally appears to them as the best solution to their difficulties, as it is felt to be an ideal state in which these patients believe it is possible to be freed from all the frustrations and tribulations of existence. Segal also draws a parallel between the 'Nirvana principle' described by Freud (1920g) as the dominating tendency of the death instinct and the wish for annihilation not only of the object but also of the self, which arises as a defence against the pain of perception of the object. Segal describes how the extreme emotional reactions of one female analysand were accompanied by a wish to annihilate both the external objects and the perceiving self, in order not to experience perceptions or instincts that might produce frustrations or anxieties. From this point of view, the objectives of the death instinct link up with those of envy, and there is in Segal's view a close connection between the two: 'The annihilation is both an expression of the death instinct in envy and a defence against experiencing envy by annihilating the envied object and the self that desires the object' (p. 10). However, Segal also shows in this contribution that a confrontation with the death instinct can in favourable circumstances mobilize the life instinct too.

How, Segal asks, is one to emerge from narcissism? In her view, it is only possible to emerge from such narcissistic structures and establish stable, non-narcissistic object relations by 'negotiating' the depressive position. For it is in the depressive position that self and object can come to be differentiated:

> The move toward the depressive position is a move in the direction of a situation in which love and gratitude toward the external and internal good object can oppose the hatred and envy of anything that is good and is felt to be external to the self. The increasing integration and separation resulting from a withdrawal of projections allow love for an object to be objectively perceived. It also means allowing the object to be out of the subject's control and acknowledging it in relation to other objects. So, by definition, the capacity to negotiate the depressive position also involves a capacity to negotiate the Oedipus complex and allow an identification with a creative parental couple.
>
> (Segal and Bell 1991)

Object-loss and symbol formation

The processes of symbolization are central to the capacity to work through separation and object-loss, and Hanna Segal (1957, 1978) has shown in particular how the symbol serves to overcome an accepted loss, while the symbolic equation is used to disavow separation between subject and object.

In her view, the process of symbolization requires a three-term relation – ego, object and symbol – and the formation of the symbol develops progressively in the course of the transition from the paranoid-schizoid to the depressive position.

During the course of normal development, in the paranoid-schizoid position which operates at the beginning of life the concept of absence barely exists; the early symbols are formed by projective identification, resulting in the formation of *symbolic equations*. Segal introduced the term 'symbolic equation' to denote the early symbols, which differ profoundly from those formed later on. The early symbols are not experienced as symbols or substitutes but as the original object itself. During the course of psychical development, disturbances in ego–object differentiation may lead to disturbances in differentiation between the symbol and the symbolized object. This explains why the symbolic equation lies at the root of the concrete thought characteristic of the psychoses (1957: 393).

In the depressive position there is a greater degree of differentiation and separation between ego and object, and after repeated experiences of loss, reunion and re-creation, a good object is reliably installed in the ego. The symbol is then used to overcome a loss which has been accepted because the ego has become capable of giving up the object and mourning for it, and it is experienced as a creation of the ego, according to Segal. However, this stage is not irreversible, because symbolism may revert in moments of regression to a concrete form, even in non-psychotic individuals.

Segal also points out that the possibility of forming symbols governs the capacity to communicate – both with the outside world and internally – because all communication is mediated by symbols. In disorders of subject–object differentiation, symbols are experienced concretely and cannot be used for the purposes of communication; this is one of the difficulties arising in the analysis of psychotic patients. Conversely, the capacity to symbolize acquired in the depressive position is used to treat unresolved early conflicts by symbolizing them, so that the anxieties which had remained split off in the ego – connected with early object relations – may gradually become able to be processed by the ego through symbolization.

Clinical implications of the contributions of Rosenfeld and Segal

Rosenfeld's and Segal's developments of the Kleinian conception of the primitive object relations which constitute narcissism have had a considerable impact on the technique of psychoanalysis. The relations between the narcissistic and non-narcissistic parts of the personality have become an essential element in the process of working through, not only in psychotic and narcissistic analysands but also in less disturbed subjects. In addition, this research has drawn attention to the wide variety of instincts and defences involved in narcissism; some of these defences are directed against separation and others against ego–object differentiation.

On the level of technique, too, this research has shown how useful it is to analyse immediately, *during the session* and in detail, the narcissistic mechanisms that arise in the analysand–analyst relationship – in particular, those deployed to counter the anxieties of separation and differentiation – so as to avoid the appearance of sometimes catastrophic reactions outside the sessions.

The transition from narcissistic tendencies to recognition of the object by no means follows a linear course, but is essentially made up of incessant progressive and regressive movements, advances and retreats. As omnipotence and envy gradually decrease, the analysand comes to be less persecuted by his envious objects; he acquires a more trusting relationship with his good internal objects, and he gradually moves away from the paranoid-schizoid position towards the depressive position. A feeling with a different quality then appears: the experience of frustration and desire in relation to the parental sexuality, in the context of the Oedipus complex.

4 Bion: vicissitudes of the container–contained relationship

Bion contributed some new and fundamental ideas, and his concepts of the container–contained and the 'capacity for reverie' may be regarded as necessary preconditions for the toleration of anxieties – in particular, separation anxieties. Bion considers that, in order for the analysand to be able to tolerate separation anxiety and to introject this function, it is essential for him to have had the experience of a psychoanalyst who can understand and contain him. What is important is for the analyst to receive the projective identification and to know how to use it. Take the example of an analysand who arrives late and makes the analyst wait: if the analyst is capable of listening to the communication value of this lateness and interpreting everything the analysand believes the analyst has felt during his absence, he allows the analysand in turn to introject an analyst who is capable of tolerating and working through anxiety.

Projective identification as a means of communication

Bion developed Klein's (1946) concept of projective identification in an original way, enriching it with a new meaning. He not only distinguished normal and pathological forms of projective identification

75

but also considered it to be the child's first means of communication and the starting point for the activity of thinking and working through anxiety.

For Klein, projective identification is a primitive defence that is operational from the first months of life and forms part of the emotional development of the infant. It is for her an omnipotent phantasy whereby the infant gets rid of certain undesirable (or sometimes desirable) parts of its personality and its internal world by projecting them into the external object. Melanie Klein had described the role of the mother as an external object – the object on to whom the death instinct is deflected, for example – but Bion was to describe much more precisely the importance of the mother's function as an external object receiving the baby's uncontrollable anxieties and emotions, transforming them and then making them tolerable to the baby.

Bion draws an analogy between the analyst–analysand situation in the session and the mother–child situation, pointing out that the analyst (and indeed the mother too) is not a mere passive receptacle but plays an active part in the processes of thinking and working through anxiety – so much so that these processes depend on the quality of the container, that is to say, of the analyst as well as of the mother.

In the mother–child relationship, the container–contained model can be used to represent not only the success but also the failure of projective identification. When there is a good fit between mother and child, projective identification is used by the infant to arouse in the mother feelings which it wishes to get rid of. For instance, when the infant feels anxious because it is hungry, it may begin to scream or cry. If the mother can understand it and act in accordance with the child's demand – for example, by taking it in her arms, feeding and comforting it – the child feels that it has got rid of something unbearable by transferring it into its mother and that she has turned it into something bearable. The infant can then re-introject its anxiety, which has now become tolerable, and also re-introject *the function* of this mother who can contain and think. The mother in this case acts as a container for the infant's sensations and, by virtue of her psychical maturity, performs the function of a good object that transforms hunger into satisfaction, loneliness into company, and 'the fears of impending death and anxiety into vitality and confidence, the greed and meanness into feelings of love and generosity and the infant sucks its bad property, now translated into goodness, back again' (Bion 1963: 31).

76

The 'capacity for reverie'

Bion used the term 'capacity for reverie' to describe the faculty of the mother whereby she accepts the infant's projective identifications. The capacity for reverie is inseparable from the contained, because the latter depends on the former, and the psychical quality of the contained is transmitted over the channels of communication which form the links with the child. Everything will thereafter depend on the nature of the mother's psychical quality and its impact on the psychical qualities of the infant. 'If the feeding mother cannot allow reverie or if the reverie is allowed but is not associated with love for the child or its father this fact will be communicated to the infant even though incomprehensible to the infant' (*Learning from Experience*, 1962: 36). Hence reverie for Bion is a state of mind that is receptive to every object coming from the loved object, a state of mind that is capable of accepting the infant's projective identifications, whether it experiences them as good or bad.

The whole complex of mother–child functioning helps to form the beginning of thought, and two main mechanisms are involved in the formation of the apparatus for 'thinking thoughts'. The first is represented by the dynamic relationship between what is projected, a *contained* (indicated by the male symbol $\male$), and an object which contains it, a *container* (denoted by the female symbol $\female$). The second mechanism is represented by the oscillating dynamic relationship between the paranoid-schizoid position and the depressive position.

If the container–contained relationship between mother and child functions well, the latter can internalize the good experiences and introject a 'happy couple', formed by a mother whose container function (α-function) acts as a receptacle for the emotions of the child, the contained, deposited in her by projective identification. This function is the source of the activity of thought, as we shall see below, because 'thinking depends on the successful introjection of the good breast that is originally responsible for the performance of the α-function' (1962: 31–2).

Bion distinguishes two functions of the personality, the α-function and the β-function, to account for certain clinical facts. The purpose of the α-function is to transform sensory impressions into 'alpha elements', which are used to form the thought of dreams, impressions of the previous day and memories. The 'beta elements', on the other hand, do not serve for thinking, dreaming or remembering, and do not perform any function in the psychical apparatus, but are expelled by projective identification; the beta elements predominate in psychotic patients with thought disorders, inability to form symbols and a tendency to act out and use concrete thought. Bion also describes the child's capacity to re-introject his anxiety, which has been made bearable, as a transformation of β into α.

In addition to the dynamic container–contained relationship, Bion describes a second mechanism, the dynamic interaction between Klein's paranoid-schizoid and depressive positions. He uses the notation PS ⟷ D to represent the constant alternations in the mind between the disintegrative tendencies of the paranoid-schizoid position (splitting, disavowal, idealization and projective identification) and the integrative tendencies that belong to the depressive position (re-integration of splitting and projection, love–hate ambivalence). Anxiety situations may lead to a dispersal and fragmentation of the ego and objects into a multiplicity of particles; conversely, an emotion or idea – which Bion calls 'the selected fact' – can restore coherence to what had been dispersed and order to disorder.

Vicissitudes of the container–contained relationship

The functioning of the mother–child relationship as conceived in accordance with Bion's container–contained model can lead to the development of the capacity to think and to communicate socially by way of normal projective identification. However, this functioning may also be disturbed in a variety of ways, either on the part of the child or on that of the mother, leading to pathological projective identification and to thought disorders such as those encountered in psychosis.

On the child's side, Bion considers *tolerance of frustration* to be an innate personality factor and a highly important element in the acquisition of the capacity to think and tolerate anxiety. The tolerance of frustration will determine the future of the processes of thought and communication with others, or their failure.

To re-capitulate briefly some of Bion's concepts, 'thought' is the union of a 'pre-conception' with a frustration. The model of this is the baby waiting for the breast: the absence of the breast that is capable of affording a satisfaction is experienced as a 'no breast', an 'absent' breast inside. If the capacity to tolerate frustration is sufficient and envy is not too great, the 'no breast' inside becomes a thought, and an apparatus for thinking thoughts develops. The impression of the absence of the object and the frustration create in the baby a 'problem to be solved'; this is the beginning of thought proper and of the possibility of learning from experience: 'A capacity for tolerating frustration thus enables the psyche to develop thought as a means by which the frustration that is tolerated is itself made more tolerable' (Bion 1967: 112).

If, on the other hand, the capacity to tolerate frustration is inadequate and envy is excessive, the bad 'no breast' within compels the psyche to decide between flight from or modification of the frustration. The inability to tolerate frustration inclines the balance in the direction of a flight from frustration. What ought to have become a thought becomes a bad object which is fit only to be evacuated, and the result is a hypertrophied development of projective identification.

> The end result is that all thoughts are treated as if they were indistinguishable from bad internal objects; the appropriate machinery is felt to be, not an apparatus for thinking the thoughts, but an apparatus for ridding the psyche of accumulations of bad internal objects.
>
> (1967: 112)

Measures are then taken to escape from perception of the 'realization' by means of destructive attacks. The predominance of projective identification blurs the distinction between self and the external object, impedes the capacity to think and may lead to omniscience – based on the principle of '*tout savoir, tout condamner*' – which takes the place of 'learning by experience'.

On the mother's side, the dysfunction may be due to an inability on her part to tolerate the infant's projections, because she reacts with anxiety or indifference. The infant is then reduced to continuing the projective identification with increasing strength and frequency, and the re-introjection takes place with comparable strength and frequency. If the infant projects into its mother the feeling that it is in the process of dying, for example, and the projection is not accepted by the mother, 'the infant feels that its feeling that it is dying is stripped of such meaning as it has. It therefore reintrojects, not a fear of dying made tolerable, but a nameless dread' (1967: 116). In analysis, this type of patient seems unable to derive any benefit from his environment, and hence from his analyst, and this obstructs the development of his capacity to think and to tolerate frustrations and anxieties.

From the very beginning of life, the child thus finds himself at the intersection of two lines of development. With increasing tolerance of frustration, he becomes able to think his thoughts and to create symbols and a language as the expression of thought; this development corresponds to the non-psychotic part of the personality. Conversely, intolerance of frustration leads to disorders of the capacity to think, symbolize and communicate, which are characteristic of the psychotic part of the personality.

Clinical consequences

If the dynamic container–contained relationship is applied to the capacity to tolerate separation anxiety, Bion's ideas may be said to allow a better understanding of the play of interrelations of normal projective identification as the basis for integration of the ego, and in particular for the sense of 'buoyancy', which I shall define later as the capacity to endure and work through separation anxiety. To tolerate this type of anxiety, it is essential for conditions for the containment of pain and anxiety to become established in the mind. Bion's proposals take account of the various factors which make possible in the analysand not only the re-appropriation of the emotional 'contained', made bearable – i.e. the separation anxiety which had been projected into the analyst – but also the introjection of the 'container' – i.e. the 'capacity for reverie' of the analyst who is capable of tolerating separation anxiety.

5 Meltzer: the psychoanalytic process and separation anxiety

In his book *The Psycho-analytical Process*, Meltzer (1967) presents a theory of the development of the transference that is substantially based on the analysand's strategies for avoiding and for working through separation anxiety. The transformations described by Meltzer can be observed in any psychoanalytic treatment, whether of a child or of an adult, but his description of them often assumes a systematic character which may bother the clinician who may be confronted in his practice with more subtle and more complex situations. However, this book was written in the early part of Meltzer's career, and his technique later changed.

Projective identification and analytic cycles

Meltzer maintains in *The Psycho-analytical Process* that the separation of the first weekend is of primordial importance in any analysis, because it gives rise in the analysand to an infantile tendency for massive projective identification into external, and internal, objects. The 'analytic situation' thus immediately initiates a twofold process: on the one hand, the analysand experiences immense relief resulting from the understanding he encounters in the relationship with the analyst, but, on the other hand, the same analysand is confronted from the very first weekend with the shock of separation, which supervenes 'like a wolf in the fold' (1967: 7). These two processes – the relief resulting from understanding and the shock of separation – 'set in motion the rhythm which is the wave-form, as it were, of the analytic process, recurring at varying frequencies, session by session, week by week, term by term and year by year' (1967: 7).

In Meltzer's view, this recourse to massive projective identification will be reproduced subsequently upon every experience of routine separation during the treatment, and it will recur later in response to any unforeseen interruption in the continuity of the analysis. For a long time, therefore, the course of the analysis will be dominated by this dynamic, until the underlying anxieties can be worked through, although this process of working through never finally comes to an end.

Meltzer bases his ideas on those of Rosenfeld, and stresses that the massive use of projective identification to counter separation anxiety has the consequence that the anxious part of the self unites violently with an object (external or internal), so that the analysand appears not to be anxious and interpretations remain ineffective until such time as the projective identification is reversed. This intrusive penetration into an object may give rise to a state of confusion – it is not then clear who is the analysand and who is the analyst – even resulting in some cases in the establishment of a virtually delusional structure which reinforces omnipotence and narcissism. Again, according to Meltzer, massive projective identification 'can function to counter any configuration producing psychic pain at infantile levels, [and] no other problems can really be worked through until this mechanism has been to some considerable degree abandoned' (1967: 23).

This initial phase, described as 'the gathering of the transference processes', may persist for several months to a year in the analysis of neurotic analysands, but, according to Meltzer, its working through constitutes the essence of the analytic work throughout the treatment in borderline and psychotic analysands.

The stages of the psychoanalytic process

Meltzer then describes a chronological succession of phases in the unfolding of the analytic treatment, as well as the specific characteristics of each; by the gradual reduction of the massive initial projective identification and the transformations in the analytic relationship, these stages eventually lead to the resolution of the transference.

Without going into the details of these different stages, we may recall that the initial phase is followed by that of the 'the sorting of geographical confusions', characterized by progressive differentiation of self and object and a better distinction between the inside and the outside of the object. The relevant working through is made possible by systematic investigation of the projective identification as intensified in the transference in connection with separation. At the same time there arises a limited form of infantile dependence on the external object, which Meltzer calls the 'toilet-breast' – a dependence which has the character of expulsion and of a part-object relation, inherent in which is a substantial and persistent splitting of the object.

Later, the reduction of the tendency to identify projectively leads to 'the sorting of zonal confusions', which will gradually introduce order into the chaos arising out of the overstimulation which swamps the transference relationship. This development leads to the introjective experience of the 'feeding breast', which in turn makes it possible to tackle the Oedipal situation in its pre-genital and genital guises.

The next stage is that of the 'threshold of the depressive position', and it is followed by the final stage, 'the weaning process'. As the termination of the analysis approaches, the analysand begins to become aware that the analyst is important to him, and that he can lose him, but he develops a new interest in his introspective capacity, which offsets the inescapable perception of the end of the analysis.

Anal masturbation and separation anxiety

Meltzer (1966, 1967) also stressed the part played by the phantasies of masturbation with anal penetration and the deployment of massive projective identification as defences against separation.

Anal masturbation involves a number of different libidinal and aggressive components, such as jealousy, envy and guilt associated with unconscious attacks on the primal scene, each of these components representing specific defences against separation. In less disturbed analysands, anal masturbation may be cryptic in character, and if the analyst uses this theoretical conception, he must seek the relevant material in phantasies and dreams.

Adhesive identification

Bick (1968) and Meltzer (1967, 1975), whose research has much in common with that of Anzieu (1974), postulate that there is a mode of identification which is more archaic than projective identification and which gives rise to particularly intense reactions to separation: this is adhesive identification. In projective identification, the subject places himself 'inside' the object, whereas in adhesive identification the subject 'clings' to the object – putting itself so to speak in 'skin-to-skin' contact with it. This constitutes a type of personality characterized by superficiality and inauthenticity ('pseudo-maturity').

Adhesive identification, according to Bick (1968), results from the failure of a very early phase of development, during which the infant needs to experience an introjective identification with the 'containing' function of its mother. The failure of this introjection causes some children – in particular, autistic children – to display an excessive need for dependence on an external object, which is used as a substitutive container for their self. This produces an extreme intolerance of separation from the external object concerned: every separation gives rise to the terror of psychical disintegration, the feeling of falling to pieces, and thought disorders.

In *Explorations into Autism*, Meltzer et al. (1975) describe four fundamental types of object relations, each of which they locate in a corresponding dimensionality of psychical space. These authors also postulate the existence of a unidimensional space of non-separation, in which space and time dissolve into a linear dimension of the self and the object, a psychical world which they consider to be characteristic of autism. If even more archaic modes of identification than projective identification exist, the problem again arises as to whether there is an initial state of non-differentiation between ego and object, as Freud supposed; this would once again call into question Klein's views on this point.

A return to the concept of primary narcissism?

One of the fundamental postulates of Klein's theory is, of course, that object relations exist from the beginning of life; in this respect she disagreed with Freud, who thought that there was at first no differentiation between the ego and objects – i.e. that there was a state of primary narcissism. The post-Kleinian psychoanalysts subsequently described narcissistic states of ego–object non-differentiation, either including them in a concept such as projective identification and envy (Rosenfeld 1964a) or resorting to the concept of 'agglutinated nuclei' (Bleger 1967); however, these conceptions presuppose that object relations exist from the beginning of life.

Bleger (1967) maintains that Klein's paranoid-schizoid position is preceded by an earlier stage of ego–object 'nuclei of agglutination', formed from the most primitive infantile experiences. According to

83

this author, ego and object gradually come to be discriminated as the child develops, progressing from the symbiotic link towards a perception of the object as distinct and separate.

The new hypotheses of Bick and Meltzer, as well as those of Resnik (1967) and Tustin (1981) in the field of autism, appear to call Klein's fundamental postulate into question. For Meltzer, the clinical material of certain autistic children described in *Explorations into Autism* (1975) suggests that these children have not been able to reach the stage of adhesive identification, let alone that of projective identification (the primordial stages of psychical development). The reason why these two stages have not been attained is that they were 'either lost or inadequate to begin with' (p. 240). It is only after a certain period of analysis that the development of a narcissistic organization proper, involving 'hardness and cruelty with consequent persecutory fears', becomes possible. It may therefore be wondered whether the phase of 'primal object–self integration' considered by Meltzer (1967: 98) to be a necessary preparation for the subsequent stages of development – adhesive identification and then projective identification – is not an indirect way of re-introducing the concept of a lack of differentiation between ego and object at the beginning of life, and at the same time of re-introducing the Freudian notion of primary narcissism which has been the subject of so much controversy.

6

The place of separation anxiety and object-loss in the other main psychoanalytic theories

We shall turn now to other psychoanalytic theories of object relations and the place accorded by each of them to separation anxiety and object-loss. I have chosen to present the theories which seem to me to be foremost among those which have influenced and still influence the practice of psychoanalysis today.

I shall begin with the theory of Fairbairn, who distinguishes between levels of dependence on objects according to the degree to which differentiation and separation anxieties have been worked through. I shall then present the views of Winnicott on early anxieties and the holding function which he attributes to the psychoanalytic process – a function which he describes as helping to strengthen the 'capacity to be alone in the presence of someone'. We shall examine later the place of separation anxiety in the ideas of Anna Freud and the related ones of Spitz, as well as in Mahler's concept of separation-individuation and in Kohut's technique. The positions of Anna Freud, Spitz and Mahler, as well as those of Klein and the post-Kleinian analysts, can in fact be seen as *models* for the understanding of separation and object-loss anxieties in both adults and children. Each of these models belongs to an individual line of thought, whose originality lends internal coherence to each of the relevant theories and has the effect that they are not readily comparable with one another. This review ends with a discussion of the particular place of Bowlby, whose research on separation and object-loss is authoritative, but whose conclusions departed from the specific field of psychoanalysis.

1 Fairbairn: dependences and differentiation anxieties

The libido in search of objects

Fairbairn's emphasis on separation anxiety from the end of the 1930s follows directly from his insistence on utilizing object relations in the theory and technique of psychoanalysis. His original research was, of course, based on a revision of certain of Freud's views: according to Fairbairn, Freud placed too much stress on a libido in search of pleasure and not enough on its search for an object. 'Libido is primarily object-seeking . . . rather than pleasure-seeking', he was wont to repeat (1941).

His conception is based on the notion of phases of libidinal development – in the sense of the term used by Abraham (1924) – and on the idea that the nature of the object and the nature of object relations differ according to the libidinal stage. He distinguishes two main phases in infantile development, the oral phase and the genital phase, as well as a 'transitional' phase between the two (this was to give rise to Winnicott's concept of 'transitional phenomena'). During the oral phase, the object is first the breast, and then the mother who gives the breast; in the genital phase, however, the object which represents the individual as a whole with his or her specific sexual organs is now cathected as a whole object.

These two extreme object stages – oral and genital – have their counterparts in two fundamental forms of object relations during the course of libidinal development, according to Fairbairn: (1) a primitive form of object relations characterized by an *infantile dependence* and based on oral incorporation of the object; and (2) a developed (mature) form of object relations characterized by a *mature dependence* based on the capacity to form object relations and entailing ego–object differentiation. For Fairbairn, *acknowledgement of the differentiation between ego and object is a fundamental stage of libidinal development*, as it allows the transition from an object relation based on primary identification (oral incorporation) to a genital type of object relation with separate and differentiated objects, loving and loved.

This development takes place through the gradual abandonment of the primitive relationship based on primary identification and the gradual adoption of an object relation based on differentiation from the object. In this process, 'separation from his object becomes the child's greatest source of anxiety', as Fairbairn (1952: 145) puts it. In the early stage of 'infantile dependence', it is the oral nature of the object relation – based on incorporation – that determines the predominance of primary identification and narcissism (this being a reference to Freud [1921c, 1923b], for whom identification is the earliest form of object-cathexis). Fairbairn explains that he uses the term 'primary identification' to define the cathexis of an object which is hardly, if at all, differentiated from the subject that cathects, but that this usage is inappropriate. In his view, the term 'identification' should be reserved for the emotional process in which the relationship is established with an object that has already been differentiated, at least to a certain extent. This latter process corresponds to what is generally meant by secondary identification, a characteristic of the stage of 'mature dependence'. Mature dependence is defined as 'a capacity on the part of a differentiated individual for co-operative relationships with differentiated objects' – i.e. a capacity for ego–object differentiation. Fairbairn speaks of mature dependence because no one is ever completely independent of their objects.

The passage from infantile to mature dependence during the course of development confronts the individual with the *separation anxiety that arises in the face of ego–object differentiation.* This process is indeed generally accompanied by considerable anxiety, expressed in dreams of falling and symptoms such as acrophobia or agoraphobia; anxiety about the failure of this process is reflected in the feeling of being imprisoned or confined.

The role of separation anxiety in psychopathology

Fairbairn notes that the analysis of schizoid patients – whom he studied particularly closely – shows how difficult it is for them to give up infantile dependence and how they tend to remain fixated on the transitional phase, characterized by a variety of defensive techniques (paranoid, obsessional, hysterical and phobic) (1940). These fixations prevent the individual from attaining the genital stage, which signifies assurance that he is genuinely loved as a person by his parents and that his parents accept his love. 'In the absence of such assurance his relationship with his objects is fraught with too much *anxiety over separation* to enable him to renounce the attitude of infant dependence' (1941: 39). In consequence of the foregoing, Fairbairn considers that the conflict of the schizoid subject ('to suck or not to suck' = 'to love or not to love') is earlier than the depressive's conflict ('to suck or to bite' = 'to love or to hate'). Fairbairn's concept of the schizoid factor was later taken up by Klein (1946) in the development of her concept of the paranoid–schizoid position.

Fairbairn was later to develop his ideas on the quality of the objects contained in the primary identifications, taking the view that painful infantile experiences give rise to a dependence on 'bad objects', and that this is one of the major forms of resistance to analysis. The analyst must establish a sufficiently good object–relationship in the transference for the patient to be able to break the libidinal bond with objects which, although 'bad', have hitherto been indispensable.

In conclusion, I would add that, in Fairbairn's view, the crucial factor in war neuroses is separation anxiety (based on his experience of the 1939–45 war).

Fairbairn's propositions, often expressed in trenchant and incisive formulations, have had a lasting impact on psychoanalytic thought. For all the criticisms inspired by the particular positions he embraced or the lacunae in his hypotheses (Klein 1946; Pontalis 1974; Segal 1979), his influence has not waned, although, as Padel (1973) pointed out, it is exerted more unconsciously than consciously. Many authors do indeed refer implicitly to Fairbairn's thought in their psychoanalytic writings without realizing it. It very much surprises me that so far only his 1940 paper has been translated into French and that his *Psychoanalytic Studies of the Personality*, a classic of the psychoanalytic literature, still awaits a French translation.

2 Winnicott: holding and disorders of primitive emotional development

Early anxieties and lack of maternal care

For Winnicott, separation anxiety is connected with disorders of early emotional development and calls for a modification of the analytic situation, and sometimes of the setting, rather than the use of interpretation.

Winnicott distinguishes two contrasting levels in disturbances of psychical development: a primitive level and a neurotic level. The analyst's response will differ according to the level of the analysand's disturbances: if the disorders lie on the level of disturbances of primitive emotional development, these analysands are unable to communicate verbally and are not accessible to interpretation. The analyst must then respond by a 'management' of the analytic situation and adopt 'an attitude' towards his analysand, because, according to Winnicott (1945, 1955), interpretation is deemed ineffective at this level of regression. If, however, the emotional disorders are located on the neurotic level and the analysand has attained the stage of concern for the object, he will be able to communicate verbally, and the analyst will be able to use interpretation validly and apply the classical technique of analysis.

The presence of disorders on the level of 'primitive emotional development' – such as excessive separation anxiety – is regarded by Winnicott as a sign of a failure in the early mother–child relationship during the first six months of life. This initial period is decisive for the rest of the subject's life, and in this initial situation the primitive development of the infant is wholly dependent on maternal care or 'holding'. In Winnicott's view, although the baby possesses a spontaneous impulse to grow, it depends entirely on its mother's care for its development. Maternal care is essential to it for the purpose of negotiating the difficult stages from primary narcissism to object relations – i.e. to the acknowledgement of its mother as a separate and different object.

If conditions are favourable – i.e. when the mother is 'good enough' – she provides her child with an 'area of illusion', which has a twofold function. First, the area of illusion will allow the child to retain a narcissistic continuity with its environment, so that the baby experiences hardly any difference between the uterine medium and the real world; and secondly, she will also induce progressive disillusionment in the baby, so as gradually to bring it into contact with reality: 'The mother's eventual task is gradually to disillusion the infant, but she has no hope of success unless at first she has been able to give sufficient opportunity for illusion' (Winnicott 1953: 238). However, the illusion to which Winnicott refers is only a semi-illusion, and he explains that total illusion would be hallucination. Again, he uses the term 'transitional phenomena' to denote the processes which take place in the area of illusion and which lead the infant to 'accept similarity and difference' (1953: 233–4).

Winnicott also describes how the processes of maturation progressively lead the child to develop a capacity to be alone, first of all in the presence of the mother. After this, the environment which acts as a support for the ego is gradually introjected, and the child acquires the capacity to be truly alone, although unconsciously there is always an internal presence which represents the mother and the care she has devoted to her child (1958: 39).

In unfavourable circumstances, if the mother fails to supply her child with an appropriate environment and to satisfy its needs, the child reacts with excessive anxiety. The mother's incapacity to identify with the baby prevents her from perceiving what the baby is able to tolerate, and this gives rise to the emergence of rigid defences with the aim of not perceiving the differences between the ego and objects. In this way there forms a 'false self' to make up for the deficiencies of maternal care, instead of a 'true self' (1960).

Holding and the analytic situation

Having arrived at these views on primitive emotional development, Winnicott applied them to the analytic situation and equated the function of the analyst with maternal care. He suggested at the Geneva Congress of the International Psychoanalytical Association in 1955 that the analyst can respond to the failures of primitive emotional development by offering the analysand the possibility of making good these deficiencies. For Winnicott, the classical technique of inter-pretation suitable for neurotic analysands is inadequate for subjects with deficiencies of primitive emotional development: these analysands need to undergo a concrete affective experience whereby they can regress in order to set off along a new path ('Clinical varieties of transference', 1956). Since the false self is a consequence of deficiencies in maternal care, Winnicott believes that if the analyst provides the analysand with favourable external conditions, in the form of an equivalent to primary maternal care, this will allow the wish to grow to re-gain the upper hand.

For these various reasons, Winnicott considers it essential for the analyst not to interfere with the regression, but instead to encourage it by all possible means, because it is the precondition for a new departure. The analysand's regression in the analytic setting has the significance of a return to early infantile dependence, in which analysand and setting dissolve into a primary narcissism, out of which the true self will be able genuinely to develop.

Regressing in order to progress

Winnicott (1955) thus considers that it is the positive aspect of analytic holding that is the determinant of regression: holding in his view provides a permissive and gratifying experience, creating conditions favourable for the commencement of a process of regression which will, through the re-living of infantile dependence, lead to cure. In the case of analysands with disorders of primitive emotional development, the analyst must for a longer or shorter time forgo the classical technique of interpretation and content himself with accompanying the regression and observing its results. These are the analysands with whom Winnicott proposes modifications of the classical analytic technique, but he is not very explicit about what he means by these. In a clinical example, he mentions the case of a female analysand who experienced such intense anxieties at the end of sessions that he felt it necessary to extend certain sessions for several hours until the analysand was able to express what she did not have enough time to tell her analyst in a session of normal length:

> She had had a long treatment on a five-times-a-week basis for six years before coming to me, but found she needed a session of indefinite length, and this I could manage only once a week. We soon settled down to a session of three hours, later reduced to two hours.
>
> (Winnicott 1971: 56–7)

The ideas of Balint are in many respects similar to those of Winnicott, especially on the role of regression as a factor of progress and on the distinction between two classes of analysands, those who have reached the genital level and those who have not. When the Oedipal level has been reached, analysand and analyst have a common language of communication which allows interpretation to function and to solve intrapsychic conflicts. Conversely, where the analysand has not overcome the regressive level of the 'basic fault', there is a gap, likened to a geological fault, between analysand and analyst, defined by Ferenczi as a confusion of language between adult and child, and the use of verbal language and interpretation is inappropriate. For Balint, in the case of an analysand at the primitive level of the 'basic fault' (1968), the analyst must make a 'new beginning' in his development possible (1952).

Balint also describes two fundamental types of personality, the *ocnophile* and the *philobath*, which he distinguishes according to their object relations, as well as the anxieties corresponding to each. The ocnophile tends to cling to objects and is afraid of spaces, which generate anxiety in him: 'Fear is provoked by leaving the objects, and allayed by rejoining them' (1959: 32). The philobath, for his part, feeds on the opposite illusion, that of being able to do without objects. Finally, Balint attempts to explain the 'ocnophilic needs' of some analysands to be physically close to the analyst, to touch him and to cling to him during the treatment. In his opinion, this need for bodily contact is the expression of the fear of being let go or abandoned, and corresponds to the need for a return to 'primary [object] love', which is for Balint the equivalent to a return to primary narcissism: 'The aim [of the need to be near is] the restoration by proximity and touch of the original subject–object identity' (1959: 100). It may be wondered here whether Balint might thereby be trying to establish a theoretical

91

basis not only for some analysands' intense need for bodily contact but also for certain aspects of the active technique recommended by Ferenczi, responding to the analysand's concrete demand for contact by action instead of interpretation.

3 Anna Freud and René A. Spitz: stages of development and separation anxiety

The ideas of Anna Freud, and in particular those on the place of separation anxiety in infant development, lie at the source of an important current of thought in child and adult analysis; the ideas of René A. Spitz can be included in the same current.

Anna Freud: the consequences of separation anxiety for development

Anna Freud came to the problem of separation and object-loss relatively late in her long career as a child psychoanalyst: the problem is not mentioned in the first part of her work, and did not truly come to the fore until later, although she was one of the first psychoanalysts to observe infants in situations of separation (Bowlby 1973).

In the works of Anna Freud which do deal with anxiety, such as those on child analysis published in 1927 and 1928, or *The Ego and the Mechanisms of Defence* (1936), there is no mention of separation anxiety and no reference to Freud's last theory of anxiety as put forward in *Inhibitions, Symptoms and Anxiety* (1926d). Anna Freud began to take an interest in the problem of separation during the war, when observing infants separated from their parents (Freud and Burlingham 1943). Although her observations of infantile helplessness are precise and her descriptions eloquent, Anna Freud fails to connect these manifestations systematically with anxiety in general, let alone with separation in particular.

In her later writings, Anna Freud turns to the clinical and theoretical aspects of the problem of separation anxiety in children (*Normality and Pathology in Childhood*, 1965). She describes the different forms assumed by anxiety during the early years, including separation anxiety, each form of anxiety being stated to be characteristic of a particular stage in the development of the relation to the object. The various stages she describes can be summarized as follows.

The first stage is qualified as symbiotic: it is the stage 'of biological unity between the mother–infant couple' and is an undifferentiated narcissistic state in which an object does not exist. The second stage is marked by the appearance of the relationship with the object which satisfies physiological needs (anaclitic relationship). The third stage is that of the ambivalent sadistic-anal relationship, in which the child seeks to dominate and control its object. The fourth stage is that of object constancy, in which a positive stability of the internalized object is acquired regardless of situations of satisfaction and non-satisfaction. The fifth stage, or phallic phase, is entirely centred on the object.

Separation will therefore have different consequences according to the stage at which it occurs. Separation anxiety proper arises in the first stage, that of biological unity of the mother–infant couple, and corresponds to the separation anxiety described by Bowlby. Forms other than separation anxiety arise in the subsequent stages: the anaclitic depression described by Spitz corresponds to the second stage, while the characteristic anxiety of the stage of object-constancy is the fear of losing the love of the object.

Abnormally intense separation anxiety in later years is attributed by Anna Freud to a lasting fixation to the symbiotic stage.

The reactions to interruptions in the analysis are of great interest to Anna Freud because they throw light on the 'stage of development' attained by the child and the point of regression, while at the same time revealing the nature of its psychical organization, as Manzano points out in connection with the 'Anna Freud model' (1989). The child's reactions can be compared with the responses to a psychological test which measures changes in the subject during the course of the analysis, either in consequence of the analytic work or as a result of the process of development. A child who has not yet attained the stage of object-constancy cannot allow the analyst a significant role in its internal world.

With regard to separation anxiety in the transference, Anna Freud emphasizes the importance of the relationship with the analyst as a real person in addition to the transference relationship, and the part played by repetition in the transference of real experiences of early separation (Manzano 1989: 8).

René A. Spitz: the psychopathology of separation and of real object-loss

The work of René A. Spitz on the consequences of separation and object-loss is based principally on the observation of situations of separation from the real object (1957, 1965), from which he draws conclusions on child and adult psychical development. The views of Spitz are comparable with those of Anna Freud, and both can be accommodated in the framework of the 'Anna Freud model'. Like her,

Spitz describes various stages in the development of the ego and of object relations in accordance with the child's age, a particular type of reaction to separation corresponding to each of these stages.

Spitz distinguishes the following stages in early infant development: the narcissistic stage (the first three months of life), the pre-object stage (three to six months) and the stage of establishment of the actual object-relationship (six to nine months). Spitz was particularly interested in 'the eight-month anxiety', which he described – i.e. the anxiety of the infant reacting to his mother's absence when he perceives a stranger's face. Spitz also describes the 'anaclitic depression' which arises when the child has been separated from his mother in the second part of the first year, and which may turn into 'hospitalism' in the case of a long-term separation.

Spitz maintains that the psychopathology of separation which he observes in children is unconnected with that encountered in adult psychoanalysis and that the two cannot be equated. He postulates that disorders arising in the period of mental formation can have sequelae in the psychological structure of the child, adolescent and adult. In analysis, these disturbances are the source of narcissistic forms of transference and act as points of fixation to early affective wounds. In his view, these excessively narcissistic patients are unable to form a transference, but the analytic technique could be modified, so that 'what has been lacking in the patient's object relations should be provided by the therapist'. This might subsequently encourage the emergence of a transference (Spitz 1965: 295). However, Spitz's conclusions from his observations of children are of a general nature; he has little to say about the effects of these early disturbances on the transference, and also fails to explain what he means by modifications of psychoanalytic technique. On these latter points, his psychoanalytic teaching was in fact mainly oral, as we saw particularly in the courses he gave in Switzerland, and specifically during his stay in Geneva from 1963 to 1968.

4 Mahler: the concept of separation–individuation

Psychological birth

Mahler considers that separation anxiety appears during normal infant development at the end of the symbiotic period – i.e. at a relatively late stage, at the beginning of the struggle for individuation, at about twelve to eighteen months (*The Psychological Birth of the Human Infant*, Mahler *et al.* 1975). She distinguishes the moment of biological birth from the later moment of psychological birth and calls the latter the *process of separation-individuation*: this process comprises the acquisition of the feeling of being separate and related, and it takes place between months 4-5 and months 30-36 in the child's life. If anything goes wrong with the decisive stages of separation-individuation in early infancy, the relevant conflict is reawakened as long as the subject lives, with each new cycle of life re-activating the anxiety-inducing perception of separateness and putting the sense of identity to the test.

The normal process of separation-individuation entails the acquisition by the child of autonomous functioning in the presence of the mother and requires the latter to be emotionally available. If conditions are favourable, the child can thus confront the minimal threats of object-losses inherent in each stage of the maturational process, and gradually attains the pleasure of genuine autonomous functioning, in the sense of the autonomous functions defined by Heinz Hartmann.

Separation and individuation are two complementary but not identical developments: separation concerns the child's emergence from symbiotic fusion with the mother, while individuation has to do with the development of the sense of personal identity, with the characteristics proper to it.

Lest there be any misunderstanding about her ideas, Mahler explains that for her the term 'separation' or 'sense of separateness' refers to the *intrapsychic* achievement of a feeling of being separate from the mother, and hence from the universe as a whole, and not of being separated from a real object. Development of the consciousness of separation entails differentiation, distancing, the formation of boundaries and detachment from the mother. Mahler further extends Edith Jacobson's study of the processes of self–object differentiation and notes that the sense of separateness leads to clear intrapsychic representations of the self as being distinct from object-representations. Real, physical separations from the mother are important contributions to the child's sense of being a separate person. Regarding the term 'symbiosis', Mahler also explains that she uses it to denote an *intrapsychic* condition and not a behaviour. Symbiosis for her means that the differentiation between the self and the mother has not yet been accomplished, or that there has been a regression to the state of self–object non-differentiation characteristic of the symbiotic phase. Finally, for Mahler, the sense of identity does not correspond to the sense of *who* I am, but to the sense of *being*, involving a libidinal cathexis of the body.

The inability to separate: symbiotic psychosis

In observing the panic of psychotic children at any perception of a genuine sense of separateness, a panic which arises from the threat to the delusion of a symbiotic unity, Mahler developed the concept of 'symbiotic psychosis'. She had already postulated in 1952 that in some children the maturational thrust occurs while the child's ego is not yet ready to function separately from its mother. The result is a panic which, being pre-verbal, is all the more incommunicable, so that the child is incapable of having recourse to 'the other'. This helplessness blocks the structuring of the ego and may be severe enough to give rise to the fragmentation characteristic of infantile psychosis. This psychical fragmentation may occur at any time from the end of the first year and during the second; it may result from a painful, unforeseen trauma, but is often triggered by an insignificant trauma, such as a short separation or a very minor loss.

The difficulty of psychotic children in developing beyond a symbiotic phase on which they remain fixated, or their inability to do so, subsequently led Mahler to enquire how the early processes of separation–individuation take place in normal children. She thus came to postulate the existence of a *normal symbiotic phase*, through which she considers that every child passes. For Mahler, the object relation develops out of symbiotic or primary infantile narcissism, in parallel with the achievement of separation and individuation. In her view, both the functioning of the ego and secondary narcissism arise out of the relationship with the mother, which is at first narcissistic and later an object-relationship. The maturational and developmental thrust gradually leads the child to confront, first, differentiation, and then, during the process of separation–individuation, separation anxiety, which is overcome with a greater or lesser degree of success. This phase of infantile development is, as it were, the expression of a second birth, an 'emergence from a symbiotic fusion' common to mother and child. Such an emergence is in Mahler's opinion as inevitable as biological birth.

As it is worked through during the sub-phases of trials and *rapprochement*, the child is led to the period of 'object-constancy', which corresponds to the culmination of this process. Mahler places the onset of object-constancy at about the third year, which is relatively late compared with the views of other developmentalists. The introjection of object-constancy has a twofold meaning: on the one hand, it signifies the acquisition of an internalized and sustaining image of the primary love-object, the mother, while, on the other, it is a sign that a whole object has been introjected, with its good qualities

96

and imperfections. The acquisition of 'object-constancy' goes hand in hand with that of the sense of 'self-constancy'.

The process of separation-individuation in clinical psychoanalysis

This research, based principally on direct mother–child observation (observation of the dual mother–child entity by participating and non-participating observers, individual films of children, observations of groups of children, tests, interviews with fathers and home visits – Mahler *et al.* 1975: 236–8), demonstrated the important part played by contact between the infant and its mother at different stages of the process of separation–individuation. In psychotic children who had been unable to use their mother as a real external object and support for development, the appearance of a stable sense of separateness and relationship was observed, with the maintenance of contact helping to reduce the symbiotic tendency. This work also highlighted the specific function of the mother not only in facilitating the child's separation but also in helping them to achieve their own personal identity.

Margaret Mahler's ideas were subsequently applied in practical psychoanalysis in the context of psychoanalytic ego psychology in both children and adults. Pine (1979), one of the co-authors with Mahler of *The Psychological Birth of the Human Infant*, drew attention to two dangers in the clinical application of the latter's ideas: *excessive* use and *insufficient* use of these ideas. In this paper, Pine applies a number of concepts derived from those of separation–individuation to clinical practice with children, adolescents and adults. He stresses the existence of an attachment to the mother prior to the consciousness of self–object differentiation, but points out that this attachment is not yet a true relationship. The perception of the mother comes later, as a differentiation that is experienced painfully and not only as a gain. Interpretation of separation–individuation must take account of these two forms of attachment: the former is an attachment to 'the undifferentiated other' and genuinely belongs to the phase of separation–individuation proper, while the latter is an attachment to 'the differentiated other' and gives rise to a different transference pathology.

In applying the concept of symbiosis to psychical development, Mahler made it a central phase in the process of separation–individuation, accompanied by the transformations of separation anxieties and attempts at a return to fusion. However, her intention to describe intrapsychic phenomena was to some extent thwarted by the limits of direct observation, an approach which does not afford the same access to phantasy contents as psychoanalytic investigation. As Cramer (1985) pointed out, Mahler deserves credit for her emphasis on the development of the self and the relationship to the object, but a better integration of her views with the psychoanalytic data might have been desirable.

Much recent work has in fact been devoted to this task; this work is reviewed, for example, in a book on self- and object-constancy in which a wide variety of theoretical and clinical standpoints are compared (Lax *et al.*, *Self and Object Constancy: Clinical and Theoretical Perspectives*, 1986).

5 Heinz Kohut: separation and working through in narcissistic disorders

At first sight, the concepts of separation anxiety, object-loss and mourning seem to be lacking from Kohut's theoretical ideas about narcissistic disorders of the personality. However, it is surprising to note that, when he expounds his views on therapy, he assigns a central position to separation in the clinical aspects of the working through of narcissistic disorders. In his opinion, real or phantasized separations from the analyst, by disturbing the transference union with the 'idealized self-object', are a crucial element in the process of working through narcissistic disorders. Kohut (1971) considers that object-loss is the main threat that mobilizes for therapeutic purposes not only the grandiose self in the mirror transference but also the omnipotent object in the idealizing transference.

Separations and mobilization of the idealizing transference

Kohut distinguishes two phases in the treatment of patients with narcissistic disorders, and in particular those who form an idealizing transference: an initial phase of regression to primitive narcissism, and then a phase in which this type of transference is worked through.

He holds that, from the very beginning of the treatment, the analytic situation gives rise to a regression to an archaic level of 'narcissistic equilibrium', which is experienced by these patients as an ideal state of perfection and unlimited self-object union with the analyst. Following this therapeutic regression, 'the analysand experiences the analyst narcissistically, i.e. not as a separate and independent individual' (1971: 91).

Once the idealizing transference is established, the period of working through can begin. This new phase of the psychoanalytic process is triggered by the fact that the fundamental narcissistic equilibrium which the patient seeks to establish and then to maintain in the treatment situation is sooner or later disturbed. Unlike the situation in the transference neuroses, according to Kohut it is the disturbance of this initial equilibrium that characterizes the narcissistic disorders, and it 'is here, in essence, caused by certain external circumstances' (1971: 90). This therapeutic disequilibrium occurs in the circumstances described below.

As long as this transference is not disturbed, the patient feels intact, potent and secure, because he feels that he is in possession and control of the analyst, who is included in the experience of self. However, having attained the stage of a narcissistic union with an idealized archaic self-object, the patient will react with extreme hypersensitivity to any event that interrupts his narcissistic control. In Kohut's view, these reactions are essentially the result of 'the traumatic impact of the analyst's physical or emotional withdrawal' (1971: 92), this 'withdrawal' being connected with real or phantasized separations from the analyst. He mentions the disturbances caused by real separations at weekends and during holiday breaks, changes in the times of sessions or late arrival by the analyst, even if he is only very slightly late (1971: 92). He attributes the phantasized separations to the feeling of incomprehension or coldness which the patient perceives in the analyst. These 'transference interruptions' – which correspond to the feeling of having lost control of the analyst – give rise to powerful emotional reactions of dejection or narcissistic rage. A number of clinical examples are given to show how Kohut interprets an analysand's reactions to the analyst's absence and the relations between real and phantasized separations. He presents the psychological 'withdrawal' of the analyst as equivalent to a real absence (1971: 92), and considers that the analysand's reproaches to the analyst 'are meaningful and justified, even in instances where the separation is realistically minute or when it was initiated by the patient himself' (1971: 92).

In Kohut's view, the essence of the process of working through consists in a succession of regressive phases in the analysand in his disappointment with the idealized analyst, and of returns to the idealizing transference resulting from appropriate interpretations based on the analyst's empathy (1971: 98). The proper use of empathy has the aim of ensuring that the analysand feels understood whenever he regresses to archaic narcissism, comes forcibly into contact with the reality-ego and is subjected to the frustrations of perceiving the analyst as separate and independent. Kohut recommends that interpretations of separation be given 'with correct empathy for the analysand's feelings' and not mechanically (1971: 98). He considers that encouragement of the development of a narcissistic transference is the only possible strategy with analysands of this kind. When successful, this prolonged and laborious process ultimately leads the analysand to tolerate the analyst's absence better, thereby allowing 'the transmuting internalization of the narcissistic energies as the idealized self-object is relinquished' (1971: 101).

A self-contained psychoanalytic psychology?

There are seeming parallels between Kohut's clinical description of the process of working through and the views of other psychoanalysts who have studied the narcissistic disorders. However, disappointment quickly sets in, as Kohut's theoretical elaborations differ so profoundly from other psychoanalytic models that any attempt at comparison fails.

For instance, concerning our subject, I would be tempted to discuss Kohut's views in the light of the various psychoanalytic conceptions we have examined in the previous chapters. I should like, for example, to compare the concepts of empathy and working through with Winnicott's (1953) ideas of holding and progressive disillusionment. I should like to compare the notion of separation from the real object in Kohut with its counterpart in Anna Freud or René Spitz. Another comparison I should like to make is between Kohut's ideas on primary narcissism and narcissistic libido and the corresponding ideas of Grunberger (1971). It would likewise be interesting to discuss in detail the place of idealization or the role of libidinal and aggressive instincts in theory and clinical practice in both Kohut and Melanie Klein. Kernberg (1975) attempted to do this when he put forward his own ideas on the analysis of narcissistic disorders.

However, comparison ultimately always proves to be impossible with Kohut, not only because his theory is highly personal but also because he employs psychoanalytic concepts without reference to the authors who used – or even proposed – them before him. Although the contributions of self psychology have been beneficial in drawing our attention to important problems, we may agree with Wallerstein (1985) that these contributions can unfortunately only be integrated in the current of contemporary psychoanalytic thought as a 'self-contained psychoanalytic psychology' (p. 402). Could it be that Kohut wanted to go it alone?

6 The concepts of attachment and loss in Bowlby

An attempt at synthesis and re-evaluation

The work of John Bowlby is an essential reference for any psycho-analyst grappling with the problem of separation anxiety and object-loss. Although Bowlby's conclusions may be disputed from the psychoanalytic point of view, he nevertheless recorded most of what is currently known about the problem of separation and object-loss, as well as normal and pathological mourning, in the three volumes of his *Attachment and Loss* (1969, 1973, 1980).

Having reviewed the various hypotheses advanced by psychoanalysts to account for separation and object-loss, Bowlby admits that his interest has been aroused, but claims to be more than anything disappointed at not having found a method capable of separating the wheat from the chaff. He considers that Freud himself does not give a satisfactory answer: in his view, Freud adopted one theory after another, all of them completely different, to explain separation anxiety before ultimately, in 1926, coming to see it as the key to the problems of neurotic anxiety, but by then it was too late for him to be understood. Bowlby also considers that the psychoanalytic research on the subject is full of contradictory speculations and that 'each theory gives rise to a different model of personality functioning and psycho-pathology and, in consequence, to significantly different ways of practising psychotherapy and preventive psychiatry' (volume 2, 1973: 32). He ascribes what he regards as a failure of psychoanalysis to the fragmentation of views: the studies that exist are isolated and fail to give a coherent overall account of the phenomena of attachment, separation and loss.

Bowlby therefore suggests a different method of research, the prospective method, based on direct observation of young children: 'In the light of these data an attempt is made to describe certain early phases of personality functioning and, from them, to extrapolate forwards' (1973: 26). He finds the prototype of his method in the work of Anna Freud and D. Burlingham (1943), who observed infants separated from their parents in a nursery.

Bowlby describes three main phases of fundamental reactions in a child separated from his mother, for whom the child feels an attachment: protest, despair and detachment. In his opinion, these three phases constitute a characteristic behaviour sequence. He links each phase to one of the essential points of psychoanalytic theory: the protest phase corresponds to the problem of separation anxiety, despair to that of grief and mourning, and detachment to the mechanisms of defence. Bowlby considers that these phases make up a coherent whole, constituting one and the same process.

A conception more biological than psychoanalytic

With the commendable intention of overcoming contradictions and controversies, Bowlby puts forward a new theory which is in his opinion the common denominator of all the others. Attachment for him is an instinctive behaviour: the child becomes attached not to the person who feeds him but to the one who has the most interactions with him. The child's attachment to his mother develops or fails to develop according to the degree of understanding achieved. Bowlby's picture is to all intents and purposes devoid of the concepts of instincts and defences, phantasies and infantile experiences repeated in adult life.

Having expounded his views on attachment and then on separation, Bowlby studies the onset of fear and anxiety. His basic thesis is that phobia and separation anxiety, deemed by Freud and the psycho-analysts to be the result of neurotic conflicts on the boundaries of the pathological, are actually normal instinctive behaviours indicative of fear, a 'natural' tendency present in both animals and man, at all ages. He clearly asserts that the tendency to react with fear in the presence of strangers, fear of the dark or of loneliness is not at all the result of unconscious conflicts but primarily the expression of 'genetically determined biases', which ultimately lead to an ability to confront real external dangers (1973: 86). Hence separation anxiety for him is a purely instinctive reaction to an external danger.

Bowlby's conclusion may surprise the psychoanalysts, for he considers that the attachment between a child and its mother is purely biological in nature, as is the resulting separation anxiety. Again, the experiences of separation and loss occurring in childhood are 'events' in the external environment which divert the course of development into an unfavourable channel, just as a 'train is diverted from a mainline to a branch'. In his attempt at a re-evaluation of psychoanalytic theory by the introduction of theories of control systems and instinctive behaviour, Bowlby departs from the specific field of psychoanalysis and comes closer to experimental psychology. As Wiener (1985) points out, Bowlby's approach is perfectly legitimate, but only 'provided that it is not taken for psychoanalytic theory' (p. 1600).

The challenge of Bowlby: a spur to the psychoanalysts

Bowlby is aware that his ethological approach to attachment, fear and human anxiety differs from that of Freud and his successors, and that such an evolutionary theory is, as he himself puts it, very much a 'challenge to psychoanalytic theory'.

Although Bowlby's conclusions are disputable from the psychoanalytic standpoint, he must take the credit for having aroused the interest of the psychoanalysts in a major field which they had not sufficiently investigated. The arguments to which Bowlby's work gave rise among the psychoanalysts caused them to throw their customary caution to the winds and to set out their views clearly, as, for example, Anna Freud (1960) did in her controversy with him.

PART THREE

Technical considerations

7

Transference interpretations of separation anxiety

'Ce qui embellit le désert, dit le petit prince, c'est qu'il cache un puits quelque part . . . '

'What adds beauty to the desert', said the Little Prince, 'is that hidden somewhere in it there is a well . . . '

Antoine de Saint-Exupéry, *Le Petit Prince*, p. 72

What theory should be taken as the basis for interpretation?

Following our examination in the foregoing chapters of the position assigned to separation anxiety by the principal psychoanalytic theories of object relations, the present chapter will be devoted to the problem of interpretation of this type of anxiety when it arises in the analysand–analyst relationship during the course of psychoanalytic treatment.

Nowadays, most psychoanalysts surely recognize the crucial function performed by the working through of separation anxiety in the psychoanalytic process. However, the way each analyst interprets depends on a large number of factors and varies not only with our personal training, theoretical preferences and clinical practice but also with our personal experience of separation anxiety – i.e. our own experience of it in our lives, in our own psychoanalysis and in the analysis of our counter-transference with our analysands.

Again, the sheer diversity of psychoanalytic theories constitutes a problem for today's psychoanalysts, and especially those in training, having regard to the bewildering array of psychoanalytic schools and theories which have mushroomed since Freud. This poses the following practical question: what foundation is a psychoanalyst faithful to Freud's thought to take as the basis for his interpretations in his clinical work? As we have seen, Freud left us with a number of indicators, and many other analysts have made their own contributions within the framework of psychoanalysis, although often adopting original paths of their own. This question of the multiplicity of psychoanalytic currents within one and the same organization – the International Psychoanalytical Association (IPA) established by Freud in 1908 – is certainly a difficult problem for us all today. It is no coincidence that the 'common ground of psychoanalysis' was the subject of the Rome Congress of the IPA in 1989, in response to the question asked by Wallerstein in Montreal in 1987: 'One psychoanalysis or many?' (1988: 5).

In my opinion, notwithstanding their differences and even divergences, all the various psychoanalytic theories of object relations mentioned, for all their varied approaches to separation anxiety, have a fundamentally Freudian conception of psychoanalysis in common. This common ground includes agreement on the following points: the role of the unconscious, the importance of infantile sexuality in the origination of psychical conflicts, acknowledgement of the compulsion to repeat in transference phenomena, and acceptance of the central part played by the Oedipus complex as the organizer of psychical life. I would add, however, that, to be a Freudian analyst, it is not enough merely to accept the above theoretical points; it is also important to agree on the establishment of a psychoanalytic setting that will allow the satisfactory functioning of the analytic experience and facilitate the interpretation of the transference. As Chasseguet-Smirgel put it: 'It is differences in the setting that cause the common ground to be lost' (1988: 1167). I shall return to this point in a later chapter.

Although each of the object-relations theories I have mentioned falls within the common ground as defined above, each has a specificity and coherence of its own within the field of 'classical' psychoanalytic practice, and full advantage can be derived from a given theoretical framework only if one's own thinking conforms to it. Embracing all of them would be equivalent to not embracing any: although there may be different routes to one and the same destination, that destination can only be reached by choosing a particular route and accordingly renouncing the others, although in the knowledge that they exist and also have their own value. This does not therefore mean that the other routes are less valid; they are different routes, and it would be wrong to rule out one theory in favour of another, even if they cannot both be applied simultaneously by the same analyst.

For instance, depending on his preferred theory, a psychoanalyst may in his clinical practice decide not to interpret separation anxiety and to remain silent on this aspect of the process, or alternatively he may interpret it when he sees fit. A psychoanalyst may perfectly well take account of separation anxiety in his theory and practice and still decide not to interpret it because, having regard to his theoretical references, he feels that this type of anxiety must be re-lived by the analysand at infra-verbal level and that the analyst must accompany this regression without necessarily interpreting it. This is the approach of the followers of Winnicott, for example, for whom the narcissistic phase is a normal stage of early development – the equivalent of the 'primary maternal preoccupation' – and who therefore prefer a holding attitude to an interpretative one. In this connection, Palacio (1988) correctly pointed out in his study of narcissism that psychoanalysts who regard narcissism as a normal phase of development deem the narcissistic phenomena arising in the treatment to be relatively normal and place little stress in their interpretations on the conflictual aspects of the narcissistic transference. This is all the more striking in a comparison with those psychoanalysts who see narcissism in the context of aggression, destructiveness and envy. For them, narcissism is the result of a whole complex of instincts and defences which can be interpreted in detail in the here and now of the transference relationship, especially when there are interruptions in the analytic encounter.

So my answer to the question posed at the beginning, as to what theory should be taken as the basis of interpretation, is that the most important thing is for the psychoanalyst to be able to acquire sufficient creative freedom in relation to his own models – theoretical, technical and clinical – for his interpretations to reflect mainly what the analysand is experiencing. It is this that makes the work of the psychoanalyst a difficult and exciting art, in which nothing is ever acquired once and for all.

The value of interpreting separation anxiety

I myself believe that when separation anxiety arises in psychoanalytic treatment, it is essential for me, as the analyst, to detect and interpret it so that the analysand can work through it. The main reasons why I consider this to be so are as follows.

In my view, the principal aim of the interpretation of this kind of anxiety is to *restore verbal communication* between the analysand and the analyst, which is often broken off by separation and object-loss anxiety. This is because end-of-session, weekend and holiday breaks tend to disturb the process of working through by occasioning anxiety reactions and recourse to regressive defences, which have the effect of interrupting verbal communication between analysand and analyst for a greater or lesser period. Freud had pointed out that 'even short interruptions have a slightly obscuring effect on the work', and he referred to these resistances as a 'Monday crust' following the rest on Sunday (1913c: 127). For Greenson (1967), the reactions to separations are a major source of resistances, which constitute an obstacle to the therapeutic alliance and to the effectiveness of interpretation; for this reason he recommends first and foremost the re-establishment of 'a working alliance so that one can analyze the patient's reaction to the separation' (p. 335). In my opinion, unless we interpret these reactions, they often tend to persist and may disturb both analysand–analyst communication and the process of working through for quite long periods in some cases. Conversely, when we interpret these reactions in the transference relationship, they are often found to be reversible, and communication can then be restored more or less quickly, as the analysand is able in this case to resume the process of working through that had been interrupted by anxiety. This is why it seems to me useful to interpret this type of anxiety, not systematically but whenever the analyst considers it necessary and for as long as the analysand is unable to become conscious of it and to work through it himself.

A second reason for interpreting anxieties connected with interruptions in the analytic encounter, in my view, is that anxiety of this kind *reveals latent aspects of the transference* and provides information on the state of the analysand's object relations, his modes of defence, aspects of his personality which have remained split off, and his capacity to tolerate psychical pain, anxiety or mourning. These myriad facets of the transference, often hitherto concealed, emerge at these privileged moments under the pressure of anxiety, which in effect compels them to show their colours. The reactions to interruptions are tinged with characteristic libidinal and aggressive tendencies specific to each analysand, to each phase of the treatment and to each transference situation. I therefore consider manifestations of separation anxiety to be particularly favoured moments for interpretation of the transference. Greenson (1967) expressed the same view in his book on technique, noting that Friday and Monday sessions are certainly the ones that give rise to reactions that are the most demonstrative and significant of the transference relationship. The importance of reactions to separations is also implicit in the views of the analysts of the English school, in that most of the clinical examples chosen by them to illustrate their contributions have to do with end-of-session breaks or sessions immediately before or after a weekend or holiday break. This is evident from a large number of papers and books – for instance, the majority, if not all, of the clinical examples chosen by Segal to illustrate her *Introduction to the Work of Melanie Klein* (1964) are associated with interruptions in the analytic encounter.

Finally, the interpretation of separation anxieties assumes an even more specific significance for those psychoanalysts who consider *the psychoanalytic process from the point of view of the vicissitudes of the working through of separation and object-loss anxieties in the transference.* In this context, interpretations of separation anxiety are valuable not only in re-establishing analysand–analyst communication when it is disturbed and highlighting certain aspects of the transference, but also in punctuating the overall process of the working through of object relations in the transference, starting from dependence and ego–object non-differentiation (narcissism) and proceeding in the direction of greater autonomy and better differentiation between the ego and objects, both internal and external. For all these reasons, the interpretation of separation anxiety in my view lies at the very heart of the unfolding of the psychoanalytic process, as I maintained in my paper presented at the Geneva Congress in 1988 (J-M. Quinodoz 1989a).

I personally have been influenced considerably by the thought of Melanie Klein and her school, both as regards the use of the transference as a total situation, as Betty Joseph (1985) puts it, and in a conception of the psychoanalytic process in which the working through of separation anxieties plays a central part. My transference interpretations – in particular, those of separation and object-loss anxieties – are always related to this context.

Different analysands and their different universes

Before continuing, I should like to illustrate the diversity of the manifestations of this kind of anxiety with which we psychoanalysts are routinely confronted, by describing without commentary the varied reactions of several of my analysands to one and the same long weekend. Each analysand will be seen to be a universe in himself, completely different from another.

That weekend, Alexia was once again overcome by a painful and anxious feeling of loneliness:

> I try to give myself reasons for living, but I cannot really make them convincing; I can't manage to live by myself. At such times it is also too much for me to confront my thoughts and feelings: they will kill me, because those thoughts are like a maelstrom in which I feel trapped. I have such an emotional desert around me. When I think of that, I have iron in the soul; I feel that I am producing only bad ideas and bad feelings. All this makes me tend to destroy myself: I tell myself that there is nothing more for me to do on this earth and

that the whole tendency of existence is towards destruction. It is like the menstrual cycle: when a period comes, it is a sign that no life has been given . . . before, there was the hope that something might be born, and then, it is gone, and there is only a bloodbath. When I am faced with these questions, I cannot expect anything from you or ask anything of you. I have to be satisfied with what I have not got.

Alice's tone, by contrast, was quite different. On the eve of this break she was very calm, although she told me she felt very jealous. She would have liked to share the intimacy that my family and friends shared with me, but felt that she was 'only' an analysand as far as I was concerned. She then thought of a female friend of whom she had just dreamt, who was coming along to me just at the moment when Alice was leaving. The idea that her friend also came along to me, just after her, had aroused a powerful sense of jealousy and exclusion in Alice, but also the feeling that she could come to her sessions with the same positive attitude that she imagined in her friend, and take more advantage of the intimacy I offered her by receiving her four times a week.

Tom had been in analysis for several years, and told me after the weekend break that he had quarrelled and then made it up with his partner. He had got very angry with her, and had then realized that he had 'unconsciously displaced' his anger towards me on to her; he had been annoyed with himself over this, but had made things up with his girl-friend.

Esther had just begun her analysis, and the prospect of this break had a powerful effect on her, having caused her to feel tired for several weeks: 'I am getting more and more tired, but I do not know why, it has been like this for some time. All of a sudden I just feel totally knackered.' However, she did not consciously connect this with the imminent separation: 'I hope that things will be better next week. I am fed up to the back teeth with it. Yet all I need is to get into a stinking temper, and then I could let off some steam, but I can't even do that.' In the session immediately prior to the break, she was still furious, but a memory arose in the midst of the tempest. Esther told me that she had been like that since she was a baby: when something went wrong, whatever it was, she would start yelling until she got what she wanted. As a baby, she would scream in the night until her parents took her into their bed. 'Today I am angry with you because I am not getting any benefit from you; that's reasonable, isn't it?' she said as she stepped out through the door.

I could go on describing how each of my analysands experienced this break in his or her own way, but I shall stop here. We can, however, see how varied the reactions are, with each individual living in a different universe from the others. This demonstrates to us the importance of taking account of the particular personality of each analysand and of interpreting in accordance with the specific transference, considered as a total situation.

The transference as a total situation

The contributions of Melanie Klein have enormously increased our understanding of the nature of the transference and of the transference process. When Freud first discovered the transference, it was considered to be an obstacle, but it then became an essential instrument of psychoanalysis; for a long time it was understood in terms of direct, explicit references to the analyst. It was later realized that the totality of what the analysand reports – not only his associations and dreams concerning the analyst, but *everything* he reports (for example, material from his daily life or relating to the people around him) – gives access to the unconscious anxieties aroused by the transference situation. This is the sense in which Melanie Klein describes the transference as a total situation: 'It is my experience that in unravelling the details of the transference it is essential to think in terms of *total* situations transferred from the past into the present, as well as of emotions, defences, and object-relations' ('The origins of transference', 1952: 437). Again, considering also Klein's discoveries about early object relations and psychical functioning, the transference appears not only as a displacement of the original objects from the past on to the person of the analyst but also as a constant exchange based on the play of projections and introjections of internal objects on to the person of the analyst. All this makes the transference a continuous back-and-forth current of experiences which are often infra-verbal and which we sometimes succeed in picking up through our counter-transference – i.e. through the feelings aroused in the analyst by what the transference has brought.

During the course of the psychoanalytic process, we can often see how greatly end-of-session, weekend and holiday breaks may disturb communication between the analysand and the analyst; these movements and changes are fundamental aspects of the transference. Hence, if the relations between the transference and interpretations are viewed as a communication in a constant state of displacement and development, our interpretations must be a living reflection of this. For this purpose, 'no interpretation can be seen as pure interpretation'; our interpretations must also be understood in depth and 'resonate' inside

113

the analysand, as Joseph (1985: 447) puts it. They must therefore be constructed from whatever is moving the analysand at that particular moment, reflecting his words and phantasies and the entire situation he brings, having regard to his current level.

Within these fluctuations it is very difficult to keep the channels of communication open, both for the analysand and for the analyst; their working depends not only on the analysand's capacity to communicate or his mode of communication – which varies considerably from one individual to another – but also on the particular point where the analysand happens to be in the psychoanalytic process, and indeed in the current session.

When an analysand is close to the depressive position, he is more in contact with himself and with others, and is able to communicate in words what he experiences towards the person of the analyst, whom he sees as a whole person. The following example concerns a female analysand who, while experiencing intense anxieties at weekend breaks – which re-activated very early separation experiences in her – nevertheless proved capable of expressing her most powerful transference emotions to me in words, of accepting my interpretations and of working them through:

> What hurts me each time are your absences at weekends or during holidays: I am afraid of being too demonstrative, of showing you my attachment or anger too much . . . when I am together with a person and look at him, I think he is going to disappear. I then shrink back inside myself, I do not give anything of myself any more, and I refuse to forge links. I tell myself that nothing is final and I prepare for the break . . . and if it does not come, I make it come. When I was small, my mother went away for a time; when she came back, I did not recognize her. Since then my mother has remained a stranger to me, and I told myself that *I* made her go away and that it was entirely my fault . . . . I think all these things about *you* every time you leave me.

In these circumstances, the transference experiences of anxiety and psychical pain are contained and communicated verbally to the analyst, whose interpretations will then be received and accepted in a way which increases insight.

Conversely, when separation anxiety is less well tolerated, analysands have recourse to primitive defences such as disavowal, splitting and projective identification, often resulting in a breakdown of verbal communication with the analyst in favour of more regressive modes of communication. These analysands then unconsciously seek to *act* on the analyst rather than communicate with him verbally. In such a case, if we conceive of the transference as a total situation, we can identify the latent or dispersed elements that are seemingly very remote from the verbal expression of the transference and gather them together in our interpretations. Here is an example in an analysand who almost always had the greatest difficulty in feeling his emotions, in putting them into words and, in particular, in seeing any connection between them and his relationship with my person. During the sessions immediately following a short holiday break, this analysand became profoundly silent, remaining completely motionless and frozen, unable to emerge from his silence by his own efforts. Eventually, after several days, he uttered a single sentence to me, in an almost inaudible voice and while covering himself with the rug: 'It is cold in here.' This sounded to me so concrete and realistic that I wondered if the heating had gone off without my noticing it, and I was at first tempted to check the thermometer to see if the temperature had fallen. When on the point of doing so, I realized that this was a counter-transference reaction and that I was about to perform an act in response to the action contained in the words of my analysand, who was in fact blaming me very indirectly for having left him out in the cold during my holidays. In this way he was telling me, in actions rather than words, that he felt abandoned and alone, left by me in a state where he was incapable of by himself connecting the physical sensation of cold with the experience of separation. My absence or presence were not perceived by him in the context of a relationship with me as a whole person but through part-sensations of 'cold' or 'warmth'. At this stage of his analysis, only interpretations which expressed the fragmentary and partial sensory quality of his experience of separation from me were able to restore life to him and warm up the relationship, with a view to re-establishing verbal and symbolic communication between us.

A particularly favoured moment for transference interpretation

The onset of anxiety in connection with discontinuities in the analytic encounter is for me a particularly favoured moment for interpretation there and then, in the session, of the crucial aspects of the transference which are manifested in especially demonstrative form on these occasions. For the repeated separations during the analysis allow the emergence of a wide variety of affects, anxieties, resistances and defences which are aroused by experiences of separation and object-loss. We may justifiably enquire why such moments are so rich in psychical phenomena.

Answers to these questions are to be found both in Freud and in

Klein. As we know, according to Freud's (1926d) second theory of anxiety, the fear of separation and object-loss constitutes the ultimate source of the onset of anxiety, whatever the libidinal level, and discontinuities in the therapeutic encounter may be expected consistently to arouse such fears. Melanie Klein, for her part, does not ascribe such a specific role to separation in the causation of anxiety, but she extends its origin to all external and internal sources. Whether the ego is threatened by an excess of stimulation which it cannot master, according to Freud's view, or threatened with annihilation as a direct consequence of the death instinct, as Klein holds – this conception being not far removed from Freud's – the ego defends itself by the production of anxiety and the erection of defences having the aim of protection from both external and internal dangers. This explains why repeated experiences of separation and object-loss at the time of discontinuities in the analytic encounter are such a productive source of transference phenomena.

In thus emphasizing reactions to breaks, I am not asserting that they represent the whole of the transference but, in particular, that they give rise to particularly intense transference experiences in the analysand, which can in consequence be more directly connected with the transference.

To interpret these transference phenomena, it is a matter of identifying what the analysand is experiencing at the present moment, taking a number of factors into account – in particular, the specific moment in the treatment and also in the session, his mood and the state of his relationship with the analyst; the analysand reacts differently according to whether he is sad or happy, angry or anxious. Account must also be taken of the topographic, dynamic and economic aspects of the experience of separation. Each time, we must ask ourselves whether the anxiety is experienced in a form close to or remote from consciousness, and in the latter case whether it is repressed or disavowed (topographical point of view). What is the quantity of anxiety involved (economic point of view)? What are the instinctual level and the nature of the predominant conflict 'here and now'? Is the anxiety experienced at oral, urethral or anal level, or at phallic or genital level (dynamic point of view)? According to the point of urgency dictated by the anxiety, the analyst can show *in statu nascendi* the link between the transference and the emergence of particular kinds of affects, libidinal or aggressive impulses, specific defences present in the associations or dreams, instances of acting out or particular psychical or somatic symptoms appearing at this point in the treatment. The analyst can also draw attention to what the analysand produces in order to avoid psychical pain or anxiety, the resistances and the hostile reactions, which may go as far as a negative therapeutic reaction, as we shall see later. Note that the countless unconscious stratagems, demonstrated by us, deployed by the analysand in order to be one with the object and avoid perceiving separation, are not mere expressions of regression but often also original creations of the ego, which should be interpreted as such (Ellonen-Jéquier 1986).

It is also important for us to establish links between the transference and the analysand's past, so as to give him a sense of continuity and allow him to detach himself from the compulsion to repeat, which overburdens the present with the weight of the past. When and how are we usefully to interpret the relationship between past and present, in order to reconstruct it? This is another delicate task, to which we shall return in connection with infantile psychical trauma, because if the analyst interrupts the continuity of the session by connecting past and present, he is liable to supply an explanation only and not genuinely to induce consciousness. It is sometimes better to wait for the analysand to be sufficiently in contact with himself and with the situation before such connections are made in our interpretations.

In addition to the basic requirements, examined above, for interpretations intended as a living reflection of the transference – topographic, economic and dynamic factors and factors concerned with the relationship between past and present – we can be even more precise in our interpretations when we take account of the principal psychoanalytic object-relations theories which assign an important position to separation and object-loss anxiety in psychical development.

As we have seen in the previous chapters, psychoanalytic research in the last few decades has emphasized the vicissitudes of separation and object-loss anxieties in normal psychical development and in psychopathology, and this work has had clinical repercussions in the analysis of the transference. No matter whether he personally prefers a framework based on the concept of separation-individuation, projective identification or any one of the other main psychoanalytic models I have mentioned, the contemporary psychoanalyst has sufficient references to enable him to determine the significance assumed by separation and object-loss anxieties during the psycho-analytic process, with a view to their interpretation in the transference so that the analysand can work through them.

The role of projective identification

If account is taken of the discoveries of Melanie Klein on early object relations and psychical functioning, and of the subsequent developments accruing from the concept of projective identification, the phenomena of separation and object-loss can be conceived of and interpreted as taking place within an unceasing exchange of projections and introjections in the transference. This exchange between analysand and analyst is in effect a living weft, in a process of constant movement and transformation, and it includes the counter-transference (i.e. the feelings aroused in the analyst), which is also an essential instrument of the psychoanalytic process.

Freud was the first to describe the ego's reactions to object-loss (identification with the lost object, splitting of the ego and disavowal of reality; 1917e [1915], 1927e) and then to separation (production of anxiety and defences, 1926d). The subsequent contributions of Klein, based on the working through of her own bereavements and her studies of manic-depressive states, threw light on the nature of the anxieties and intrapsychic conflicts involved in separation, object-loss, normal and pathological mourning and developmental mourning, and made it possible to apply her views to analysis of the transference during the psychoanalytic process. Some of the decisive contributions of Klein are her conception of object relations, whose starting point was the concept of the relation to the object featuring in 'Mourning and melancholia' (Freud 1917e [1915]), her conception of the splitting of the ego and of projective identification in the paranoid–schizoid position, her ideas on the splitting of affects and on the resolution of ambivalence at the time of the integration of love and hate in the depressive position, and her research on the role of envy in psychical life.

On the basis of the above developments, we can understand, for example, not only how the ego can split in order to disavow the reality of a loss, as Freud had shown, but also how the experience of the loss can be split off and projected and/or introjected within the continuous relational exchange of the transference/counter-transference: the parts of the ego split off in this way may be deposited either in external objects (acting out) or in parts of the subject's body taken as objects, in which case they may give rise to somatic disorders or accidents (J–M. Quinodoz 1984), or else they may be projected into the analyst, who experiences them in his counter-transference, sometimes to the extent of yielding to these projections (projective counter-identification; Grinberg 1964). A conception of the analysis as a total situation then makes it possible to identify the parts thus dispersed, so that they can be drawn together in our interpretations with a view to bringing about a better integration of the ego and of object relations.

Where the anxiety is excessive and insufficiently contained by the analysand, it may be so massively projected that the analysand no longer experiences the separation: verbal communication is then temporarily interrupted by the excessive use of projective identification. It is then a matter of, first, 'bringing the analysand back into the session' (Resnik 1967) in order to re-establish verbal communication, and only then of interpreting separation. Here is an example.

A clinical example: re-establishing the 'red thread' cut by separation anxiety

I should now like to present a clinical example to show how an analysand's very creative process of working through was suddenly unconsciously disrupted by a separation, and how I was able to interpret this to him so that, once verbal communication had been restored, we could re-establish the 'red thread' that had been temporarily broken.

The analysand concerned was usually capable of becoming conscious of and communicating his transference feelings directly and subtly. However, at the beginning of a particular week preceding a pre-arranged break for my holidays, he suddenly experienced such intense anxiety that, shortly after the beginning of the session, he was reluctant to leave. He had completely lost the thread of the analytic work in progress, saying that he felt confused and fragmented, unable to gather together his ideas, but did not know why. However, he once again began to associate during the session, mentioning various people he had met and spoken to just before he arrived: there was 'one who clings to life, even if he has thoughts of suicide', another 'who smelt so bad that he ought to be thrown out', a third 'who simply cannot remain himself and goes away in pieces', and finally one 'who feels like an invertebrate that has lost its shape'. Having regard to the context of the session and his associations, I thought that my analysand was probably reacting to the forthcoming holiday separation, and that this anxiety-laden transference experience had given rise to a regression that had gained the upper hand over the more integrated process of working through that had been in progress. As his anxiety about the break had grown stronger, my analysand had reacted by resorting to the mechanism of projective identification: he had become in effect absent from the session, incapable of expressing what he was experiencing in the relationship with me and as it were deprived of his sense of identity. This transference experience had been split into many different fragments, scattered outside the session and projected into the people he had met, whose words, mentioned in the associations, were expressions of the fragments of the transference relationship existing

119

between my analysand and myself. How was I to bring my analysand back into the session so as to enable him to recover his own transference experience – i.e. his ego?

In this case, a single interpretation sufficed to bring this analysand back into the current situation of the transference: I pointed out to him that, after having been so present in the last few days, he suddenly seemed to me to be absent and, as it were, to have taken leave of himself, but I felt that I was actually hearing *him* speak to me in relating what the people around him had said; what powerful reason could he have thus had for taking leave of himself in this way and not telling me what was on his mind today? He pulled himself together and told me that when he had come along that morning he had thought he would find no one in, and this had reminded him for a moment of my holidays, which he had then forgotten again. He then told me that he was at present feeling very alone, and that my absence did not suit him at all at this time. Suicidal ideas had passed through his mind, as well as thoughts about me that were so aggressive that I would eventually throw him out like the stinker he was. He added that, if he could tell me that, he would perhaps be able to recover his shape. Having elaborated this transference experience concerning my forthcoming absence in a few words, he resumed the thread of the analytic work at the point where it had been cut at the end of the previous session.

Immediately after this first interpretation, which emphasized the mechanism of splitting and projection on to external objects of the content of the transference relationship, I had the feeling that my analysand had returned and was truly present in what he was in the process of experiencing with me. A second interpretation on the content of the anxiety proved superfluous, as my analysand had himself become conscious of the link between anxiety at my forthcoming absence and the mechanism of projective identification. The point of urgency in this case had seemed to me to be the interpretation of the mechanism of defence, in order to reverse the projective identification, prior to any interpretation of the content of the anxiety. Once the analysand had resumed his place in the session and then become capable of working through the content that currently induced the most anxiety, he could return to the higher level of integration he had attained before the disruption caused by the separation anxiety and link up again with the thread of working through and of communication.

This example also illustrates the fact that separation anxiety, when not excessive, can be contained and worked through by the analysand. However, if the anxiety is too intense, various defence mechanisms may be deployed to avoid psychical pain; the use of the mechanism of projective identification by this analysand convincingly illustrates how ego-loss is often connected with object-loss. It is therefore vitally important for interpretation to be aimed first of all at allowing the analysand to recover his ego and its lost aspects, in order to restore his sense of identity (Grinberg 1964) and allow him to re-own his real feelings about the separation; this is a condition precedent for the rejoining of the – temporarily broken – red thread of the process of working through.

A profound knowledge of psychical mechanisms is not only useful for enabling us to interpret at the appropriate level and at the right time but also essential in order to indicate where interpretation is ineffective, so that it can be directed to a place where it is more likely to strike home. The interpretation given succeeded in reversing the projective identification in the above example, but this is not always the case. Where massive recourse is had to projective identification to avoid separation anxiety, especially at the beginning of an analysis (Meltzer 1967), the loss-of-self anxiety may be so intimately and almost delusionally bound up with an object (or objects) that no interpretation can be effective as long as the mechanism of projective identification is not reversed. Consequently, according to Etchegoyen (1986), an inexperienced beginner in analysis may be tempted to interpret on too optimistic a level: if you tell an analysand who resorts massively to projective identification that he misses the analyst at the weekend, you are very unlikely to be understood by him, as this type of interpretation implies that the analysand can distinguish subject from object. How can an analysand who does something specifically in order to ensure that he does *not* miss the analyst, in fact miss the analyst?

Everything I have described above takes place at different levels and on different scales both during the prolonged course of the psychoanalytic process and in the microcosm of the session. We shall now turn to the latter.

In the microcosm of the session

Many psychoanalysts today – especially the post-Kleinians – place the emphasis on a detailed consideration of the fluctuations of the transference within the actual session, with a view to following the affective movements of the analysand and maintaining as close as possible a contact with his psychical functioning. For this purpose, it is not enough for our interpretations to be correct and to correspond to the personal associations of the analysand; what is particularly important is for us to keep a close eye on how we, the analyst, are used unconsciously at each moment by our analysand. By analysing the current reactions in the here and now of the session and taking account of the analysand's response to our interpretations, we can gain better access to the earliest affects and object relations.

From this point of view, it seems to me essential to identify and interpret all the defences against differentiation during the session, so that they can be worked through and the analysand can confront the separation. In the constant fluctuations of the transference and the counter-transference, we can show the analysand how he uses us by resorting to projective identification, for example, in order to avoid perceiving ego—object differentiation and to disavow separation. In the moments when the analysand succeeds in detaching himself from this, we can draw attention to the changes brought about by his mode of communication with us — for instance, how better communication gives rise to a painful feeling of loneliness, but how this experience is at the same time a sign of the re-discovery of a sense of identity and of a more differentiated relationship. If this detailed work of differentiation is not performed in the here and now of the fluctuations of the session, separation is likely to become difficult or even catastrophic. Eskelinen-de Folch (1983) showed how painstaking analytic work during the sessions succeeded in reversing a female analysand's general unconscious tendency to split off the feeling of loss and loneliness and project it into the analyst by colluding with him: detailed analysis of these phenomena in the sessions allowed increased tolerance of separation and restored a form of 'I' and 'you' functioning in communication between two persons now more readily perceived as distinct from each other. The 'we', which was initially used by the analysand for the defensive purpose of denying her separateness from the analyst, ultimately came to be a 'we' corresponding to an alliance of cooperation.

Some psychoanalysts have also laid great stress on the importance of identifying the effects of the beginning or end of the session on the content of the session itself, and also on the transference and counter-transference (Wender *et al.* 1966). According to these authors, each session has a 'pre-beginning' phase, during which the analysand expresses the unconscious phantasy which will dominate the session, and a 'post-final' phase, which triggers other phantasies which have remained latent during the session but come to the surface only after the moment when the analyst says that time is up. Etchegoyen (1986) considers it to be more useful and effective for the psychoanalyst to concentrate his attention on the moments of contact and separation at the beginning and end of the analytic hour than on weekend or holiday reactions, as the latter are often too emotionally charged for the analysand to be able fully to accept and work through the relevant interpretations.

In the long term: a conception of the psychoanalytic process

Over and above what takes place in the immediate present of the session, we must also take account in our interpretations of the evolution of separation and object–loss anxieties *in the long term*, over the course of the psychoanalytic process as a whole. From this standpoint, as we have seen, the psychoanalytic process as a whole can be considered in terms of the transformations and working through of this type of anxiety. I shall now present some other hypotheses which I find useful for understanding the significance assumed by the evolution of separation and object–loss anxieties in the unfolding of the transference, with a view to identifying and interpreting them.

Etchegoyen (1986) draws the analyst's attention to the need to recognize how far he himself is involved in the link of transference dependence: in his view, the separating of the analysand from the analyst gives rise to anxiety in the analyst too (unless he denies or displaces it); we need only consider how far a session missed by an analysand can, depending on the circumstances, disturb our working day. In this work on technique, Etchegoyen places Meltzer's conception of the psychoanalytic process in a wider context, including within it the ideas of Bick and Meltzer on adhesive identification and dimensionality. For Etchegoyen, the working through of this kind of anxiety has a fundamental impact on the psychoanalytic process, because it is an essential component of the proper functioning of the transference and must be interpreted accordingly. In his view, the analyst has the twofold task of containing and interpreting separation anxieties when manifested from session to session, from week to week, at holidays and in the approach to the termination of the analysis. The containing function of the analyst, which he regards as decisive, is felt through his holding function, in Winnicott's sense, and at the same time on the level of Bion's container–contained relationship. Etchegoyen also points out that this type of anxiety arouses powerful resistances and counter-resistances throughout the treatment, and that analysands tend to minimize or disavow separation anxieties and to trivialize or reject the analyst's interpretations of this aspect of the transference.

In his study of separation and object–loss anxiety in children, Manzano (1989) puts forward a hypothesis that is useful for interpretation of transference phenomena in both child and adult analysis: he postulates the existence of a 'double transference', reflecting the disavowal and splitting of the ego that are the specific defences of object–loss, *within* the relationship with the analyst. He considers that disavowal and splitting are revealed by a mixture of variable proportions of an early 'narcissistic' transference – comprising the development of narcissistic defences expressing the vicissitudes of separation and object-loss – and a 'neurotic' transference as conventionally defined. Manzano also emphasizes the vital part played by the manic defence in this type of transference. In his view, the analytic relationship immediately gives rise in the child to a relationship with the analyst as an idealized object, whose presence generates the first separation anxiety: the first defence to be used will therefore be an introjection of the idealized object and an identification with it (projective identification with an internal object), thus organizing a manic defensive system. This early manic defence – earlier than in Klein's conception – specifically 'crystallizes' the loss of the idealized object, constituting 'anti-mourning' *par excellence*. During the psychoanalytic process, the gradual dismantling of the 'fortress of manic defence' allows the integrative tendencies of the ego to become stronger and facilitates a decrease in the severity of the split and a 'return of the disavowed'; this gives rise to a process of mourning and working through whereby the two aspects of the transference are integrated.

I should now like to draw attention to a further point which seems essential to me and which must be allowed for in our interpretations throughout the psychoanalytic process: I believe that it is of crucial importance in the interpretation of separation anxiety not to set a dyadic level of relationship – i.e. one involving only two persons, to the exclusion of a third – against a triangular or Oedipal relationship level in which the third member is included. This opposition between a dyadic and a triangular level is postulated explicitly by Winnicott and in particular by Balint, and has created the impression that the predominantly narcissistic transference implied mainly a two-person relationship and should be interpreted in this context, the analyst being introduced as the representative of the third party only when the Oedipal level is attained. In my view, it is essential for the analyst interpreting separation anxiety always to take up a position in which he is also involved as the third party. This will allow him, for example, to interpret the failure to acknowledge the third party as the result of an active and aggressive disavowal and not as mere ignorance. Of course, a triangular relationship does not imply interpretation in genital, Oedipal terms alone: there are different levels of three-person relationship which vary according to the libidinal level, and many analysts currently lay stress on the importance of early triangulation.

My intention in this chapter has not been to draw up an inventory of the manifold reactions of analysands to separation and object-loss anxiety, or to enumerate the infinite variety of possible ways of interpreting them. My principal aim has been to put forward a number of reference points for the detection of this type of anxiety and its interpretation in terms of the session and of the unfolding of the psychoanalytic process, allowing for the fact that each analysand is effectively a universe in himself. The theories do not therefore by themselves account for what an analysand experiences individually from one session to the next, or from one year to the next, and it is essential for us to pay attention to what is experienced by him in the transference as well as to our own experiences – in our counter-transference – if our interpretations are to be not generalities but the living reflection of the originality of the analysand's person.

The various reference points I have mentioned are present in every psychoanalytic treatment and provide us with an understanding of the unfolding of the transference, as it develops from a predominantly narcissistic state of dependence towards greater autonomy and a more differentiated perception of the ego and the object, allowing the Oedipal situation to be worked through and the final separation from the analyst to be tackled. I have formulated these different points on the basis of my own references, in the knowledge that other psycho-analysts may in turn conceptualize them in different terminology. I hope that I have thus been able to show that the working through of this type of anxiety belongs fully within the realm of the analysable, because the object-relations phantasies involved in it are by no means concerned solely with the relations between the ego and external reality, but have to do with the interrelationship between external reality and psychical reality, which form an inseparable combination.

Loss of the real object and the working through of mourning in the transference

I should like to conclude this chapter by discussing the function of the psychoanalytic process in the working through of mourning, in particular in persons suffering the conscious and unconscious consequences of the real loss of a loved one. The repercussions of the death of a loved one on psychical life often induce people to ask for analysis and constitute an indication for the treatment; many analysts have studied the process of psychoanalysis in persons who have sustained a real loss of this kind before coming into analysis or during the analysis itself.

To recapitulate briefly, any loss of a real object results in the initiation of a work of mourning, which may be normal or pathological depending on the individual. As stated earlier, Freud considered that normal mourning work has to do with the relationship to the reality of the loss and occurs 'under the influence of reality-testing; for the latter function demands categorically from the bereaved person that he should separate himself from the object, since it no longer exists' (1926d: 172). As for pathological mourning, Freud describes its intrapsychic consequences in melancholia (or depression, as we would now call it): introjection of the lost object and identification with it on an ambivalent basis (1917e [1915]), and splitting of the ego with disavowal of the reality of the loss, by a mechanism similar to fetishism (1927e). Since then, many psychoanalytic contributions have been devoted to the consequences of a real loss, which may be accompanied by a depressive or manic state: excesses of sadness or disavowal of sadness, guilt and ambivalence (conscious idealization of the lost person and unconscious hate of that person, turned back on to the ego in the form of self-punishment), disavowal of the death and identification with the lost person. On this subject, a comprehensive critical review of the psychoanalytic literature concerning adults will be found in Haynal's *Depression and Creativity* (1985), and, in the case of children, in Manzano's 'La séparation et la perte d'objet chez l'enfant, une introduction' (1989). Like many other authors, Manzano considers that the normal process of mourning does not take place in childhood and early adolescence, defences instead being erected in order to disavow the death and maintain the attachment. During adolescence, problems of abandonment are experienced very intensely, an important part being played in adolescent suicide attempts by the difficulty of coping with losses in both the external and the internal world (Ladame 1987).

In the analytic situation, relations with internal and external objects are reproduced in the transference and re-lived in the constant exchange of projections and introjections between analysand and analyst. Again, the real separations from the analyst which regularly punctuate the analytic encounter repeatedly re-activate object-loss phantasies, and a mourning process which can be interpreted in all its aspects gets under way. In this way, mourning in respect of real losses sustained by an analysand may be experienced in parallel in the transference with the analyst and then carried through to its resolution, as we shall see later in connection with the termination of the analysis.

Mourning reactions to the loss of real persons prove to be analogous to the reactions to the early losses suffered by the infant and later the child in the course of his development, according to Melanie Klein. The different stages of infantile development may be conceived of as a succession of repeated losses and separations, which reactivate the depressive position. In anxiety states, the baby or child feels that he has not only lost his mother in the external world but also that his good

126

internal object has been destroyed. In this connection, Klein considers that depressive anxieties form part of normal development, that they are an inevitable corollary of the process of integration and that they are revived to a certain extent in all subsequent loss situations. In the event of a real loss, for instance, psychical pain and anxiety give rise to a regression and recourse to primitive defences; in this sense, the defences used to cope with real mourning are the same as those deployed to confront mourning during development.

This means that there is a difference between the Kleinian and the classical conceptions, as Segal has pointed out: in the classical conception of Freud and Abraham, melancholia involves an ambivalent relationship to the internal object and a regression to the oral stage, whereas normal mourning concerns only the loss of an external object. In the Kleinian conception, ambivalence towards the internal object and the associated depressive anxieties constitute a normal stage of development and are re-activated in normal mourning:

> It is often contended by classical Freudian analysts that when a patient is actually mourning it is usually an unproductive period in his analysis; Kleinian analysts, in contrast, find that analysis of mourning situations and tracing them to their early roots often helps the patient greatly in working through the mourning and coming out of it enriched by the experience.
>
> (Segal 1967: 179)

8

Psychical pain and negative transference

'On risque de pleurer un peu si l'on s'est laissé apprivoiser . . .'

'You are likely to cry a little if you have allowed yourself to be tamed . . .'

Antoine de Saint-Exupéry, *Le Petit Prince*, p. 83

Transference hatred of the loved object

'I did not come here for you to make me suffer, but for you to rid me of my suffering,' one of my analysands would protest in response to a transference interpretation of separation anxiety which had struck home. He could no longer deny his suffering, but was becoming able to contain it and express it to me.

The explicit and implicit content of this analysand's words tellingly illustrates how exacting a task it is to become conscious of the painful quality of the transference link; it is a painful experience which causes hostility towards the analyst to flare up again and reinforces the negative transference. It is also understandable that the analysand resists becoming conscious of separation anxiety, and that the analyst hesitates to interpret it – or even resists doing so.

We here touch upon a central point in the psychoanalytic process: emergence from narcissism and recognition of the object. All analysts since Freud agree that it is when the object is not there that the subject notices that the object exists; this discovery is frustrating because the subject becomes aware that he is not himself that object and that the (wished for) presence of the object is independent of his will; however, this discovery is at the same time structuring, because the analysand becomes conscious of his identity as a subject precisely when he comes up against the limits of the object.

The painful experience of absence and its positive counterpart constitute a fundamental component of psychical development, which has been conceptualized in various terms by different authors. For Freud, 'wishing' arises in the absence of the satisfying object, by way of hallucinatory satisfaction: the totality of this primal experience gradually allows the ego to distinguish hallucination and perception, phantasy and reality (1895: 326; 1900a). In 'Negation', Freud (1925h) again draws attention to the importance of early satisfaction in the seeking of objects: he considers that the condition for the establishment of reality testing is to 'refind' a lost object, which would in the past have afforded a real satisfaction (p. 237). This experience of the lack of the important object is essential for the formation of symbols and of verbal communication: the word replaces the absent object, as Gibeault (1989) pointed out. The experience of absence has been discussed from a number of different points of view. For Bion (1963), the experience of the absent breast and the development of tolerance of frustration lead to the capacity to think one's thoughts. For Green (1975), absence is half-way between silence and intrusion and is the bearer of 'potential presence'. Finally, for Laplanche (1987), the 'empty space' resulting from the enigmatic character of the object is the engine of psychoanalytic treatment.

Melanie Klein's description of the conflict of ambivalence and its resolution was certainly a decisive contribution, because of its possible applications to the technique of transference interpretation. In her description of the dynamics of the conflict of ambivalence in the process of mourning and its relations with anxiety, Klein goes further than Freud and Abraham: she provides us with the basis we need for interpretation of the negative and positive part-aspects of the transference, allowing integration of the affects of love and hate felt in respect of the analyst when experienced as a whole object.

I have already discussed the details of Klein's conception, and would recall here only that, in her view, experiences of loss re-activate sadistic wishes at the time of separations and reinforce conflicts of ambivalence, because hate is accentuated and projected on to the lost loved person, represented by the analyst in the transference. When the psychical pain and anxiety resulting from separation are excessive, the intensity of suffering gives rise to a regression and a return to the primitive defence mechanisms characteristic of the paranoid-schizoid position; hatred is then stronger than love. For defensive purposes, the object is split into an idealized object and a persecutory object and, by virtue of the projection and deflection of the death instinct, the threat of annihilation of the ego is experienced as coming from the bad part-object situated outside, while the idealized part-object is introjected in order to keep the persecutors at bay.

Conversely, when good experiences predominate, projections

decline, persecution is reduced, and the split between the ideal and the persecutory objects also diminishes. The subject is then drawing near to the depressive position – i.e. the integration of objects and the ego, as well as the synthesis of love and hate in ambivalence, the object now being experienced as a whole entity. Klein does, however, consider that the depressive position is never acquired once and for all, and that there is a constant fluctuation between the persecutory anxiety, when hatred is stronger, and the depressive anxiety, when love comes more to the fore (Segal 1979: 80).

Returning to Freud's ideas on the genesis of love and hate while also taking into account the post-Freudian contributions (Delaite *et al.* 1990), we find that the primordial split described by Klein closely corresponds to Freud's own description ('Instincts and their vicissitudes', 1915c). He considers that objects which give rise to unpleasure generate hate, so that, while the good is taken into the self (the 'purified "pleasure-ego"', p. 136), what is hated is expelled: this in his view explains why 'hate, as a relation to objects, is older than love. It derives from the narcissistic ego's primordial repudiation of the external world with its outpouring of stimuli' (p. 139). 'Not until the genital organization is established does love become the opposite of hate' (p. 139). As for love–hate ambivalence, Freud uses this term in two different senses during the course of his career and, as D. Quinodoz has pointed out, nowhere explains the distinction. According to D. Quinodoz, the contributions of Klein enable us to distinguish two different senses of the concept of ambivalence:

> It is in my view important to distinguish two kinds of ambivalence of affects: *a pregenital ambivalence in which loving and hating cannot be connected together because they are fused*, and *a genital ambivalence in which loving and hating are connected together because they are distinguished from each other*, thus making possible *the love of the whole ego for the whole object*.
>
> ('"J'ai peur de tuer mon enfant" ou: "Oedipe abandonné, Oedipe adopté"', 1987: 1591)

A trial for the counter-transference

The re-activation of psychical pain, depression and the conflict of ambivalence, involving the conscious and unconscious expression of hate towards the analyst, who represents the loved and hated object in the transference relationship, constitutes a severe trial for the psychoanalyst's counter-transference.

The hostile feelings, as well as the accompanying death anxiety, whether projected on to the analyst or turned back on the analysand himself in the form of aggression against himself and self-destructiveness, demand from the analyst a soundly based capacity to receive and contain the negative aspects, so that he can interpret them and link them to the positive aspects that are always present. While the predominance of hostile feelings on the part of the analysand towards the analyst is described as 'negative transference', it is important not to forget its positive counterpart – i.e. the love implied by hate, and the wish that lies concealed behind envy.

Whether the analyst will or will not allow the negative transference to develop depends partly on his theoretical references and partly on his counter-transference resistances. According to his conception of object relations, he may interpret the negative transference in terms of resistance to the working alliance, as we have seen (cf. Greenson 1967). If his orientation is Kleinian, he will allow for the fact that anxiety gives rise to the projection on to the analyst of the phantasy of the hated bad object and the idealized object. In this case, the analyst's capacity to receive and interpret these projections and to connect the feelings of hate with the idealization of the object permits the split between the ego and objects to be gradually overcome, thereby encouraging the synthesis of love and hate in an ambivalence towards one and the same object, experienced as whole, corresponding to the ambivalence of the genital level.

There is, however, no doubt that the main obstacle to interpretation of the conflicts of love and hate connected with separation anxiety is our own counter-transference resistance to accepting the hostile projections of the analysand and his destructiveness towards ourselves, the analyst, whom the analysand considers to be responsible for and guilty of the awakening of psychical pain. Yet it is the analyst's capacity to accept these projections in the transference that will allow him to distinguish aggression from destructiveness and to link it with positive feelings, in order to restore the connection between love and hate.

Grinberg (1962) introduced the concept of projective counter-identification to draw attention to the danger of the analyst's unconsciously identifying with the parts projected into him by the analysand by projective identification; such concepts are particularly valuable in preventing unconscious collusions from arising between the analyst and the analysand. An analyst who represses anxieties about his own death, for example, might well be thrown off balance by an analysand who tells him that, for him, when the analyst is absent, he might as well be dead, and might even have difficulty in interpreting this to his analysand.

131

It is also essential to distinguish psychical pain from masochism, because an analysand sometimes tells us: 'I do not want to suffer, because I am not a masochist.' Psychical pain is not masochism, because it involves perception of external and internal reality as painful and not as pleasurable. Masochism, on the other hand, entails unconscious enjoyment of pain, based on a need to practise sadism on the object and to take pleasure in it, sadism and enjoyment being turned back upon the subject in the form of masochism, as Freud showed (1917e [1915], 1924c).

Interpretation of the positive concealed behind the negative

I should like at this point to give a brief example of interpretations which draw attention to the positive aspect of a manifestation of hostility associated with a holiday break, in an analysand whom we shall call René.

On my return from a week's holiday, I had been surprised by the change in René's tone: he began to hurl obscene abuse at me, in a way that was unusual for him, telling me that I was a turd who made him sick and that he was 'fed up to the back teeth' at the mere thought of coming to the sessions. He became more and more irate, raising the pitch of his frenzy a little more whenever I ventured to ask him why he was so angry. He presumably did not know himself, as he often had a good capacity for introspection, and was this time quite obviously swamped by anxiety. Nor did I have any clues in terms of phantasies to put me on the track of what was the matter, and I did not want to supply an over-general interpretation – for instance, to the effect that his anger might be connected with something he had felt about me during my holidays – as I felt that this would not have added anything to what he already knew. I wanted to be more precise. Instead of subsiding with time, René's anxiety was increasing all the while, and an intervention on my part seemed to me to be urgently necessary. A dream gave me the opportunity.

In this dream, René saw a couple travelling in a white car; suddenly there was a mountain torrent in spate, whose surging waters came flooding down the valley, threatening to drown the couple. The torrent was made up of a strange mixture of muddy and yellowish water and a clear, milky water which reminded him of milk, or rather of semen.

René, who had several years of analysis behind him, hazarded a number of different interpretations of his dream, all of them reasonable, but one-sided: I noticed that his interpretations related solely to the

132

hostile, envious or destructive aspects of the dream – i.e. negative instinctual aspects. I interpreted this to him first, asking whether he might not also have some more secret reasons for feeling so anxious and guilty, and for accusing himself so openly of hostility towards me, and that only.

My comment reminded him that he had, unbeknown to myself, recently seen me together with my wife, and that he had been so disturbed by this that he had not dared to mention it to me. I then completed my interpretation by saying that I now understood his rage better, as it seemed to me to be a mixture of intense stimulation and a positive state of confusion, to which the dream offered us the key. I considered that my absence had aroused in him an intense state of sexual stimulation, which he knew well because he had often experienced it in relation to the parental couple when he was a child. However, in his excited state, all his sensations merged into one another, and he could no longer distinguish what it was that was causing the excitement: was it the need to urinate, to defecate or to ejaculate? For urine, faeces and semen were all mixed up together, just like the surging waters of the torrent (muddy, yellowish and milky) in the dream, which threatened to swamp the couple (myself and my wife, representing his parents in his phantasy). The distinction between urine and semen introduced by the interpretation enabled him to identify the wish that lay hidden behind his envy. The destructive, guilty rage he had experienced towards me had hitherto swamped his wish to identify with the creative aspect of the couple and of the man whom I represented – the couple who had in his dream escaped drowning.

The hypothesis contained in my interpretation proved to be accurate, and I soon observed a profound change in René, following the distinction he had gradually been able to make in his mind between semen, urine and faeces and the functions corresponding to each. Not only did his anger quickly subside, but he also began to feel full of new creative possibilities and less and less submerged in sterile conflicts.

The presence of the object as a source of psychical pain

Just as the *absence* of the analyst may be experienced by the analysand with a pain that is tolerable to a greater or lesser extent, so too can the perception of the analyst's *presence* be a cause of more or less tolerable psychical pain and anxiety: the analyst may be perceived in a myriad of ways, all of which give rise to pain and suffering – for instance, when his presence is perceived as that of a person who is free (i.e. capable of going away) and who has a sex (i.e. is capable of sexual union with another person).

Generally speaking, analysands who react powerfully to separations involving the absence of the analyst are also the ones who have the least tolerance of his presence, which for them is an unconscious source of frustration, stimulation and envy, all of which are not readily tolerated. With the progress of the analysis, the analyst's presence comes to be better perceived and endured, and separation anxiety gradually gives way to the specific anxieties of the Oedipal situation and to the wish to know the analyst instead of possessing him. However, when an analysand is intolerant of the presence of the analyst, this is accompanied by a reinforcement of hate and of the conflict of ambivalence – i.e. a recrudescence of the negative transference.

The negative transference resulting from perception of the positive qualities of the object has been the subject of research by a number of authors: whereas Segal (1956) showed that psychotics tend to avoid the painful feelings associated with the depressive position, Rosenfeld (1971) demonstrated the role of envy at the perception of the positive qualities of the object. Meltzer (1988), for his part, arrived at the concept of the 'aesthetic conflict'. In his view, a child who discovers his mother finds himself confronted with a person who is an enigma to him; he may suffer at not knowing everything about the object, but may also be reassured when he discovers that the object's behaviour has a meaning even if he also discovers that he will never manage to discover it fully: the pleasure of knowing the object will have supplanted that of possessing it (Meltzer 1988).

When the analytic encounter is interrupted, we often observe manifestations of regression and flight induced by feelings connected with the depressive position, by a recrudescence of envy of the analyst, or by the 'aesthetic conflict'. I consider that these reactions must be carefully distinguished from anxiety reactions to separation: it is essential to distinguish in our interpretations between manifestations of psychical pain resulting from *absence* and associated with separation anxiety, and ones connected with the keen perception of what the *presence* of the object represents for the subject, precisely when it is lacking.

Separation anxiety as a syndrome?

Is the typical, repetitive clinical picture presented by analysands suffering from separation anxiety a specific psychopathological entity? Some authors have attempted to define a clinical picture, such as Guex in his *La Névrose d'abandon* (1950), later retitled *Le Syndrome d'abandon* (Quinodoz *et al.* 1989).

I have had a number of analysands whose principal symptoms were connected with separation anxiety. These symptoms had invaded the analytic process to such an extent that they appeared to have relegated other transference conflicts to the background. Although it was possible to attribute the totality of these analysands' manifestations to one and the same origin, I do not think that they can be regarded as a psychopathological entity in its own right; they can at most be regarded as a syndrome.

Some analysands exhibit such intense manifestations of separation anxiety that the analyst may wonder how far these symptoms can be contained and worked through in the analytic setting. In my experience, however, a meaningful correlation cannot be made between the intensity of this type of anxiety and the prognosis for these analysands. I have found that the noisiest and most spectacular manifestations do not necessarily give rise to a less favourable prognosis and do not prove to be the least analysable.

The negative therapeutic reaction and separation anxiety

The onset of the negative therapeutic reaction has been ascribed to a number of different factors. Among these factors, separation anxiety is foremost for a large number of authors at present, albeit with different theoretical approaches.

The importance of separation anxiety – in the sense of differentiation anxiety – as a source of the negative therapeutic reaction was stressed by analysts of different schools at the 1979 London conference of the European Psychoanalytical Federation on this subject. Although each speaker invoked different mechanisms to explain the need to be one with the object and not to separate from it, their clinical conclusions did not differ fundamentally from each other. For instance, for Pontalis (1981), the negative therapeutic reaction is a way of preserving the union with the analyst: 'Breaking with one's analyst is a way of keeping him, and is not the same thing as separating from him.' Bégoin and Bégoin (1981) showed that several different kinds of negative therapeutic reactions can be distinguished according to the nature of the prevalent anxiety. In addition to the form in which envy predominates, they consider there to be one based on a catastrophic separation anxiety connected with adhesive identification:

This anxiety is deemed to result from the experience of separation of the subject from an object which appears to him to be both inaccessible and non-distinct from himself, owing to the predominance of an adhesive mode of relationship in which the physical and the psychical are not experienced as being different from each other.

(Bégoin and Bégoin 1981)

Grunert (1981) considers the common denominator of the negative therapeutic reaction to lie in the process of separation–individuation described by Mahler *et al.* (1975), to which she refers. In her view, the negative therapeutic reaction results from problems in separating out from the mother–child dyad, which is reproduced in the transference but is not only negative in value.

Attention has also been drawn by other authors to the importance of separation anxiety as a factor in the negative therapeutic reaction. For instance, Gaddini (1982) holds that the tendency towards integration entails confronting the anxiety of recognizing that the subject is separate for ever. Limentani (1981) refers to the catastrophic reactions sometimes observed in analysands at the end of their analysis, which proved to be attributable to the persistence of a phantasy of fusion which had dominated the transference but had escaped analysis, but which came to the fore when the patient suddenly became conscious of his separateness from the analyst.

The concept of the negative therapeutic reaction has now been expanded to such an extent that it is often difficult to distinguish it in clinical practice from other factors that disturb the unfolding of the psychoanalytic process, such as the negative transference, insuperable resistances or the therapeutic impasse. The broadening of this concept is very likely to create confusion in evaluating the different components involved in a particular transference situation.

In a recent contribution, Maldonado (1989) endeavoured to distinguish the negative transference, the negative therapeutic reaction and the impasse situation in connection with separation anxiety. For him, the negative transference does not interrupt the analytic dialogue, and the relationship with the analyst remains positive even if the analysand displays a negative, hostile attitude. Conversely, in the negative therapeutic reaction, the analysand's negative attitude destroys the former positive elements of the relationship, by an insidious process under the sway of the repetition compulsion. According to Maldonado, the negative therapeutic reaction is particularly strong in certain patients who have insuperable difficulty in confronting the separation anxiety resulting from the regular breaks in the analytic treatment. With these analysands, the danger of the positive being destroyed by the negative increases as the end of the analysis draws near. Maldonado considers that an unconscious counter-transference collusion on the part of the analyst is more important in the impasse situation than in the negative therapeutic reaction.

In my experience, the wish to be one with the object and not to separate from it is frequently involved in the negative therapeutic reaction. I have seen many analysands retreat repetitively after making progress, because progress represented intolerable loss and separation, according to the material of the dreams and associations. In some analysands, the unconscious wish not to separate from the object was manifested by the persistence of attachments to objects or object-substitutes that were particularly resistant to change. In other analysands, the fear that progress might entail the irretrievable loss of the object is connected with a need for omnipotent control and domination of the object, which may find expression in a somatic illness or an accident. The somatic lesion then has the significance that the analysand, in a split-off part of his ego, unconsciously continues to be one with the object and not to separate from it, under the dominion of the death instinct and of instinctual defusion, as I have shown in a paper on the subject (J-M. Quinodoz, 'Implications cliniques du concept psychanalytique de pulsion de mort', 1989c).

The problems of the infantile psychical trauma

An analysand suffering from excessive separation anxiety often reports a real event − separation from the bosom of the family in early infancy, a real loss, or loss of the love of a parent or of a significant person in his circle − to which he ascribes his anxiety. 'Since he or she went away, nothing has gone right for me,' we are told.

In analysis, this event may be presented in different ways by the analysand. He may speak of it as a shock in the crude state, from which he cannot recover, which comprehends past, present and future and paralyses his ability to think. In a word, the analysand presents himself as the victim of a trauma in almost pure form, in which it is impossible to distinguish the contribution of phantasy from that of reality: 'If I am not well, it is because my husband (my wife, or another significant person) abandoned me . . . . It is because my parents abandoned me when I was five years old . . . or it is since so-and-so's death.' In some cases, the analysand is unable even to express his feeling of abandonment and to associate it in words with the separation or an event in his life, such as the loss of a loved person, or with a decisive moment in his existence. He can express this only at infra-verbal level, by acting it out in the present of the transference through reproduction of the situation already experienced in the past: for instance, the analysand may perform meaningful unconscious acts whereby he is liable to make the analyst abandon him in the present, just as he felt abandoned by his parents in the past. In such cases, the analysand often resorts to the mechanism of projective identification by abandoning the analyst, or at least to repeated instances of acting out in which the analyst may feel abandoned, while the analysand is identified with the abandoning person (the analysand arrives late, frequently absents himself, or remains silent during the session, which can also be a form of absence). In other cases, the analysand is more capable of containing his anxiety; he is then able to express in words the suffering resulting from his fear of separation and can more easily distinguish the present from the past, and inside from outside, without feeling swamped by anxiety. The traumatic event may also have been forgotten as a conscious memory and may be acted out in silence, to be remembered only during the course of the analysis.

These traumas raise in psychoanalysis the problem of the relations between external reality and internal or psychical reality; when confronted with them, it is difficult for us to decide what is real and what is phantasy. As we know, Freud's position on this central point changed. His original model was one of mechanistic causality, the appearance of hysterical symptoms in adult life being attributed to a real event in childhood – generally a seduction. Later, realizing that the seduction scene reported by patients was often imaginary and not always real, he arrived at a more comprehensive and more complex conception of the relations between external reality and psychical reality and between present and past. This psychoanalytic conception takes account of the 'traumatic situation' in its totality, in which phantasies predominate (Freud 1926d).

To sum up the present-day psychoanalytic position on the question of trauma, it may be said that what applies to seduction applies equally to the traumatic situation of separation. Just as, in seduction, the analysand has a memory of a scene which he believes to be real but which actually existed only in his imagination, there are cases in which the abandonment event reported by the analysand does not correspond to a reality on the level of actual events but to an imaginary scene belonging to his own psychical reality, or else to a real scene which is in itself trivial but which subsequently became traumatic by virtue of frightening phantasies projected on to it. However, there are, of course, also cases in which there is no doubt about the real abandonment, but ultimately, even in such a case, it is always the phantasy element which is decisive and which makes the experience 'traumatic' or otherwise. The expanded concept of the infantile psychical trauma, including both actual experiences *and* phantasies, thus assigns a central role to psychical life and to phantasies. This may be observed, for example, in children who have to be placed in isolation in hospital: some exhibit more or less severe regressions at the separation from the family environment, while others are capable of tolerating the separation; this raises the question of the influence of the phylogenetic factor, as pointed out by Guillaumin (1989). The state of orphanhood may sometimes even constitute an existential stimulus (Rentschnick 1975).

It may be added that there is no such thing as a traumatic situation in which objects and object relations are not involved, and that the tendency to repeat the trauma entails a relationship of identification with the object of the loss (Andréoli 1989). As Baranger *et al.* (1988) put it:

> The anxiety-inducing object, by virtue of its internal or external presence, of its hyperpresence, is always subjectively present, insofar as it is always possible to attribute the trauma to someone who failed to do what ought to have been done, or who did what ought not to have been done.
>
> (1988: 123)

The psychoanalytic concept of the traumatic situation inserted into object relations, in which a dialectic causality between past and future structures the present, makes the therapeutic action of psychoanalysis possible. If it were not possible to retrace our steps along this backward path and thereby reconstitute the trauma, we should not be able to modify the course of our personal history.

An example of the compulsion to repeat a traumatic situation

The following clinical example will help us to understand the nature of the problem of a traumatic separation situation, as presented by an analysand, and to see how it can be worked through in the transference relationship.

I remember Paul, an analysand who despaired because he systematically caused himself to be dismissed by his employers in his professional life, and also by women in his love life. Paul would describe these events without being aware that he himself had any part in these dismissals. He had few memories of his childhood, except that he was annoyed with his mother, and also with his father, who had

139

been the first employer to give him the sack. Yet Paul's enterprises, both professional and emotional, always began with excellent prospects, but suddenly everything became spoilt and he did not know why. He was therefore afraid of the future, and this was why he had come to me for analysis.

Paul embarked upon his analysis with interest and commitment. After a year, however, he began to tell me that his work more and more often prevented him from coming to sessions, and that there were imperative professional obligations to which he had to give precedence over his analysis. He began to miss sessions frequently. Paul never gave me advance warning of his absences; he would tell me on his way out through the door at the end of the session, as if his absences had nothing to do with his analysis. When I brought up the subject during the session, he would reply that it was a matter of professional obligations which concerned him only, and had nothing to do with me. Having regard to the difficulty, and indeed the impossibility, of bringing this conflict into the relationship between us, I began to feel more and more irritated by Paul's absences, and by his threats to break off the analysis, which were becoming increasingly frequent. I felt my anger gradually rising within me, and in view of Paul's seeming lack of interest in our work, I began to think that he might do better to devote himself to his profession and that he should make a choice: either to come regularly to his sessions or to give up the analysis.

I then realized that I was in the process of allowing myself to be caught up in his unconscious game, and that I was running the risk of dismissing him, in exactly the same way as his successive bosses or girl-friends. It became clear to me at this point that Paul was in the process of unconsciously projecting on to me the image of a boss who was threatening to give him the sack: the risk of dismissal did not come from me but in fact from himself, and he was *doing* something unwittingly in order to induce me to dismiss him. I interpreted this to him from various different aspects, showing him how he was acting indirectly on me without being aware of it, turning me into an angry boss who was likely to dismiss him, or a girl-friend who would reject him, that this was a repetition of a form of behaviour which he acted out with every new relationship of his, and that he had been doing this since his childhood. Paul had the greatest difficulty in discerning any involvement of his own in the timing of his professional meetings which made him miss so many sessions. He was convinced that the other party 'just happened to' impose on him times that coincided with his sessions, which he accepted without protest, thereby performing an unconscious act that translated into action his secret wish to be given the sack by me.

140

This transference conflict was extremely trying, as it represented a struggle between himself (or at least a part of himself, for he continued to come) and myself over which would prevail: phantasy or reality. During this period, at the end of almost every session, Paul told me that he would not be coming tomorrow, adducing a fresh argument drawn from 'reality'. I was often impressed by the realism of his grounds for not coming again, and I sometimes felt quite impotent with my interpretations, when confronted with the compelling 'reality' situation. One day, Paul told me that he had accepted a new job and that he was going to move to a place 300 kilometres away on the very next day. Instead of yielding to the wave of discouragement which threatened to overcome me, I interpreted to him once again that he was acting out his wish to be abandoned by me, and at the end of the session I said to him: 'Goodbye, see you tomorrow', while at the same time thinking that if he was really moving away on the following day, I would never see him again. The next day, notwithstanding his shattering announcement, Paul came along to his session punctually and told me a dream whose subject was abortion, and I never again heard him talk about moving away.

This significant dream awakened a memory in him: as a child, he had several times been told by his mother that she had tried to interrupt her pregnancy while she was carrying him, and that, on the day Paul was born, she had said she did not want this child. We realized from this memory associated with the abortion dream that, by threatening to break off his analysis, Paul was unconsciously turning me into an analyst-mother who was trying to get rid of her analysand-child. All this incidentally rekindled Paul's rage towards his mother, which he ascribed to this rejection, and he began to accuse her of having ruined his life, forgetting that, although his mother had sometimes tended to reject her son, she had nevertheless been a loving and caring mother. Paul also became capable of expressing his anger and grievances, not only towards his family but also towards me and 'the analysis', so that the threats to break off the analysis in reality were superseded by verbal threats, which it was possible to interpret and work through. Paul also came to understand that he himself played an active part in these dismissals and, by analysing his relations with his father, he became conscious that his father had done everything possible to keep him, until Paul himself had forced him to send him away. He realized that it was exactly the same with women, who eventually left him, because he repetitively projected into each the image of a mother interrupting her pregnancy.

By becoming increasingly conscious of his phantasies and their impact on reality, Paul gained a better perception of the external world and of his internal world, and of the relations between reality and phantasies. He could distinguish better what belonged to the past and to the present, and what had to do with the compulsion to repeat a traumatic situation, in which we shall never know to what extent reality is involved. Paul also realized that the hate for his mother, as long as it was connected with a situation felt to be traumatizing, had prevented him from imagining her at the same time as a loving and loved mother, and that the same applied to his feelings towards his father.

9

Acting out and separation anxiety

'Les hommes, dit le petit prince, ils s'enfournent dans des rapides, mais ils ne savent plus ce qu'ils cherchent. Alors ils s'agitent et tournent en rond . . .'

'You know', said the Little Prince, 'people throng into express trains, but then they forget what they are looking for. Then they get excited and go round in circles . . .'

Antoine de Saint-Exupéry, *Le Petit Prince*, p. 80

Close links

This chapter is concerned with the close links between separation anxiety and acting out. I should point out that I am here using the term 'acting out' in its original sense, as defined by Laplanche and Pontalis (1967: 4), without distinguishing between acting in and acting out as some authors have done. While there is a relatively substantial body of psychoanalytic literature on the various aspects of acting out, contributions on acting out as a manifestation of separation anxiety are far less numerous considering how common this phenomenon is. This is surprising, as clinical experience shows that the frequency of acting out increases particularly at the time of between–session, weekend and holiday breaks, and especially in the event of an unforeseen interruption such as a missed session.

I believe that the relationship between separation, acting out and transference is so obvious and familiar to us psychoanalysts that most of us are accustomed to interpret it in our practice without paying attention to certain technical and theoretical aspects of these phenomena.

Analysts, after all, conventionally interpret acting out as a sign of the emergence of the repressed and, when it occurs in relation to the transference, as 'a basic refusal to acknowledge this transference'

143

(Laplanche and Pontalis 1967: 4), but they disregard its timing. If account is taken of the timing, acting out proves, by virtue of its intensity and frequency, to be one of the principal manifestations of separation anxiety in the treatment.

For this reason, every instance of acting out, being closely bound up with interruptions in the analytic encounter, contains within itself not only the characteristics of acting out in general but also specific aspects connected with the separation. These will first be examined from the clinical standpoint and then discussed in terms of theory.

Acting out and separation in clinical practice

As a characteristic manifestation of separation anxiety, acting out combines in its expression most of the components of the transference manifestations of separation anxiety as described in the previous chapters. These include: failure to acknowledge the relational link with the analyst, action taking the place of thought, a regressive tendency or even one of psychical disorganization, the use of pre-verbal forms of communication, and the displacement of affects (by projection of hate, attachment, idealization and so on) or parts of the ego (by projective identification) on to a person or persons other than the analyst. All this has the unconscious aim of repressing, and above all disavowing, the separation from the analyst and the associated feelings. In general, when acting out occurs at the time of interruptions in the analytic encounter, its purpose may be said to be primarily defensive; namely, to disavow the affects aroused by repeated separations from the analyst – i.e. psychical pain, anxiety and the entire range of corresponding feelings.

Acting out in connection with separation may not only assume a wide variety of forms but also occur at any point in the treatment, more particularly when there is a discontinuity due to an interruption. For instance, before or after a holiday break, we often find that the analysand arrives late or misses one or more sessions. The analysand may mistake the dates of departure and return, so that he comes back before or after the intended resumption of the sessions, but not on the day and at the time arranged, because he has for unconscious reasons misunderstood the date fixed by the analyst. The analysand may also arrange a business meeting at the time of his session for reasons signifying his wish to find a substitute for the analyst, thereby expressing his dissatisfaction or any of countless other feelings whose unconscious meaning needs to be discovered. Displacements onto persons other than the analyst, suppression of affects and parapraxes are benign responses to separation. However, the consequences of acting out may be more serious where they are expressions of the death instinct and the defusion of instincts: splits and break-ups having damaging effects on the life of the analysand may then occur. For instance, the analysand may cause himself to be dismissed by his partner or his employer, because he unconsciously feels that the analyst has dismissed him; alternatively, the analysand may express his unconscious attachment to and hate for the analyst by an accident (D. Quinodoz 1984) or a physical illness (J-M. Quinodoz 1984, 1985), or by a delusion − all of these being to a greater or lesser degree regressive manifestations of his struggle against separation anxiety.

It is not easy for the analyst to tell whether a given instance of acting out has to do with separation, and what transference significance an analysand's request may have. I recall one female analysand who, whenever sessions resumed after a holiday, would ask me to change the time of the next one or two sessions, so that, for example, she could come in the morning instead of the afternoon, or the afternoon when she normally had a morning session; these changes always drastically disrupted my schedule, and also that of the other analysands. On each occasion she would present me with compelling and seemingly incontrovertible arguments, to do with her work or family, or so at least it appeared at first sight. I needed time and experience before it became possible for me not to fall into the trap of her manifest request. We eventually understood that, beyond the level of words, a request of this kind, coming after my holiday, concealed a latent need, combining affection and aggression, to make me *do* something special for her, to restore her to a predominant position in the midst of my family, because she had felt that I had sent her away.

In his paper entitled 'Separation: a clinical problem', Brenman (1982) drew up an impressive list of the types of separation-related acting out in which an analysand may engage during the treatment:

> He may indulge in loveless sexuality, stuff himself with food, drink, hatred, criticisms and grievances to comfort himself. He may become excessively intrusive or, by virtue of projection, feel excessively intruded into by others. . . . He may contrive menaces that need constant attention, occupy himself with paranoid activity, physical fitness, hypochondriasis and various kinds of masturbation. Separation is not consciously recognized. In order not to experience separation, compulsive attachments take place with various objects; exciting, hateful, idyllic, etc., which require constant pathological attachment to avoid realization of what is missing.
>
> (1982: 14–15)

Brenman here lays emphasis on the masochism and hate-based attachment to objects which deprives these analysands of a 'good enough' relationship. He mentions patients whom he describes as 'separated' in the relationship. He uses the term 'separated' in what seems to me to be an uncommon sense: he does not mean that the subject is separate from the object, but that he is 'separated from a good enough relationship' with the object – i.e. deprived of such a relationship. Brenman also stresses the importance of the analyst's counter-transference ability to cope with his own depression if he is to be able to interpret separation anxiety: this capacity

> can only be established if the analyst keeps his own contact with separation anxiety and withstands the pain of maintaining this course when bombarded with rejection, contempt and reproach and is able to analyse and link these attacks with the experience of separation.
>
> (1982: 23)

When we psychoanalysts interpret acting out in relation to separation, it is helpful for us to conceive of the transference in terms of a total situation. We can then place cases of acting out within the dynamic, constantly evolving pattern of relations between the analysand and the analyst. If we can ascertain the meaning of a given instance of acting out at a particular point in the treatment, we shall then also be able to evaluate how the analysand is using us in the present as an analyst, and shall thereby obtain a snapshot of the current state of his anxieties and object relations, which can then be interpreted in the transference.

Acting out as a search for a psychical container

With the progress of our knowledge of the mechanisms involved in object relations and the transference, it has in the past few years become clearer why acting out is such a frequent consequence of interruptions in the analytic encounter. Bion's (1962) concept of the container–contained, Rosenfeld's (1964b) developments of the concept of projective identification and Grinberg's (1968) work on acting out have contributed decisively to our understanding of the mechanism of acting out at the time of separations from the analyst and to its interpretation.

If the container–contained concept, discussed above in connection with Bion's contributions, is applied to the analytic relationship, it can be thought of as modelled on the mother–child relationship: the analysand seeks in the analyst a container which can receive his projections and return them to him, transformed by his 'capacity for reverie'. At end-of-session and weekend breaks or during holidays, the analysand separates from the analyst and is deprived of him not only as a person but also as a container for his projections. For example, when there is a break, the analysand not only suffers anxiety at the fear of separation from and loss of the analyst, but also no longer has the container he requires to get rid of his psychical pain, because he cannot deposit his projections in the person of the analyst during the break. It is then that acting out occurs. In his paper 'On acting out and its role in the psychoanalytic process' (1968), Grinberg states that acting out takes place within a generally narcissistic relationship, modelled on Bion's container–contained relationship, and that this is why breaks so often give rise to acting out. When the analyst is not there, he notes that 'the analyst's absence is felt to be persecutory because the patient associates it with his aggressive fantasies and fears retaliation' (p. 172). At other times, the analysand does not project the phantasy contents into a person in the external world whom he uses as a substitute in the absence of the container represented by the analyst, but projects them into a part of his own body, which is used as a container: somatic or hypochondriacal symptoms thus arise to contain the concrete 'presence' of the object, which counteracts and cancels out the absence of the analyst while at the same time preserving the intolerable painful affects connected with separation anxiety. Finally, still according to Grinberg, there is a correlation between weekend dreams and acting out: the more the analysand dreams, the less he acts out, and vice versa.

Zac (1968) has made an interesting study of analysands' reactions to the alternation of the 'analytic week' and the 'analytic weekend', pointing out that weekend separations have the significance of losing in the analyst a container for projective identification of pain. According to Zac, since the patient cannot discharge anxiety into the analyst, he finds himself compelled to re-introject it into himself. This he experiences in the form of persecution, as a forced 're-inoculation' with aspects which he has been unable to get rid of because of the analyst's absence. Zac believes that this is what gives rise to acting out, which represents an attempt to find an object in which psychical pain can be deposited. By re-projecting the contents which the ego cannot re-introject into an external object – or an internal object, or a part of the body – he can establish a new equilibrium. In Zac's view, acting out is thus not only a defensive technique but also a 'safety valve', whereby the psychotic parts of the personality can sometimes, but not always, be re-projected in order to avoid psychosis and to protect the non-psychotic part from them.

We also referred earlier to the work of Rosenfeld (1964b), which showed how projective identification is frequently used by borderline and psychotic patients to combat separation anxiety, and is often manifested in acting out. The acting out can in this case be regarded as taking place in the context of an idealized narcissistic relationship, with one or more objects representing one or more substitutes for the analyst, resulting in a confusion between the ego and the object.

In *Culpa y depresión* (1964), Grinberg made an original contribution to the problem of separation and object-loss, showing that mourning and depression give rise to experiences of loss not only of the object but also of aspects of the self. According to Grinberg, mourning is always not only for the lost object but also for the *lost parts of the self* which are deposited by projection in objects, as may be observed, for example, in acting out. Whether this process is normal or pathological depends on whether depressive guilt or persecutory guilt predominates. For this reason, the working through of mourning for the aspects of the self that have thus been lost and dispersed is a precondition for the working through of mourning for the loss of the object, because its success depends on restoration of the sense of identity. These valuable contributions by Grinberg show how our interpretations of separation anxiety must take account not only of object-loss but also of the loss of identity that is closely bound up with losses of aspects of the self: we must therefore demonstrate to our analysand in detail and in a manner designed to promote insight what aspects of the ego are experienced as lost at a given moment in the session, or what link with the object is felt to be lacking in a particular transference context 'here and now'.

Separations, session times and fees

I wish to add a technical rider to the discussion of this subject, by pointing out that acting out connected with separation anxiety is often reflected in failures to adhere to the agreed schedule, such as arriving late for sessions or forgetting to come altogether, as well as in a wide variety of parapraxes, such as miscounting the number of sessions in the payment of fees. All such instances are highly meaningful in terms of the unconscious transference.

In my practice I prefer to arrange matters so that the possible risks of acting out can be analysed while the session is still in progress; for example, by choosing to impart any communications or announcements at the beginning of the session, if possible with an ample period of notice. Similarly, I would rather have the analysand pay his bill at the beginning of a session, so that, where applicable, we can work *in statu nascendi* on the unconscious meaning of the separation-related transference phantasies contained in this type of acting out, whereby the number of sessions or the amount payable are often altered. Every analyst will have found that communications imparted at the end of a session or absences announced at the last minute tend to increase the risk of acting out and do not leave enough time for working through.

10

The psychoanalytic setting and the container function

Le lendemain revint le petit prince.

'Il eût mieux valu revenir à la même heure, dit le renard. Si tu viens, par exemple, à quatre heures de l'après-midi, dès trois heures je commencerai d'être heureux. Plus l'heure avancera, plus je me sentirai heureux. A quatre heures, déjà, je m'agiterai et m'inquiéterai; je découvrirai le prix du bonheur. Mais si tu viens n'importe quand, je ne saurai jamais à quelle heure m'habiller le coeur . . . . Il faut des rites . . .

– Qu'est-ce qu'un rite? dit le petit prince.

– C'est aussi quelque chose de trop oublié, dit le renard. C'est ce qui fait qu'un jour est différent des autres jours, une heure des autres heures.'

The Little Prince returned the next day.

'It would have been better if you had come along at the same time,' said the fox. 'If you come, say, at four o'clock in the afternoon, I shall start feeling happy as soon as three o'clock strikes. As the time passes, the happier I shall feel. By four o'clock, I shall already be getting excited and anxious; I shall discover the price of happiness. But if you come at just any time, I shall never know at what time to get myself into the right frame of mind . . . . We must have rites . . . '

'What is a rite?' asked the Little Prince.

'It is also something that is too often forgotten,' said the fox. 'It is what makes one day different from other days, one time of the day different from other times.'

Antoine de Saint-Exupéry, *Le Petit Prince*, p. 70

The conditions of the psychoanalytic experience

Since separation anxiety occurs in connection with discontinuities in the analytic encounter, it is evident that interpreting it is insufficient for its resolution, but that it is also essential to provide the analysand with a situation and setting in which the psychoanalytic process can take place in the best possible conditions. A satisfactory transference experience calls for particular conditions, which are afforded principally by the establishment and active maintenance of certain constants.

Zac (1968, 1971) considers that some constants are absolute – because they form part of every analytic treatment and are connected with the fundamental hypotheses of psychoanalysis – while others are relative. Some of the absolute constants have to do with the specificity of the transference relationship and the way it unfolds, while others are concerned with the analytic setting which makes that relationship possible. Zac considers the regularity and frequency of the weekly pattern of sessions, their fixed length, the constancy of the analytic venue and the payment of fees to be essential factors in the stability required to facilitate the process of communication between analysand and analyst. In his view, there are two kinds of relative constants: some relate to the analyst himself and have to do with his own personality, his personal and social situation and his allegiance to a particular psychoanalytic school, while others result from specific agreements between the analysand and the analyst – for example, on the level of fees or the length of holidays.

Freud used an empirical approach when he established the optimum form for the conduct of psychoanalytic treatment, with the aim of facilitating its development and minimizing interferences. Psychoanalysts have for decades taken the setting proposed by Freud for granted in their own practice, without considering that there was any need for it to be based on explicit theoretical arguments. On the whole, the analytic situation and its setting have been maintained, even if individual analysts may have disagreed with particular aspects of the setting and disregarded them in their practice, while observing the others. The aspects of the setting relating to the place of sessions, time and money have long been deemed a part of psychoanalytic technique, and there has been more interest in the content of the process than in the significance of the conditions which contain it and contribute to its specificity.

The idea has recently begun to gain currency that we should try to make our identity as analysts increasingly specific in order to arrive at a better definition of ourselves, and we have noticed that this identity necessarily involves an explicit description of the specific setting of analysis and of the function of its various aspects in the unfolding of the process. Since any change in the setting inevitably involves a change in the nature of the process, 'we need to know to which particular setting the entity which we ourselves call analysis best corresponds', as D. Quinodoz (1987a) pointed out, emphasizing the role of the psycho-analytic setting as the 'organ of the container function'. In other words, as Laplanche reminded us in his lecture in Geneva in 1987, it is a matter

151

of knowing what we wish to do with the awesome energy we unleash in establishing the analytic situation: do we want it to explode in an uncontrollable chain reaction, or would we rather channel it in a cyclotron – i.e. in the classical analytic setting?

For this reason, with a view to preserving the essence of the psychoanalyst's identity and transmitting it from generation to generation, the International Psychoanalytical Association recently published the minimum qualifications and requirements deemed essential for future psychoanalysts, laying down specific norms for such aspects as the frequency of sessions (four or five per week) and their length (forty-five to fifty minutes) (*IPA Newsletter*, 1983, 1985; *IPA Brochure*, 1987). In his foreword, R.S. Wallerstein (1987), then President of the IPA, noted that analysis had hitherto 'grown in the manner of the oral tradition', but that it had now become necessary to clarify our consensus more precisely and to codify our common purpose in the form of guidelines. De Saussure (1987) gave her own personal commentary on the criteria used by the working group which had the difficult task of laying down these minimum requirements. In her view, for analysts-to-be, a personal analysis is most likely to succeed in the precise setting of classical psychoanalysis, as this affords ongoing contacts between analysand and analyst on more than half the days in the week and makes possible the development of the type of transference experience which De Saussure describes with great subtlety and sensitivity.

The psychoanalytic setting and the container–contained relationship

An examination of the part played by separation anxiety in the analytic situation seems to me to furnish scientific confirmation of the validity of the classical psychoanalytic setting, having regard to the close links between this type of anxiety on the one hand and the setting and process on the other. A minimum frequency of four or five sessions a week, each lasting forty-five or fifty minutes, at fixed times and distributed evenly throughout the week for most of the year, helps to reduce the already numerous intervals and the reactions to separations, while at the same time allowing the work of analysis to be better contained. A reduction in the frequency of sessions or their length is a constant source of separation anxiety in many analysands who have not sufficiently acquired the sense of continuity possessed by neurotic analysands who are capable of symbolizing absence, and who have a greater need than others to feel contained. An analytic week which includes more days without than with sessions creates a discontinuity that makes it more difficult for the analyst to identify and interpret separation anxiety and for the analysand to work through the complex affective transference processes associated with it.

I personally use a frequency of at least four sessions a week in my analytic practice. On the one hand, I need this condition in order to feel able to cope with the rich diversity of transference conflicts deployed, with a view to their identification and interpretation; and, on the other, I consider that the deepening of the specific emotional and affective experience of psychoanalytic treatment is conditional upon a sufficient frequency of the analysand–analyst encounter. Hanna Segal has repeatedly expressed her conviction that only a frequency of four or five sessions a week can give access to the most hidden and fundamental affective conflicts in the transference, in particular because adequate contact allows the paranoid-schizoid and depressive anxieties which arise in connection with separations to be worked through in detail. Again, if the setting is not preserved as a place dedicated to analytic understanding, the present reality confronting the patient becomes too chaotic and troubled (Segal 1962).

There can be no doubt that the analysand's ability to confront the final separation from the analyst – i.e. the end of the analysis – depends on his capacity to cope with his own anxieties, as well as on the mobility acquired in the transition from paranoid-schizoid anxieties to the depressive position. In my view, as Segal (1988) has shown, the problem of the end of the analysis has to do not only with the disappearance of symptoms and regressive defences but also, and more importantly, with whether the analysand has acquired a sufficient capacity to move from the paranoid-schizoid position to the depressive position, even though the latter is never acquired once and for all. This mobility makes it possible for the analysand to cope with pain, anxiety, loss and separation, so that he can internalize a good affective experience.

PART FOUR

The taming of solitude

Termination of the analysis and separation anxiety

'Ainsi le petit prince apprivoisa le renard.' Et quand l'heure du départ fut proche:

'And so the Little Prince tamed the fox.' And when the time for him to go drew near:

'Ah! dit le renard . . . Je pleurerai.

'Oh!' said the fox . . . 'I shall cry.'

– C'est ta faute, dit le petit prince, je ne te souhaitais point de mal, mais tu as voulu que je t'apprivoise . . .

'It is your fault,' said the Little Prince, 'I did not wish you any harm, but you wanted me to tame you . . . '

– Bien sûr, dit le renard.

'Yes, I did,' said the fox.

– Mais, tu vas pleurer! dit le petit prince.

'But you are going to cry!' said the Little Prince.

– Bien sûr, dit le renard.

'Yes, I am,' said the fox.

– Alors tu n'y gagnes rien!

'So it will not do you any good!'

– J'y gagne, dit le renard, à cause de la couleur des blés.'

'Yes, it will,' said the fox, 'because of the colour of the wheatfields.'

Antoine de Saint-Exupéry, *Le Petit Prince*, p. 70

The question of the termination in psychoanalytic treatment poses a large number of problems at clinical, technical and theoretical level. The relevant debates and round-table discussions have been summarized elsewhere (Firestein 1980). For the sake of conciseness, this chapter will be confined to a discussion of the relations between the end of the analysis and separation anxiety. The place assigned by psychoanalysts to separation anxiety in the process of termination of the analysis varies with the termination 'model' taken as one's reference. If the end of the analysis is regarded as a separation occurring between the analysand and the analyst, the work of mourning will tend to be considered an important component of the transference/counter-transference link.

I personally believe that the analysand's capacity to cope with the work of mourning that precedes, accompanies and follows the termination of the analysis is one of the principal criteria not only of the end of the analysis but also of the psychoanalytic process itself. I also believe that the work of mourning plays an important part in the terminal phase of the treatment, and that its success or failure will substantially determine whether the analysis can be deemed to be finished or, conversely, interminable.

The end of the analysis in Freud

Freud put forward several criteria for termination at different times in his career. The first was that the patient should be capable of work and love. Later, he defined the objective of the treatment as the making conscious of what had been unconscious, in accordance with the first topography. After the introduction of the second topography, he considered that one aim of analysis was to allow the ego to function better in relation to the superego, the id and reality: '*Wo Es war, soll Ich werden*' (Where id was, there ego shall be) (1933a: 80). In 'Analysis terminable and interminable' (1937a), Freud dealt with the problem of the various causes of insuperable resistance to the termination of the treatment – in particular, castration anxiety in men and penis envy in women. In his conception of the end of the analysis, little emphasis is placed on mourning work in the transference as compared with working through, one of his favourite concepts. Freud was presumably not yet in possession of a theory of affects adequate to account for the various stages in the integration of love and hate, such as those, for example, developed later by Abraham and Klein. Again, Freud considered that mourning took place primarily in relation to reality – i.e. as a capacity of the ego to detach itself from the lost object by accepting the reality of the loss, thereby allowing new object-cathexes.

At the beginning of its history, psychoanalysis may be said to have had as its main objective the making conscious of unconscious aspects of the mind by interpretation; later, however, psychoanalysts laid more stress on the analysand–analyst relationship and its transformations, and this has given rise to changes in how the termination of the analysis is viewed.

The principal termination models

Psychoanalysts at present have a number of different conceptions of the processes which take place in the terminal phase of an analysis. Broadly, two opposing conceptions can be distinguished, one of which is concerned almost exclusively with the personality of the analysand while the other concentrates on the analysand–analyst relationship. Various termination 'models' have been described within each of these conceptions, but all of them can be assigned to one or other of these two basic groups.

The psychoanalysts who are interested mainly in the *analysand's personality* try to identify what psychological changes in the analysand can be taken as indicators of the end of the analysis. Most authors consider that symptomatic relief is not in itself a sufficient criterion, and that increasing insight and the lifting of infantile amnesia are better indicators. Other analysts, in particular those belonging to the American school, stress the importance of 'structural' changes in the personality, the resolution of intrapsychic conflicts and the achievement of a psychical equilibrium corresponding to an equal level of harmonious adaptation to reality and to the environment, in accordance with the conceptions of Heinz Hartmann and Anna Freud. Rank (1924) considered that the termination of the analysis was a symbol of birth for each patient.

Later, Balint (1952) was to describe the end of the analysis as a 'new beginning': as the analysand approaches full term, he feels that he is being born to a new life, and this new departure in his existence gives rise to mingled feelings of sadness and hope. For still other analysts, the analysis comes to a natural end, as if by exhaustion of the analysand's conflicts. For instance, Ferenczi (1927) sees the termination as gradual, and virtually spontaneous: 'The proper ending of an analysis is . . . when it dies of exhaustion, so to speak. . . . A truly cured patient frees himself from analysis slowly but surely' (p. 181).

At the end of the analysis, according to Flournoy (1979), the analyst, acting on his own behalf and on that of the absent phallic parent, expresses

> his refusal to play the game of the transference relationship. The terminal interpretation can therefore be seen solely in terms of the absent phallic parent's refusal to take this role. [. . .] The end of the secondary phase thus corresponds to the renunciation of the Oedipal aim. The analyst and the analysand are now merely two persons together in the same room, who have nothing psychoanalytically in common with each other.
>
> (1979: 232–3)

Finally, we may mention the extreme position of some analysts, for whom, at the end of the analysis, the *analyst is no longer anybody* for his analysand, as the transference link is dissolved by the disappearance of the person of the analyst: 'Then the analysand realizes that heaven is empty . . . and if anyone is to know and to know more about, he and no one else is the one' (Roustang 1976: 61).

Lebovici (1980) disagreed with this elimination of the analyst. Like many psychoanalysts, he takes the opposite view, that at the end of the analysis 'the psychoanalyst, far from not being anybody, in fact becomes a person', and that, in this authentic relationship which the analytic relationship has become, neither the patient nor the analyst has any need for the transference neurosis (p. 244).

I personally believe that although the encounter ceases, the relationship between the analysand and the analyst persists, but in internalized form. In my view, maintaining that the analyst is no longer anybody at the end of the analysis has the implication in the analyst's counter-transference of a disavowal of the reality of the separation and of the depressive feelings not only of the analysand but also of the analyst.

In contrast to the above conception, many psychoanalysts lay stress on *the analysand–analyst relationship* in the termination of the analysis, rather than on changes in the personality of the analysand alone. In this view, the final separation from the analyst is deemed to initiate a mourning process, the working through of which is decisive. The final breaking off of the relationship between the two members of the analytic couple constitutes a loss which, when overcome, tends to deepen insight and encourage the capacity for self-analysis. This process is comparable in every respect with normal mourning work, and implies that the analysand has become capable of tolerating solitude without excessive anxiety, of relinquishing omnipotence and the feeling of immortality, of accepting the reality of a finite life span, of accepting the prospect of separation between the analysand and the analyst, and of internalizing the function of the latter. The knowledge acquired through insight will help to reduce the analysand's anxieties and enable him to apply the self-understanding he has acquired to all subsequent experiences. As Grinberg (1980) puts it: 'Analysis does not terminate with the separation of the analyst and the analysand. The only thing which ends is the relationship between them, giving way to a new phase of continuation of the process through self-analysis' (p. 27).

The problems of the transference and the counter-transference are inextricably bound up with the approach of the end of the analysis, and the termination confronts not only the analysand but also the analyst with his own mourning processes. In some cases, the analysand's pathological defences and excessive projections may induce the analyst to respond with counter-transference reactions of anger or rejection, or alternatively cause him to become depressed, to the point of assuming responsibility for the mourning which the analysand cannot tolerate, by the mechanism of projective counter-identification (Grinberg 1980). The analyst may then prolong an analysis or, conversely, bring it to a premature end, for unconscious reasons.

Termination of the analysis and mourning

Successive authors have drawn attention to different aspects of the work of mourning at the end of the analysis. For instance, Annie Reich (1950) observed that the termination of the analysis involved a twofold loss for the analysand: loss of the infantile transference objects, and loss of the analyst as a real person, by virtue of the nature of the analytic relationship itself, its length and its intimacy. Hence the importance of fixing a date for the termination of the analysis several months in advance, in order that mourning for these aspects can be worked through.

The capacity to tolerate solitude is another important aspect of the end of the analysis. André Green (1975) expressed this in one of his typically memorable formulations: 'Perhaps analysis only aims at the patient's capacity to be alone (in the presence of the analyst)' (p. 17), thereby applying Winnicott's idea in original fashion to the aims of analysis.

For Melanie Klein there is a direct correlation between the infantile depressive position, on which psychical organization depends, and the termination of the analysis. In her view, the infantile depressive position is organized primarily around the experience of loss of the breast at weaning, and the experience of termination of the analysis is a reproduction of weaning. In her paper 'On the criteria for the termination of a psychoanalysis' (1950), Klein states that an analysis which takes a satisfactory course will give rise to a mourning situation in relation to the analyst, and that this mourning will re-activate all other instances of mourning in the analysand's life, starting with the prototypical mourning process of weaning.

Segal (1988) notes in a paper on termination that the imminence of the end of the analysis often has the effect of re-awakening old anxieties and defences, although the symptoms may not necessarily recur. She gives the example of a patient who was particularly sensitive to separations during the analysis. In the final phase, this patient was faced with the extremely painful task of working through not only separateness and the separation from the analyst (p. 167), but also the accompanying anxieties and depression. A few weeks before the end of the analysis, the most primitive separation anxieties re-appeared, and the patient became so obsessed by the thought of death that he felt that, if death existed, life was not worth living. Hanna Segal asks whether an analysand who resists the approach of the end of the analysis with such anxieties is ready to terminate. She considers that in this case the decision was correct, because her criterion for termination is not the resurgence of anxieties or symptoms but the psychical mobility that allows defences and anxieties, however primitive, to be contained in dreams, phantasies and the analytic sessions.

> Very broadly I could say that my criterion would be a sufficient move from the paranoid/schizoid position with predominance of splitting, projective identification, and fragmentation to the depressive position, with a better capacity to relate to internal and external objects.
>
> (1988: 173)

In the depressive position, the analysand will have to cope with separateness, conflicts and the integration of hate. He will have to endure loss and anxiety, and to internalize a good experience in order to restore good internal objects, as well as the psychoanalytic function of self-awareness, so that he can learn from experience. Another part of the process of working through is acceptance of the prospect of his own death. The depressive position is never completely resolved, and fluctuations persist throughout life; the main criteria for Hanna Segal are the degree of mobility and the severity of the resulting psychical disturbances.

A criterion for termination

Many analysts consider the transformations of separation anxiety during the course of the treatment to be one of the principal clinical criteria of the analysand's development in relation to the end of the analysis. It is indeed difficult to determine the moment when the objectives may be deemed to have been accomplished and the analysis to be approaching its end. There has been considerable controversy on this point, and the various contributions have shown how difficult it is to determine the appropriate criteria for the end of the analysis (see Firestein's bibliography [1980]). We may also mention the result of the survey of the members of the British Society conducted by Glover before World War II, in which he asked them for their personal termination criteria: he concluded that no one criterion truly stood out from the others, save that of the psychoanalyst's *clinical intuition*, as an indication of the point when the treatment could be terminated (Glover 1955).

Rickman (1950) holds that it is impossible to isolate individual criteria for the end of the analysis, but that a combination of criteria should instead be used, which would together indicate a 'point of irreversibility' beyond which the analysand would be capable of tolerating frustrations without regression or psychical disintegration. Rickman mentions the following component factors: (1) the capacity to remember past and present, to lift infantile amnesia and to work through the Oedipus complex; (2) the capacity for heterosexual genital satisfaction; (3) the capacity to tolerate libidinal frustrations and privations without regressive defences or anxiety; (4) the capacity to work and to tolerate inactivity; (5) the capacity to tolerate aggressive instincts of one's own or of others without losing the love object and without guilt; and (6) the capacity to work through mourning.

For Rickman, the best clues as to the level of integration achieved by the analysand during the treatment are afforded by weekend and holiday breaks. Breaks force transference phantasies to emerge, and changes in the nature of these phantasies faithfully reflect changes in the analysand's object relations. In his view, the determination of a 'point of irreversibility' of this kind does not rule out the clinical intuition of the psychoanalyst in fixing the time for the end of the analysis.

Rickman's paper on the importance of the analysand's reactions to breaks for the evaluation of changes during the treatment paved the way for in-depth research on the relations between separation anxiety and the psychoanalytic process. For instance, Liberman (1967) considered changes in the content of weekend phantasies to be a significant indicator of the development, or otherwise, of the analysand. Grinberg's (1981) study of the relations between the content of dreams during breaks in the analysis and transference phantasies has already been mentioned. Firestein (1980) emphasizes the importance of evaluation of the transference neurosis during breaks in the analysis, especially during holidays, to allow an assessment of the analysand's capacity for autonomy in the absence of the analyst.

In the matter of evaluation of the termination, and indeed any evaluation of the analytic encounter, I share Diatkine's (1988) view that the transference is so complex that it cannot be resolved into a kind of normality:

> In order to evaluate the significance of the ending of the analysis, beyond the experience of object-loss to which the decision to stop meeting regularly may give rise, it is better not to be captivated by too absolute a model of psychical autonomy conforming to

whatever one's conception of normality might be, for normality can never be grasped.

(1988: 811)

Separation anxiety and analysis interminable

Although it may be possible for a psychoanalysis to be terminated for both the analysand *and* the analyst, psychological obstacles do sometimes make it interminable, thus necessitating another analysis in order to achieve a satisfactory termination, as Freud showed in 'Analysis terminable and interminable' (1937c). Among the various obstacles to termination, I believe that excessive separation anxiety in relation to the final separation from the analyst is an important factor in interminability.

The approach of the end of the analysis can, as we have seen, arouse all kinds of anxieties, associated with the fear of depressive pain and loneliness, to such an extent that the work of transference mourning is impeded, thus blocking the way to the new phase of the analysis, that of 'continuing on one's own'. Psychical pain – which Bégoin (1989) distinguishes from anxiety because it masks a more hidden pain – may also be a source of interminability, in his opinion, owing to the risk of the emergence of nuclei of terror corresponding to a threat of psychical death. The end of the analysis may also reawaken anxiety concerning the discovery of the truth about oneself (Grinberg 1980), or cause the analysand to retreat in the face of progress, as in the negative therapeutic reaction, which also causes many analyses to be broken off prematurely.

The analyst must be prepared for the most unexpected reactions when the end of the analysis approaches; in order to identify and interpret them, he must draw on his experience and use his own conception of object relations and the transference as his reference point.

I recall one analysand who denied almost to the very last day the fact that we had arranged a final date for the end of our meetings and that we were going to part. However, he managed to become aware of this just in time to embark on a genuine process of transference mourning. This was a typical example of the disavowal of reality and splitting of the ego described by Freud (1927e, 1940e [1938]); when confronted with an unbearable reality, that of our separation, this analysand's ego split into two, with one part accepting the reality and the other disavowing it. As this satisfactory analysis drew towards its close, I saw this analysand apparently resigned to its forthcoming end, but I could see that he had not really accepted it. It was not until a few days before the date set for the end of the analysis that the disavowal emerged in all its force:

> Until today, I always thought that you had set a date for the end of the analysis only to put me to the test, that you did not really believe in it yourself, and that it was a bad joke on your part; I imagined that you would put off this date at the last minute. . . . It is only today that I realize that you really mean it.

We parted a few days later, but because we had talked about it, we were able at the eleventh hour to lift this disavowal and split, which had been used as a repetition of former defence mechanisms, re-activated at the end of the analysis.

It should, however, be noted that the fear of the end of the analysis not only has its effects during the terminal phase of the analysis but is in fact present from the beginning. From the very first contact, the analysand-to-be may express his anxiety about the end of the analysis: 'If I begin with you, I am afraid that I shall never be able to leave you.' The analyst, too, cannot avoid wondering, right from the time of the preliminary interviews, about the capacity of the analysand-to-be to cope with the termination. Anxiety about the end of the analysis is sometimes so intense that, after an initial contact, the person asking for analysis decides not to commit himself to an analytic relationship which is destined to come to an end, as if expressing the idea that life is not worth living because death will inevitably supervene one day.

Conversely, an analysand-to-be sometimes asks for analysis with the declared aim of successfully working through the separation of the end of the analysis. I have had more than one analysand who was aware of his difficulty in forming lasting personal relationships and who hoped that the relationship that would be forged with me would enable him to prepare to overcome the separation of the end of the analysis and to clarify his relational problems.

But what is the meaning of 'overcoming separation'? This will be the subject of the final chapter.

The capacity to be alone, buoyancy and the integration of psychical life

'Adieu, dit le renard. Voici mon secret. Il est très simple: on ne voit bien qu'avec le coeur. L'essentiel est invisible pour les yeux.

– L'essentiel est invisible pour les yeux, répéta le petit prince, afin de se souvenir.'

'Goodbye,' said the fox. 'Here is my secret. It is very simple: you can only see properly with the heart. The essence of things is invisible to the eyes.'

'The essence of things is invisible to the eyes,' repeated the Little Prince, to be sure of remembering it.

Antoine de Saint-Exupéry, *Le Petit Prince*, p. 72

Taming solitude

One of the aims of analysis is for the analysand to discover or re-discover in himself feelings which excessive anxiety about separation and object-loss may have prevented him from acquiring or caused him to lose: the feeling of autonomy and psychical freedom, internal strength and continuity, trust in himself and other people, and the capacity to love and be loved – in a word, a whole complex of feelings which characterizes what we call psychical maturity, summed up so aptly by Winnicott (1958) as the acquisition of a capacity to be 'alone in the presence of someone' (p. 32). For Winnicott, there are two forms of solitude during the course of development, a primitive form at an immature stage and a more elaborate form:

> Being alone in the presence of someone can take place at a very early stage, when the *ego immaturity is naturally balanced by ego-support* from the mother. In the course of time the individual introjects the ego-supportive mother and in this way becomes able to be alone without frequent reference to the mother or mother symbol.
>
> (1958: 32)

Contrasting with feelings of anxiety, this capacity to experience solitude as a replenishment of one's wellsprings, in relation to oneself and to other people, appears when the presence of the absent object is internalized. This progressive process of internalization is the specific result of the working through of repeated experiences of separations followed by reunions. During the course of infantile development, as in the psychoanalytic process, successive separations from the important person constantly rekindle the fear that the loss of the good object in external reality might also cause the internal good objects to be lost. The threat of this loss re-awakens the characteristic anxieties of the infantile depressive position, according to Melanie Klein, with the accompanying affects of sadness and mourning for the external and internal objects. Only positive experiences are capable of offsetting these internal beliefs that the object is lost as a result of phantasies of destruction. During the psychoanalytic process, the succession of experiences of separation followed by reunions gives rise to a work of mourning which will be overcome by means of reality testing, confirming that the destructive phantasies have not come true and reinforcing trust in good internal and external objects. The setting up of a good object within the ego then bears witness to the acquisition of an 'ego strength' that has become sufficient to tolerate the absence of the object without excessive anxiety, thereby subsequently allowing the sadness at the inevitable losses encountered in external reality to be overcome.

The appearance of this inner feeling was described by Freud; for instance, in the little boy who was afraid of the dark and who said he felt relieved to hear his aunt's voice: 'If anyone speaks, it gets light' (1905d: 224). Later, when in 1926 Freud came to examine the conditions for the allaying of anxiety, he was to note that repeated experiences of satisfaction reassure the child, soothe his anxiety and develop in him a 'nostalgic' cathexis of the mother, a token of an internal sense of security. According to Freud, the factor on which the capacity to cathect new objects and assign them their full value depends is the ability to mourn for lost objects: 'Transience value', says Freud (1916a), 'is scarcity value in time. Limitation in the possibility of an enjoyment raises the value of the enjoyment.'

A similar development gradually takes place in the course of psychoanalytic treatment, and we can observe in the analysand the effects of the progressive internalization of the analyst's presence on ego structure and object relations. These changes correspond to the installation of the good – which does not mean idealized – object in the internal world in symbolic form and an identification with it, accompanied by what amounts to a reorganization of psychical life in its relations with internal and external reality. Different authors use different terminologies: acquisition of the constancy of the object (A. Freud, M. Mahler); early internalization (W.W. Meissner, in Lax *et al.* 1986); 'being alone in the presence of someone' (Winnicott 1958); or integration of psychical life (Klein 1963).

Introjection of the good object as the foundation of integration

A number of factors contribute to integration of the feeling of solitude and to making it tolerable. Analysis of defences and object relations in phantasies and reality allows the analysand to distinguish better between the external and internal reality of the object, reducing the tendency to project and thereby putting the analysand more in touch with psychical reality. Among the factors relevant to integration, a crucial part is played by affective factors such as the synthesis of love and hate. It is this that makes the difference between 'a solitude that replenishes the wellsprings' and a 'solitude that destroys', as Dolto (1985) puts it.

Melanie Klein considers that integration is the outcome of the resolution of the love–hate ambivalence that appears in the depressive position, and that it is based entirely on introjection of the good object. *Satisfactory integration has the effect of attenuating hatred by love and of mitigating the violence of the destructive instincts.* In her paper 'On the sense of loneliness', Klein (1963) says that the sense of loneliness stems from the nostalgia of having suffered an irreparable loss, of having irrecoverably lost the happiness of the primitive relationship with the mother. This sense of loneliness, which is based on the paranoid-schizoid position, gradually diminishes with the establishment of the depressive position and the progress of psychical integration. However, it is impossible to achieve complete and permanent integration, and a painful sense of loneliness may recur at any time, when trust in the good part of oneself is lost (1963: 302–3). Among the internal and external factors which make the sense of loneliness tolerable, Klein considers that ego strength derives from the security resulting from the internalization of the good object: 'A strong ego is less liable to fragmentation and therefore more capable of achieving a measure of integration and a good early relation to the primal object' (1963: 309).

Identification with the good object also diminishes the harshness of the superego and, when a happy relationship with the primal object becomes established, the conditions for giving and receiving love are satisfied. For Klein, *loneliness, if it is actually experienced, becomes a stimulus towards object relations* (p. 311).

Transference and the psychotic and non-psychotic parts of the personality

I have tried to emphasize throughout this book that the specific conflicts of separation and object-loss are different in nature from neurotic conflicts, which are symbolic. What makes the concept of the integration of psychical life so important and enables us to account for the degree of cohesion of the ego, which may be disturbed to a greater or lesser extent according to the relevant psychopathology, is the part played by the primitive defences in response to this type of anxiety. This is because conflicts connected with separation and object-loss confront the ego with a reality – both external and internal – that is experienced as intolerable, and the ego defends itself against such a conflict not only by repression but also by disavowal. As Freud has shown, the disavowal of internal and external reality gives rise to a split within the ego itself, which divides into one part that disavows the reality and another part that accepts it. Since a conflict of this type affects the very structure of the ego, it is resolved otherwise than by the lifting of repression which characterizes the resolution of neurotic conflicts. This is also emphasized by Klein (1963) when she points out that splitting is essential to the security of the infant but may subsequently contribute to ego fragmentation and insecurity if the tendency towards integration is insufficient (p. 300).

To return to the psychoanalytic process, in very general and simplified terms we may say that the resolution of conflicts involving a disavowal and a splitting of the ego takes place in two stages: the first, by way of analysis of the transference, entails reduction of the splits, lifting of the disavowal and analysis of love–hate ambivalence in order to reduce psychical fragmentation and improve ego cohesion; while in the second, once the splits have been reduced and better communication between the different parts of the ego has been achieved, these conflicts can be analysed from the point of view of repression and their symbolic meaning.

In clinical practice, however, the situation is infinitely more complex, and is rendered all the more difficult to grasp in that the two modes of psychical functioning are juxtaposed in constantly varying proportions: while disavowal and splitting predominate in a larger or smaller part of the ego, repression preponderates in its other part. This particular psychical structure of the personality, which corresponds to the conflict resulting from a splitting of the ego (Freud 1940e [1938]), has given rise to the development of the concept of psychotic and non-psychotic parts of the personality (Bion 1957). This concept enables us to understand this type of intrapsychic conflict and to interpret it when it is reproduced in the transference relationship with the analyst.

During the psychoanalytic process, both the psychotic and the non-psychotic parts become the object of the constant projections and introjections which reflect the fluctuations of the transference. Symbolic interpretations of transference phantasies allow simultaneous contact with both levels of psychical functioning, so that disavowal and splitting can be reduced at the same time as repression is lifted.

The idea of a 'double transference' in which a 'narcissistic' transference coexists with a 'neurotic' transference, coupled with a view of the psychoanalytic process in its function of reducing the dominion of the manic defence, is extremely valuable in allowing us to take account in the transference of splitting and disavowal on the one hand and repression on the other, so as to develop the integrative tendencies of the ego and induce a 'return of the disavowed' (Manzano 1989). These structural changes should in my opinion be identified and interpreted in relation both to the overall development of the psychoanalytic process and to the rapid and instantaneous modifications observed during the session.

An example of the feeling of integration

I should like to give an impression of this trend towards integration by quoting a female analysand close to the end of her analysis, who expresses it extremely well in very simple language (*my personal inner reflections are given in square brackets*).

'For a long time', she told me, 'I thought that my difficulties were my mother's or my father's fault. Now that I am becoming aware of these matters and accept that I also have something to do with them, it is more difficult, but I can look at events and myself in a different way, and I am able to know myself better, to interpret things better and to understand better.' [*The reduction of projection in favour of a return to the self gives rise to a personal sense of responsibility which is admittedly painful, but which improves relations with internal and external reality.*] 'I shall try to find strength within myself', she continued, 'and if I ever fail, I shall say that it is my fault and not that other people are to blame, because you cannot change your environment the way you would like. Up to now I always wanted my environment to be different, and I told myself that this was the key. But I am discovering that my way of understanding reality is the result of my perception: my perceptions belong to me, I am the result of these inner conflicts, I am not manipulated, my struggles belong to me and it is not the environment that triggers them in me. That way, it is also easier, it is as if I were better armed.' [*The renunciation of omnipotence paradoxically increases her effectiveness: conflicts are no longer dealt with by imagining that everything is possible but on the basis of distinguishing between what is possible and what is not – a distinction that comes about with an increased awareness of our own limits.*] 'What amazes me', said the analysand, 'is that you can give me a positive image of myself, whereas I am merciless towards myself: it is as if you were protecting me from myself, and slowly leading me to see myself differently; this works because you do it gradually; when I get there, I am ready to accept it; your interpretations reflect back to me a good image of myself which surprises me. I feel that I am lucky, it could be quite different, the person with whom you take a different look at yourself is important. The work we do here will determine everything else: who I shall be later on, my way of reacting and interpreting. I shall keep all that inside me. When you give me a good image of myself, I feel fuller, I feel able to start taking responsibility for what happens, to manage myself better, and not always to project outside what I don't like; I can grow and manage my internal world better.' [*Note how integration is bound up with the introjection of a good, non-idealized object with which one identifies, thus strengthening trust in oneself and other people, by diminishing the violence of the destructive and self-destructive instincts.*] 'Yet my fears have not disappeared', she added; 'when there is a break, I am still afraid of no longer being able to cope with it, of tumbling out of control, of no longer being able to find enough strength in myself and clear-headedness; it is not easy to be clear-headed.' [*The aim of analysis is not, of course, to get rid of anxiety altogether, which would be the fulfilment of an omnipotent, manic wish, but to acquire an increased ability to contain anxiety, psychical pain and the feeling of loneliness.*] 'When I feel an inner void', the analysand continued, 'I have also realized that I am behaving in a way that may perhaps have been set off in my childhood, but now it is I who am setting it off: I then feel that I am identifying with the mother of my childhood.' [*She is beginning to be able to distinguish better between past and present: the past is no longer the acted-out repetition of unconscious events experienced in childhood but becomes memory, while the present belongs to us.*] 'I noticed that I had unwittingly identified with my mother,' she went on, 'I thought I had expelled her and got rid of her, and now I am discovering that I had identified with her, that the anxieties I had were also hers, that my fear of loneliness was also hers; she used to feel excluded, and I also felt excluded.' [*The 'identification'*

171

mentioned by the analysand is really more an introjection – i.e. the internalization of an object with which she had merged in a split-off part of the ego (here she had merged with her mother: 'I was my mother'); the diminution of projections in favour of increased internalization will gradually bring about a better differentiation between the ego and the object, thereby allowing the establishment of post-Oedipal introjective identifications characteristic of the working through of the Oedipal conflict.] After a silence, the analysand brought the session to an end as follows: 'I would really like to become myself again.'

To take account of the quality of the changes that represent the phases of integration of psychical life, aspects of which may be witnessed in this analysand, and to demonstrate the new equilibrium which becomes established in the relations between the ego and objects, I have introduced the concept of 'buoyancy', which I shall now discuss.

From separation anxiety to buoyancy

With the progress of the analysis, as we have seen, the manifestations of separation anxiety are reduced in intensity and frequency because the quality of the transference relationship evolves and changes. Among the many aspects of the new feelings which arise from these transformations, I should like to draw attention to a quality of buoyancy of the internalized object, which can be observed in analysands who reach this stage of psychical integration and equilibrium, which, however, not all attain. This sensation of buoyancy is perceived by analysand and analyst alike as a gain in autonomy relative to dependence, and as an affirmation of the identity of the analysand, who feels himself becoming truly himself, thus auguring well for termination of the analysis. I use this quality of buoyancy of the internalized object to denote the analysand's pleasurable sensation of managing to 'fly with his own wings' because he feels that he has acquired a self-supporting capacity that makes him independent of the object which he needed until then in order to 'be carried'. It is a new and complex sensation, in which joy mingles with a little fear, accompanied by the feeling of finally being oneself, of knowing that one can govern oneself while being aware of one's limits in time and space, and of perceiving the comings and goings of the object therein without excessive anxiety. The novelty and pleasure of this impression of being able to 'carry oneself' instead of depending on the object gives rise to a sense of jubilation, which also appears in particular dreams of taking wing or flying, which have an integrative quality, as we shall see below. However, this jubilation is not without its shadow side; it is associated with sadness, because it implies an awareness that our life and that of the object have a beginning and an end, the perception of our own death and the ephemeral character of the object, and the fact that the relationship with the analyst will also have an end. Buoyancy in my sense therefore has nothing omnipotent or manic about it.

This feeling of succeeding in 'flying with one's own wings' appears simple and, when noticed by the analysand or the analyst, tends to be experienced as a matter of course. However, like all vital processes which lead to satisfactory functioning, it is perceived at the time when it is discovered, and afterwards no further notice is taken of it. Buoyancy marks the culmination of slow and infinitely complex processes which cannot readily be grasped, and belongs to the category of emotions that are so familiar and yet so little known, to which Freud was referring when he wrote of the 'affective state, although we are also ignorant of what an affect is' (1926d: 132). It is just as difficult to describe an affect as it is to describe a musical or visual sense impression.

This hypothesis of the gradual acquisition of a feeling of buoyancy during the course of the analysis came to me as a result of various observations.

Like any psychoanalyst, I observed that the interruptions in the encounter between analysand and analyst that recur day after day, week after week and during holidays, as well as the end of the analysis, are experienced as so many instances of 'letting go' of the analysand by the analyst, with a twofold meaning. On the one hand, these lettings-go may be experienced with anxiety as so many abandonments – and may be represented in dreams of falling giddily – while on the other hand they may be experienced as meaning that the analyst has confidence in the analysand's autonomy and expects the analysand to find within himself the resources he thinks only the analyst has.

I once had a female analysand who reacted very powerfully to separations, with manifestations of despair or rage or clamorous somatic symptoms. However, quite often during the last session before a break, she would interrupt her protestations to tell me that she also knew that she had confidence in herself and her own resources in order to cope with anxiety during my absence. This analysand was thereby expressing a whole range of affects connected with the depressive position, working through her unconscious guilt and feeling gratitude and a wish to make reparation to me after her attacks on me. Yet I believe that my analysand was feeling something more: leaving her meant not only dropping her but also having confidence in her and letting her 'fly with her own wings'.

It is important to emphasize this in interpretations, because too often one tends to interpret in terms of defence – the fear of the analyst's dropping the analysand – rather than in terms of the positive feeling that is acquired through the experience. When the analysand notices the possibility of assuming his independence, he is sometimes held back by fear that this impulse might be construed as an abandonment by him of the analyst. He might then be running the risk of *confusing independence from the object with indifference towards it*. It is valuable for the analyst to make him feel that taking wing does not mean doing without the object. The analysand does indeed retain a relationship with the object, but its quality is different: the freedom he grants the other becomes a token of trust and a condition of object love. The analyst, for his part, may experience resistances in accepting his analysand's autonomy, but it is often necessary for him to express through his interpretations the positive character of this impulse towards independence.

I also have a second reason for postulating a quality of buoyancy. This is my observation of its insufficiency in many psychopathological conditions and its collapse in depressive states where the individual seems to have lost this self-supporting capacity and feels an increased need to depend on both external and internal objects. I believe that a number of symptoms described as the collapse of the ego, which are characteristic of depression, in fact have to do with the collapse of buoyancy, which is in turn connected with the loss of the supporting qualities of the internalized object: this is how I see the symptom of inhibition, the so-called lack 'of will power' – i.e. the inability of the depressive to get moving and adopt a particular direction, because he does not know who he is and what he wants for himself – the kind of feeling expressed by the phrase 'I feel reduced to a jelly'.

In addition to the psychical fragmentation associated with splitting and the crumbling of the cement which holds the subject's thoughts together, the feeling of ego loss brought about by loss of the object results in the disappearance of the feeling of being held, of being supported above the crests and troughs, and the appearance of the feeling of being at the mercy of the waves.

In describing the melancholic's inhibition in 1917, Freud had used different words to express the collapse of the ego characteristic of depression: some of these stress the moral abasement corresponding to self-depreciation and self-criticism (*er erniedrigt sich*, translated in the Standard Edition by 'he abases himself' [p.247]), while others seem to me to lay more emphasis on the collapse of the ego, its 'downfall' and impoverishment (*eine ausserordentliche Herabsetzung seines Ichgefühls, eine grossartige Ichverarmung* [*GW* 1917e, 10: 431], rendered in the Standard

Edition by 'an extraordinary diminution in his self-regard, an impoverishment of his ego on a grand scale' [p. 246]). The words chosen by Freud in his own language probably convey the idea of the prostration of the ego more eloquently than the English (and French) translation. In my view, subtle distinctions can legitimately be drawn between the forms of abasement of the ego, one of these corresponding to the loss of buoyancy, in my sense, and the other to the moral abasement of the sadism of the superego turned against the ego.

In the depressive, the attack on both the external and the internal object has the effect of destroying the supporting qualities of the good object, which finds itself disavowed and stripped of this function that belongs to the benevolent quality of the post-Oedipal superego. The lack of self-support that follows the loss of buoyancy gives rise to a regression to infantile dependence on substitutive objects. In analytic treatment, the depressive finds it more necessary than any other patient to experience the buoyancy of the analyst in order to recover and internalize his own capacity for self-support.

Whatever the analysand's level of development or psychopathology, he is confronted with the alternating pattern of separations and encounters that recur regularly and constantly throughout psycho-analytic treatment. In this way the analysand can gradually internalize the presence of the analyst, on the model of the experience of the child who internalizes the reliability of the mother's presence by way of the repetition of her disappearance followed by her reappearance (Freud 1926d), or in the game with the reel or the mirror which represent the mother (Freud 1920g). The quality of buoyancy is acquired through a similar process of internalization connected with the supporting capacity of the analyst and with his reliability, as expressed in, for instance, the reliability of the analytic setting. End-of-session, weekend and holiday breaks – provided that they take place within a stable and continuous setting – often give the analysand a chance to have the experience of being able to 'support himself' and to share the pleasure of this discovery with the analyst.

I shall now try to describe what I consider to be the exact nature of the affect of buoyancy as it may appear in the relationship with the analysand when he reaches this stage of integration – which is not always attained – and to examine its meaning from different points of view.

The result of a dynamic equilibrium

Buoyancy in the sense in which I use the word is the result of a dynamic equilibrium which is constantly re-established and never acquired once and for all. I do not see buoyancy as a static equilibrium, like the support of a foundation, for example.

It might be thought that a person who succeeds in acquiring a capacity to tolerate separation anxieties feels sure of himself because he has become stable and solid. On the contrary, in my view buoyancy gives a person a dynamic psychical equilibrium, so that he not only dominates the movement but works together with it, just as a surfer draws energy from the waves. What, we may ask ourselves, are the factors that make for the sense of dynamic equilibrium which underlies the feeling of buoyancy? I believe that it is substantially the de-idealization of the object and the forgoing of omnipotence that create favourable conditions for a mobility of psychical life whereby the analysand can find his buoyancy: he then becomes aware of his instability in an internal and external world that is fundamentally in a state of flux, realizing his own vulnerability and the need to depend on his own reliability and not only on someone else's. We saw in the clinical example given above how the analysand achieved buoyancy for herself only when she relinquished omnipotence because she recognized her limits, allowing her to distinguish better between the possible and the impossible and thereby to become more efficient.

In her paper 'Vertigo and object relationship', D. Quinodoz (1990) showed how each form of vertigo and the equilibrium corresponding to it are located at the intersection of the immutable and the changing: a person who no longer suffers from vertigo finds his security not in the static or immutable but in the ability to move along with the flux resulting from de-idealization and the forgoing of omnipotence. Conversely, the symptom of vertigo appears in immobility and in the instantaneous when frozen by the phantasy of omnipotence.

The search for a dynamic equilibrium lasts a lifetime, because this equilibrium is never acquired once and for all; it demands constant attention in order to 'feel' the movement, so that the necessary 'trim corrections' can be made immediately, allowing equilibrium to be progressively restored – an equilibrium which we know to be constantly threatened because ever changing. Omnipotence is anti-buoyancy, because it gives rise to a freeze-frame image and not to movement, taking its fixity from idealization. In this respect omnipotence – which belongs to the manic defence – seems to me to be a manifestation of the death instinct, whereas buoyancy is an expression of the life instinct.

Becoming oneself and becoming responsible for oneself

Buoyancy in my sense is also the expression of an awareness of personal responsibility: 'I feel able to start taking responsibility, to manage myself better . . . not always to project outside what I do not like,' the analysand I quoted earlier told me. This sense of personal responsibility stems primarily from the feeling of becoming master of oneself, an impression of unity corresponding to the return to the ego of parts hitherto scattered 'outside the ego' in objects and confused with them. Projection of parts of the ego – exacerbated in the struggle against separation anxiety and object-loss – gives rise not only to an impoverishment of the ego but also to an unconscious dependence on external objects which make the subject feel 'manipulated' by other people, whereas he is in fact manipulated by himself in an unconscious narcissistic relationship, through the phantasy of projective identification.

The reversal of the tendency to project and its replacement by the opposite tendency to internalize – which is very conspicuous in the example given above – is like a throwing of the entire mechanism of the functioning of psychical life into reverse: 'For a long time I felt that my difficulties were the fault of my mother or my father, or of someone else,' the analysand said. 'Now I am becoming aware of these matters and accept that I also have something to do with them, it is more difficult, but I can look at events and myself in a different way.' The ego's recovery of the hitherto split-off and projected parts strengthens the feeling of integration and of belonging to oneself, and we shall see below how this process of putting the ego back together is expressed in significant dreams.

Feeling responsible for oneself also modifies the nature of dependence on others, and buoyancy in my view implies a link of 'mature' dependence, in the terminology of Fairbairn (1941), who, it will be remembered, contrasts 'mature' dependence with 'infantile' dependence, the latter being based on incorporation, primary identification and narcissism. It is worth repeating here that the autonomy or independence characterizing 'mature' dependence and buoyancy does not mean that the object is dispensed with – that would be to remain in the paranoid-schizoid duality of clinging to/fleeing from the object – but that one allows oneself and the object a freedom to come and go.

Bayle (1989), in his paper entitled 'Discontinuités et portances', takes as his starting point the concept of buoyancy in the Oedipal sense, as defined by me, but distinguishes elementary forms of dependences on the object, which he also calls buoyancy. He suggests that the depressive does not lack buoyancy, that 'the depressive does not lack', and that 'the narcissistic object of hypochondria offers a perfectly stable partner' (p. 89). I agree that different levels of dependence can be distinguished, but I reserve the term 'buoyancy' for the movement of integration that allows freedom in interdependence at a highly developed level of relationship, retaining the term 'dependence' for less developed forms. This discussion of levels of dependence compels us to acknowledge that our psychoanalytic language is very poor in this respect, as we have only the one term 'dependence' to describe such diverse forms of links with objects.

Introjective identification with a good, containing object

Buoyancy is also the feeling that our psychical apparatus is identified with a good object and its containing capacity. To avoid any misunderstanding, I repeat that a 'good' object is not an 'idealized' object and that, in particular, a good object can withstand criticism.

Identification with a good object is conditional upon the abandonment of defences against separation and object-loss; and one of the most important of these defences is precisely identification with an idealized, omnipotent object. When a good object can be set up in the ego, with the development and synthesis of love and hate in ambivalence towards the object which is experienced as whole, a sense of security is established, eventually becoming the core of an ego that has acquired unity and strength by virtue of the trust placed in the good parts of oneself. This introjective identification with a good object therefore has nothing omnipotent about it; it is not a matter of feeling oneself to be God but, on the contrary, of finding one's way to something good in oneself, which provides a support.

In buoyancy, an introjective identification with a containing object (in Bion's sense) may be said to be added to the introjective identification with a good object. The idea of the container–contained relationship has significantly extended Winnicott's concept of holding, which, as we have seen, was introduced by him to take account of the part played by the mother and of 'maternal care' in development in the first year of life and corresponds to a kind of support. Brousselle (1989), who was interested in the problem of the spatio-temporal foundations of identity, realized that buoyancy fell within an 'evolving continuity of "support" in the *post-holding* situation, but without being located precisely at a genetic level' (p. 93). He saw it as positioned at an intersection – that is, at a preferential locus of condensation.

I consider that Bion's concept of the container–contained relationship conveys both the idea of an evolving continuity (of a diachronic development in time) and that of a psychical functioning at a given moment (synchronic functioning). This concept also gives us a broader understanding of relational phenomena by providing us with a theory that covers not only early mother–child relations but also object relations, as well as a theory of thought. For this, Bion uses the concept of 'capacity for reverie' in preference to Winnicott's idea of maternal care or area of illusion, because he is attempting to reach other levels and interactions, such as preconception and conception, the innate and experience, phantasy and reality, frustration and satisfaction, and the transition from the primary to the secondary process, there being a continuum from the most primitive layer, in which these entities have their roots, to the most highly evolved. He seeks to understand how the autonomy of thought becomes established.

As with introjective identifications, the satisfactory operation of the container–contained relationship between mother and child allows the latter to internalize good experiences and make introjective identifications with a 'happy couple' formed by a mother whose container function constitutes the dynamic receptacle for the emotions of the child (contained).

Athanassiou's (1986) paper 'Déni et connaissance' is an interesting application of Bion's ideas on attention, which comes close to my idea of buoyancy. The author stresses the part played by 'the attention "carried" by the mother to the baby, which is experienced very concretely by the baby as a "carrying" which, physically holding him through this psychical act, brings about his existence for him and confirms it'. According to this author, 'whenever the mother lets the baby go, he experiences this as a fall which abolishes his existence'. The baby's loss of the mother's attention may result in his turning away from the mother and withdrawing his attention from her with the omnipotent aim of disavowing her existence. According to Athanassiou, the baby then drops the 'true object' – his mother – who then fails to be recognized by the child. The baby may then seek a 'false object' which acts as a fetish and substitute for the mother.

> In this way the links of knowledge may be dismantled in favour of others: those of an 'anti-knowledge' (Bion's -C) present, like a fetish, only to divert attention and finally to deny that behind an absence another presence lies concealed.
>
> (1986: 1136)

Athanassiou's views, based on Bion, on the role of attention in the early mother–child relationship help in my opinion to explain why the analysands who react most strongly to discontinuities in the analytic encounter are at the same time the ones who set up the most massive disavowal against the existence of separation anxiety, as that would be tantamount to acknowledging the existence of the analyst and of the relationship with him: these analysands probably experience breaks as so many losses of the analyst's attention, to which they respond by withdrawing their own attention from him in an attempt to abolish the existence of the analyst by omnipotent disavowal. Discontinuity is experienced by them as a direct threat to their own existence and survival. Conversely, analysands who have acquired a trust in the analyst's reliability have integrated a sense of internal continuity and acknowledge the importance of the analyst. An apparent paradox is then observed: *it is when the analysand experiences the pleasant sensation of being himself that he feels the importance of the object more and is better able to accept depending to a certain extent on the analyst.*

To sum up, applying Bion's views to buoyancy, it may be said that what allows the analysand to tolerate anxiety – in particular, separation anxiety – is that, by virtue of the experience of the analytic relationship, he succeeds not only in re-introjecting the anxiety modified by the analyst's 'capacity for reverie' (contained) but also in introjecting the container – i.e. the containing function of the analyst, who can *contain* and *think*, so that, by identification, *the analysand can in his turn contain and think*. This is an essential step in the toleration of anxiety and in becoming capable of tolerating it by oneself by acquiring autonomy *vis-à-vis* the analyst.

Buoyancy, space and time

It is the combination of the perception of time and that of space which allows the feeling of buoyancy to emerge: the notion of time gives the individual the means to come to terms not only with space but also with duration, so as to create a dynamic equilibrium in object relations. Freud emphasized the part played by the appearance of the notion of time – an attribute of the sense of reality – as a step forward in the development of the ego's capacity to confront anxiety: if the traumatic situation can be transformed into a less threatening danger situation, this is because the ego becomes capable of 'anticipation', 'foreseeing', 'expecting' and 'remembering' (Freud 1926d).

I should like to make it clear that the feeling of buoyancy in my sense is not the direct opposite of separation anxiety, and that buoyancy cannot simply be regarded as the positive and separation anxiety as its negative counterpart. That would be a reductive view. For me, buoyancy is the synthesis and culmination of complex processes of integration, which have worked together to create a temporo-spatial psychical space of relationship, a space whose nature is fundamentally different from that in which separation anxiety rules. In my view, it is the creation of this radically different space which allows buoyancy to appear and operate satisfactorily. The instinctual forces prevailing at the level of separation anxiety induce the analysand to 'cling' concretely to the troughs and crests of the waves of the analyst's absence and presence. Conversely, the instinctual forces prevailing at the level of buoyancy allow the analysand to 'lift off' from the troughs and crests of the transference relationship and to experience the analytic encounter in another space, which is governed by different lifting forces. Might this be another expression of the antithesis between the death instinct and the life instinct?

The French word here translated by 'buoyancy' is *portance*, which literally means 'lift'; this is defined in physics as a force which acts perpendicularly to velocity and supports a mass (for example, an aircraft). Velocity, it will be recalled, introduces the idea of displacement (space) in time (metres per second), and the velocity acquired on the surface of water, for example, allows a surfboard to glide or a boat to rise up out of the water, radically changing its relationship with the liquid medium. A similar sensation is experienced by a child who lets go of the parental hand to walk by himself, or forsakes the water's edge in order to swim. My intention in using the term *portance* as an analogy is to emphasize the possibility of the analysand's acquiring a stability of his own *vis-à-vis* the object, using it for support but without resting his weight on it: whether the object is receding or approaching, the subject has acquired a sense of existence in a place and in time, and a feeling of self-support which makes him at one and the same time a partner and an autonomous being, without experiencing the anxieties of falling or collapse characteristic of early states of dependence. The subject does not lose his relation to the object, any more than the surfboard leaves the water, but the relationship changes in quality and comes to be governed by new combinations of forces.

Tomassini (1989) has pointed out that the term *portance*, which comes from the Latin *portare*, has two technical meanings in French. First, it is used in civil engineering to denote the maximum load-bearing capacity of a structure (such as an arch or a foundation). In the second sense, to which I referred above, *portance* means vertical lift as in aerodynamics and hydrodynamics.[1]

Although I have preferred to define *portance* in dynamic rather than static terms, Tomassini's comment is valuable in drawing attention to two complementary aspects of the concept, when applied by analogy to psychoanalysis: a dynamic aspect stressing the capacity of the ego to support itself independently of the object, and a structural aspect indicative of the ego's capacity to tolerate separation anxiety without splitting.

As stated above, the concept of buoyancy/*portance* seems to me to fit in naturally with a psychoanalytic conception of space and time. This space is not real space but that of the internalized representation of temporo-spatial space. It also reflects the four-dimensionality of psychical space as described by Meltzer (1975), a notion that appears in the mind after the stages of two-dimensionality (connected with adhesive identification) and three-dimensionality (connected with projective identification, which needs to conceive an 'inside' of the object in order to penetrate into it). Meltzer also points out that four-dimensionality makes it possible for a new type of identification to arise, described by Freud (1923b) and subsequently called 'introjective identification' (although this term is not Freud's). In this mode of identification, the subject leaves the object free in time by acknowledging the difference between generations, and leaves it free to come and go in space, because he forgoes possessing it and becoming one with it. In the context of the Oedipal situation, the subject can then become himself and see the object as it is.

Dimensionality and Oedipal triangulation

I consider that there is a close relationship between the internalization of buoyancy and the acquisition of the sense of identity and autonomy on the one hand, and the formation of a psychical object-relations space which becomes established with the Oedipus complex and allows that complex to be resolved, on the other.

It does indeed seem to me that the Oedipus complex can be resolved provided that the situation in its totality and the objects involved in it appear clearly and precisely in temporo-spatial space, in the same way as a blurred image is eventually brought to a sharp focus: the perception of objects distinct from the ego and of the difference between the sexes and generations triggers the mourning processes which shape our identity and establish our post-Oedipal introjective identifications. This forms part of the acquisition of the 'sense of reality'. Buoyancy, in my opinion, appears at the point when the object is symbolically internalized and seems to me to be an attribute of trust in good objects. This is why I consider that buoyancy belongs to the highly developed levels of integration.

To be more specific, I think it important to distinguish buoyancy from other, related concepts which their authors place in a dyadic relationship. This applies in particular to Winnicott's concept of 'holding' and Balint's 'basic fault', which their authors explicitly conceived in a relationship between two persons, a child and his mother, to the exclusion of the father. While accepting many of Winnicott's hypotheses, Green repeatedly emphasizes the earliness of the space of triangulation. For instance, he pointed out in 1979 that the internal object, 'to the extent that it is a good object, can be used as a consoling or soothing object, a "holding object" in Winnicott's sense' in the mother–child unity. However, the father is already present even before the child becomes aware of the third entity he constitutes:

> The child becomes the object of the object in the illusory relationship of the mother–child unity – until the day when this illusion yields to the disillusion resulting from the awareness of the third entity constituted by the father. The father has always been there. But he has been present only *in absentia*, in the mother's mind.
> (Green 1979: 57)

I personally see buoyancy operating in the context of a three-person or triangular relationship, whether already outlined in the early Oedipus complex with part-objects or fully developed in the Oedipus complex with whole objects. I believe that the quality of buoyancy becomes established with the first object relations and depends very early, perhaps even from the beginning, on the relationship the mother has in her phantasy with the father, as I consider that the role of the father appears much earlier in this form than has for a long time been accepted. Many analysts have stressed – and are currently stressing – the mother's need to feel herself to be in a container–contained relationship with the father in order to perform her maternal function, with the two parents and the child forming the basis on which phantasies of a primal scene with good objects can subsequently develop.

Dreams, buoyancy and the counter-transference

Freud mentions typical dreams of flying, floating, falling or swimming in *The Interpretation of Dreams* (1900a). Dreams of flying, floating or swimming are usually agreeable, he says, while falling dreams tend to be accompanied by anxiety. All these dreams reproduce impressions of childhood. 'There cannot be a single uncle who has not shown a child how to fly by rushing across the room with him in his outstretched arms.' Freud notes that children are delighted by such experiences and never tire of asking to have them repeated. 'In after years they repeat these experiences in dreams; but in the dreams they leave out the hands which held them up, so that they float or fall unsupported.' Freud claims to lack the material to explain these dreams, but points out that, with their tactile and motor sensations, they 'are called up immediately there is any psychical reason for making use of them'. These dreams of flying or taking wing must be interpreted in accordance with the context, as their meanings may differ widely. They often incorporate omnipotent or manic sexual phantasies, but may also signify buoyancy and express the mixture of pleasure and fright that accompanies the feeling of being able to fly with one's own wings.

I think it is very important in this case for the analyst to be able to give a positive interpretation of the internalization of buoyancy. After all, the fright accompanying the pleasure corresponds to the analysand's legitimate anxiety at letting go of the object in order to partake of a new experience. To the extent that taking wing is seen as equivalent to loss of interest in the object, the analysand may feel guilty towards the analyst. This unconscious guilt on the part of the analysand might block the unfolding of his buoyancy function and keep him in his situation of dependence on and fusion with the object.

I personally have often noticed the appearance of these typical dreams of flying or taking wing at particular points in the analysis corresponding to phases of integration of the sensation of buoyancy, when the analysand becomes agreeably aware of the feeling of being himself and of being able to 'fly with his own wings'.

I should like to illustrate this by a clinical sequence from a period when a female analysand who had hitherto been very dependent was discovering her potential to think by herself, a process whose different stages appeared successively in dreams. This analysand had never managed to decide what she wanted for herself and had done everything possible to discover what other people would do or think in her place. In the transference, she had striven above all to cling to me and my thoughts rather than to communicate: for this purpose she had used every possible trick and set traps for me to find out what I would think, say or do if I were her. Breaks, especially at the beginning of the analysis, had been experienced each time as wrenches, and this form of dependence had been a considerable impediment to her life.

After prolonged analytic work, this analysand embarked on a period of significant change, and I noticed that she was beginning to think for herself and develop her creative capacity. I had the feeling that she was in the process of acquiring a sense of identity and that she could rely more on herself – that is to say, in my terms, she was internalizing the supporting quality of the object.

184

In one dream she was holding fast to the wall of a tall building that was very old and was about to be demolished. She had to decide to release her grip because she could no longer continue to cling to the wall, nor could she get inside. She suddenly noticed that there was a caretaker living inside the building, which she had thought to be empty, who helped her to climb down unscathed.

After this dream, which illustrated her tendency in the transference to cling to a two-dimensional space (adhesive identification), followed by her discovery of a space with an inside and an outside – i.e. a three-dimensional space (projective identification) –

the analysand had a new dream in which she had hurt a bird, which could not fly away.

For reasons I cannot go into here, this dream was connected with her hatred of her brother, and the resulting guilt feelings, turned against herself in the form of a self-punishment that prevented her from 'flying with her own wings', were the aggressive element that stood in the way of the creation of a symbolic space. Interpretation of her libidinal and aggressive instincts brought about a change in her feelings for her objects and made for a trust which was also reflected in a dream:

this time she was sitting in a chair lift, with a man beside her, and everyone had his place. In spite of the height she had no sensation of vertigo and felt comfortable. She had a map on her knees to tell her where she was and in which direction to go.

This does not seem to me to be a dream of omnipotence because, in her associations, the presence of the cable represented the acknowledgement and acceptance of dependence, used for the sake of greater freedom.

I believe that dreams of departure, flying or taking wing, in which the taking along of luggage is involved, may also be included among the typical dreams of these moments of integration of buoyancy. For me, *the sense of identity stemming from integration and the accompanying sense of buoyancy result from the gathering together of the essential aspects of the ego and their continuous re-organization in a unified ego, or rather an ego in constant search of unification.* As long as essential parts of the ego remain split off and confused with the objects on to which they are projected, the ego remains unbalanced. During analysis we are able to feel how the ego acquires an equilibrium when the analysand re-discovers crucial aspects of himself, takes them with him and makes them his own, while at the same time becoming capable of detaching himself from important aspects of himself which have remained tied to objects (Grinberg 1964). At one and the same time, therefore, there is a *recovery* of essential aspects of the ego which had previously been 'lost', in particular by splitting and projection (on to external objects, internal objects or parts of the body seen as objects), a constant *re-organization* of these re-discovered aspects of the ego in a unified ego, and a preparedness to *forgo* taking everything with one.

This process of working through and mourning often features in dreams where the analysand has to catch a train or plane and sort out the luggage it is essential to take from the luggage to be left behind. In these cases the train or plane may represent an ego capable of containing (container), while the luggage represents the scattered parts of the ego which must be sorted: some of them are to be abandoned (mourning for the lost parts of the self), while others – felt to be essential – are taken on the journey (contained). The phantasy material of dreams of this type gives us valuable information about the unconscious significance of what is essential to the ego and what binds it to its objects. As for the context of the dream (associations, phase of the analysis and so on), this gives us an impression of its quality (omnipotence, integration and so forth) and allows us to interpret appropriately: for instance, when an analysand dreams that he cannot take some luggage with him, this may mean that he finds himself unable to give up certain parts of himself that have remained attached to his objects and that in this case feelings of integration, identity and buoyancy are lacking. This type of dream often tells us about the hidden aspects of the ego that have remained attached to objects, constituting unconscious 'narcissistic welds' which cannot easily be detected otherwise and which stand in the way of integration and buoyancy (Athanassiou 1989).

Finally, I should like to mention a particular type of dream whose often frightening content may be experienced by the analysand – and also by the analyst – as a turning back rather than a step forward indicative of a tendency towards integration. I have called these 'dreams which turn over the page' (J-M. Quinodoz 1987), to indicate that the interpretation should emphasize their positive side. For when the totality of the transference situation is taken into account, we understand that the frightening content corresponds to phantasies that have hitherto been acted out and have not been representable, which come to be represented in the dream once the analysand has become conscious of them, ceases to act them out and integrates them into his psychical life.

For instance, an analysand may dream that he is about to set off by train or plane and finds himself in the extreme anxiety situation of not managing to take his luggage with him. The analysand may be very frightened by the regressive content of the dream (the impression that he cannot leave) and may be surprised to have a dream accompanied by such anxiety just at the moment when he is showing signs of autonomy in his life: 'I do not manage to get away,' the worried analysand says. 'Is that where I still am?' He may communicate his anxiety, and if the analyst does not pay sufficient attention to the context of the treatment, he is liable to assume that the analysand is regressing and to interpret only the regressive aspect of the dream, thus yielding to the danger of projective counter-identification (Grinberg 1962). It is only the totality of the analytic situation – the dream, associations, phase of the transference, movement in the session and so on – that will enable the analyst to place the dream correctly and distinguish between a regressive and an integrative tendency. It is in my view essential, when an analysand brings a dream with regressive content accompanied by anxiety at a time of progress, for the analyst to place and interpret it positively, not only in order to avoid a regression but also to emphasize the process of psychical integration that is under way, with the dreamer succeeding in representing aspects of himself he has not hitherto integrated because they were previously unrepresentable.

Although a sense of buoyancy is never acquired once and for all, it is still the sign that the analysand has tamed solitude and become capable of separating from the analyst with a sense of unity and re-discovered personal identity.

Note

1 The French term *portance*, with the penumbra of figurative associations accompanying its literal connotations, has no direct equivalent in other languages, except in Italian (*portanza*); the English word chosen to translate it here is 'buoyancy', while the Spanish equivalent would be *auto-sustentación*.

Recapitulation and conclusions

Why I wrote this book

There are several reasons why I felt it appropriate to write this book.
One was my wish to communicate my past and present experience as
a psychoanalyst confronted each day with a register of feelings of which
the analytic relationship is capable of making sense. Another was the
idea that such a project might satisfy a need, because to my knowledge
there is not yet any general work which sets out the various
psychoanalytic viewpoints on this crucial aspect of the psychoanalytic
process.

I believe that such a work may also be of interest to all who have
recourse to psychoanalytic thought in their practice – for instance,
psychotherapists, who also encounter the phenomena of separation
anxiety in both individual and group therapies. Finally, I am addressing
all who face the challenge of the anxiety aroused by solitude and
mourning, to tell them what the psychoanalytic experience in the
therapeutic setting can offer. The clinical examples are intended not
only as a demonstration to psychoanalysts of how theory and technique
in my view combine but also to create an awareness in people with
little or no acquaintance with psychoanalytic concepts, giving them a
living insight into the exchanges between analysand and analyst
whereby this affective evolution becomes possible.

It is very difficult to express in words the result of the transformations which we observe in psychoanalytic therapy and which
eventually induce the analysand to contemplate terminating his analysis
because he feels able to leave his analyst and continue on his own.
Winnicott succeeded in conveying this idea when he wrote that the
capacity to be 'alone in the presence of someone' is an essential
component of psychical maturity (1958). Changes in the experience of
solitude do indeed constitute a barometer of affective evolution and of

188

the level of psychical integration attainable, both during each individual's psychical development and in the course of the psychoanalytic process, as shown by Melanie Klein ('On the sense of loneliness', 1963). However, many other factors must be taken into account if we wish to understand, with a view to influencing them, the complex mechanisms underlying the transformations observed in therapy.

For the analytic situation allows the analysand to re-discover the emotional experiences he had with important persons of his childhood by reproducing and remembering them in the transference relationship which is formed with the person of the psychoanalyst. In the transference, the analysand re-lives the anxiety of being separate and alone, especially at end-of-session, weekend or holiday breaks and with the approach of the termination of the analysis. At the same time, however, the psychoanalyst's interpretations of the transference will stimulate the analysand to work through these experiences so that he can benefit from them. The alternation of meetings and separations is therefore a fundamental aspect of the transference link. For this reason, many analysts now consider that the psychoanalytic process, regarded from the point of view of the working through in the transference of separation and object-loss anxieties, creates conditions whereby the analysand may become capable of experiencing a structuring sense of solitude. The capacity to cope with the termination of the analysis is then an expression of the capacity to lead one's life alone while forging links of communication with others and with oneself.

If we wish to go further, beyond a purely descriptive approach to the psychical phenomena we observe, we must resort to genuine psycho-analytic models for understanding, in order for our interpretations to be effective and to lead to profound changes in the relational lives of our analysands. Since a high proportion of these transformations escape the conscious perception of the person concerned, only a method of investigating the unconscious such as psychoanalysis makes it possible to tackle these unconscious phenomena in such a way that they can be modified.

It is perhaps surprising to see how little published material is devoted precisely to the clinical manifestations of separation anxiety. That such a widespread phenomenon is so relatively little discussed is paradoxical. I suppose that this is part of the general tendency to take the familiar for granted: from this point of view, the manifestations of separation and object-loss anxiety are so frequent that they may easily pass unnoticed, because they are so much a part of our everyday work. Yet a large number of psychoanalytic publications exist on various individual aspects of separations which lead to the changes observed in psychoanalytic therapy. I realized that any attempt to take account of all these contributions would be liable to degenerate into a tedious encyclopaedic listing, and have therefore confined my critical presentation to the theories which constitute the models for understanding separation and object-loss anxieties in the principal psychoanalytic schools of today. Other contributions are incorporated in the discussion and not presented systematically. The relevant references may be found in the index and bibliography.

Structure of the book

I have divided this book into four parts: (1) an introduction centring on a clinical example; (2) a critical presentation of the principal psychoanalytic models for understanding the phenomena observed in clinical practice; and (3) an account of how I interpret the phenomena of separation anxiety in the transference relationship, followed by (4) a discussion of my personal hypotheses.

After recalling that anxiety at being separate and alone is a universal feeling bound up with our condition as human beings, I show that these affects can accompany many different psychopathological conditions and give rise to psychical symptoms and disorders of greater or lesser severity. There is a view that the problems of separation, object–loss and mourning are merely reality conflicts and therefore fall outside the field susceptible to analysis. Like many psychoanalysts today, however, I consider that they are psychical conflicts which *are* accessible to analysis. After all, the affects of separation anxiety, mourning and loneliness are not only related to external reality but are located at the very heart of psychical life, at the junction between phantasy and reality, past and present, unconscious and conscious, and therefore satisfy all the conditions for being transferred and worked through in the analytic relationship. To illustrate my argument, I describe the progress of the treatment of an analysand who had suffered from excessive separation anxieties since her childhood, showing how they evolved until they were eventually worked through in the resolution of the Oedipus complex.

I considered it important to begin with a clinical example because the experience of meetings between psychoanalysts has convinced me that it is on the basis of our observations with analysands that we can find a common psychoanalytic language, and that divergences appear in theoretical discussions as soon as the clinical field is departed from.

This example then enables me to ask a number of the questions which occur to a psychoanalyst concerning the significance of the vicissitudes of separation and object-loss anxiety not only during the course of the psychoanalytic process itself but also in normal individual psychical development, which the psychoanalytic process resembles in a number of respects. In this way, in observing the changes occurring in object relations, we note that one element of progress is when the analysand moves on from states in which the other is seen as hardly, if at all, different from himself (narcissism) to a perception of other people as different from himself, separate and having a well-defined sexual identity (object relation). In this transition from narcissism to a better established object-relationship, we find that the working through of differentiation and separation anxieties plays a central part; how then are we to explain this transition and to encourage these changes by way of our interpretations? This is the basic question that confronts us, and I have presented here the attempts to answer it made by the various psychoanalytic schools from the earliest days. These transformations can be discerned particularly in the conditions of the classical psycho-analytic setting, which, following Freud, are those recommended by the International Psychoanalytical Association (1983), in order to establish a common psychoanalytic practice as a basis for the theoretical hypotheses underlying our interpretations.

In the second part of the book I discuss the position of separation and object-loss anxiety in the main psychoanalytic theories, starting with the contributions of Freud. This review clearly shows how far psychoanalytic ideas in this field have progressed, especially since the 1920s and 1930s. Since Freud, no revolutionary idea has – as is sometimes asserted – made psychoanalytic therapy obsolete or 'out of date'; its foundations (the concept of the unconscious, the central role of infantile sexuality and the Oedipus complex, and the repetition of childhood experiences in the transference) have remained unchanged. However, psychoanalytic theory, technique and practice have been enriched over the years with many innovations which have extended their field of application and substantially deepened the affective dimension of the experience of psychoanalytic treatment.

In the third part of the book I dwell at greater length on various aspects of the transference manifestations of separation and object-loss anxiety – in particular, their relations with psychical pain, the negative therapeutic reaction and acting out – giving a detailed account of how I interpret them, having regard to the influence on me not only of Freud's thought but also of the ideas of Melanie Klein and her followers. In the fourth part I develop my hypothesis about the sense of buoyancy which is the token of the process of integration of psychical and relational life.

The frequent contacts between psychoanalysts today confront us with the many streams of contemporary psychoanalytic thought and with conceptions that differ from our own, these varying from region to region and school to school. If we are to respect the thought of others and to benefit from these encounters, it seems to me important to realize that the different theoretical models now current are not always readily reconcilable with one another and that any attempt to combine them into an integrated whole would be liable to create confusion.

Finally, having regard to the wealth and diversity of present-day psychoanalytic ideas, it is more than ever essential for each psychoanalyst to find his personal way through the different schools of thought, most of them original, so as to arrive at his own synthesis. This is a thrilling proposition, demanding an unending learning process and the capacity to call oneself into question over and over again.

From separation anxiety to the taming of solitude

What solution can psychoanalysis offer a person to whom solitude is a nightmare? This is a vital question when it is realized that our lives are a fabric of constant separations, each of which may re-activate our sense of solitude. If solitude is experienced as a nightmare, then it is life as a whole that is thereby wrecked.

My intention with this book has been to show that for the psychoanalyst the solitude experienced by some people as wrecking can change in quality and be tamed. When experienced in the analytic relationship, it can not only allow the analysand to tolerate better the painful awareness of being a separate individual who is alone but also enable him to develop its potentialities and riches. Solitude may then be experienced by him as life-giving, becoming a source of personal creativity and a stimulus to affective relations.

Solitude can become life-giving when the distrust and anxiety aroused by the inescapable transience of our own existence and that of those dear to us can be overcome in favour of bonds of trust, when love becomes stronger than hate. It is paradoxically this awareness and knowledge of our limits that enable us to benefit truly from them: we can appreciate the infinitely precious worth of each being all the more because he is ephemeral, and savour each instant of life to the full because it will never be repeated. Hence, to all those who believe, on the contrary, that life is not worth living because it has an end, the analytic encounter presents nothing less than a challenge: the challenge of life to non-life.

From another point of view, solitude tamed can become a source of personal creativity when we succeed in remaining in contact with that which is most true and most secret within us – but for this purpose we must be constantly on the lookout, as we are perpetually changing. Solitude, creativity and the sense of identity are therefore linked indissolubly in a state of flux, each being conditional upon the others: solitude is essential to the replenishment of our wellsprings, this replenishment in turn being responsible for the unique character of our creation, while our creativity expresses our identity – that is, the true nature of our ego. All creative life, its movement constantly renewed and never accomplished once and for all, is a reflection of the *ego* as I see it: an entity in the process of becoming, constantly searching for its identity. Some may tire of this never-ending search, but others may discover the whole excitement of life within it, because one never finishes 'becoming what one is'.

As long as it remains founded on distrust and hostility, solitude leads to isolation and withdrawal into oneself; it is the solitude of the ivory tower. When tamed, solitude becomes a stimulus to knowledge of self and others, and a call to communicate with others on the most authentic level. It is for this reason that I have been concerned in this book to devote as much space as possible to the views of other psychoanalysts, considering that the originality of each benefits from the thought of the others and contributes to the richness of psychoanalysis. This is how I experience my solitude as a psychoanalyst in relation to the presence of the others.

Solitude is not the forgoing of relationship with others. On the contrary, it allows each individual to define himself, and the confrontation with the originality of the other brings out the preciousness and irreplaceability of what each person alone can contribute. The worth of the object and of the subject derives from the fact that each is unique; it is born of their solitude.

Bibliography

Abraham, K. (1919) 'Some remarks on Ferenczi's paper on Sunday neuroses', in *Clinical Papers and Essays on Psycho-Analysis*, London: Hogarth Press (1955), pp. 55–6.
—— (1924) 'A short study of the development of the libido, viewed in the light of mental disorders', in *Selected Papers*, London: Hogarth Press (1949), pp. 418–501.
Abraham, N. and Torok, M. (1975) 'L'Objet perdu – moi', *Revue Française de Psychanalyse*, 39: 409–26.
Andréoli, A. (1989) 'Le Moi et son objet narcissique', report on the 48th Congrès des Psychanalystes de Langue française des Pays romans, Geneva, 1988, *Revue Française de Psychanalyse*, 53: 151–96.
Anzieu, D. (1974) 'The skin ego', in S. Lebovici and D. Widlöcher (eds) *Psycho-Analysis in France*, New York: International Universities Press, pp. 17–32.
Athanassiou, C. (1986) 'Déni et connaissance', *Revue Française de Psychanalyse*, 50: 1125–44.
—— (1989) 'La sondure narcissique: une impasse therapeutique', *Revue Française de Psychanalyse*, 53: 75–85.
Balint, M. (1952) 'New beginning and the paranoid and depressive syndromes', in *Primary Love and Psycho-analytic Technique*, London: Hogarth Press and the Institute of Psycho-Analysis.
—— (1968) *The Basic Fault*, London: Tavistock.
Balint, M. with Balint, E. (1959) *Thrills and Regressions*, New York: International Universities Press.
Baranger, M., Baranger, W. and Mom, M. (1988) 'The infantile psychic trauma from us to Freud: pure trauma, retroactivity and reconstruction', *International Journal of Psycho-Analysis*, 69: 113–28.
Baranger, W. (1980) 'Validez del concepto de objeto en la obra de Melanie Klein', in W. Baranger, E. del Campo, R. Goldstein, E.C. Merea, J.M.

Mom, B. Resnicoff, L. Ricon, E. Romano and B.A. Schutt, *Aportaciones al concepto de objeto en psicoanálisis*, Buenos Aires: Ed. Amorrortu.

Bayle, G. (1989) 'Discontinuités et portances', *Revue Française de Psychanalyse*, 53: 87–91.

Bégoin, J. (1984) 'Présentation: quelques repères sur l'évolution du concept d'identification', *Revue Française de Psychanalyse*, 2: 483–90.

—— (1989) 'Introduction à la notion de souffrance psychique: le désespoir d'être', report on the 48th Congrès des Psychanalystes de Langue française des Pays romans, Geneva, 1988, *Revue Française de Psychanalyse*, 53: 457–69.

Bégoin, J. and Bégoin, F. (1981) 'The negative therapeutic reaction, envy and catastrophic anxiety', *Bulletin of the FEP*, 16: 21–32.

Bick, E. (1968) 'The experience of the skin in early object-relations', *International Journal of Psycho-Analysis*, 49: 484–6.

Bion, W.R. (1957) 'Differentiation of the psychotic from the non-psychotic personalities', in *Second Thoughts*, London: Heinemann Medical (1967); Maresfield Library (1984), pp. 43–64.

—— (1962) *Learning from Experience*, London: Heinemann Medical; Maresfield Library (1984).

—— (1963) *The Elements of Psychoanalysis*, London: Heinemann Medical; Maresfield Library (1984).

—— (1967) *Second Thoughts*, London: Heinemann Medical; Maresfield Library (1984).

Bleger, J. (1967) *Symbiose et ambiguïté*, Paris: PUF, 1981.

Bowlby, J. (1969, 1973, 1980) *Attachment and Loss*, 3 vols, London: Hogarth Press and the Institute of Psycho-Analysis.

Brenman, E. (1982) 'Separation: a clinical problem', *Bulletin of the British Psycho-Analytical Society*, 1(2): 14–23.

Brousselle, A. (1989) 'Portance et assise de l'identité', *Revue Française de Psychanalyse*, 53: 93–7.

Chasseguet-Smirgel, J. (1988) 'Autres commentaires (questions de Cléopâtre Athanassiou)', *Revue Française de Psychanalyse*, 52: 1167–79.

Cramer, B. (1985) 'Les psychoses infantiles et les étapes du développement de la séparation et de l'individuation chez Margaret Mahler', in S. Lebovici, R. Diatkine and M. Soulé (eds) *Traité de psychiatrie de l'enfant et de l'adolescent*, Paris: PUF.

Delaite, F., Nicollier, D. and de Senarclens, B. (1990) 'Brève étude sur l'amour et la haine chez Freud', *Bulletin Société Suisse de Psychanalyse*, 30.

Diatkine, R. (1988) 'Destins du transfert', *Revue Française de Psychanalyse*, 52: 803–13.

Dolto, F. (1985) *Solitude*, Paris: Vertiges du Nord/Carrère.

Ellonen-Jéquier, M. (1986) 'A propos de la signification de certains mécanismes psychotiques', in J.J. Baranes, R. Cahn, R. Diatkine and J. Philippe, *Psychanalyse, adolescence et psychose*, Paris: Payot.

Eskelinen-de Folch, T. (1983) 'We – versus I and you', *International Journal of Psycho-Analysis*, 64: 309–20.

Etchegoyen, R.H. (1985) 'Identification and its vicissitudes', *International Journal of Psycho-Analysis*, 66(1): 3–18.

—— (1986) *The Fundamentals of Psychoanalytic Technique*, London: Karnac (1991).

Faimberg, H. (1987) 'Le Téléscopage des générations', *Psychanalyse à l'Université*, 46: 181–200.

Fairbairn, W.R.D. (1940) 'Schizoid factors in the personality', in *Psychoanalytic Studies of the Personality*, London: Tavistock/Routledge & Kegan Paul (1952), pp. 3–27.

—— (1941) 'A revised psychopathology of the psychoses and psychoneuroses', in *Psychoanalytic Studies of the Personality*, London: Tavistock/Routledge & Kegan Paul (1952), pp. 28–58.

—— (1952) *Psychoanalytic Studies of the Personality*, London: Tavistock/Routledge & Kegan Paul.

Ferenczi, S. (1919) 'Sunday neuroses', in *Further Contributions to the Theory and Technique of Psycho-Analysis*, London: Hogarth Press (1950), pp. 174–7.

—— (1927) 'The problem of the termination of the analysis', in *Final Contributions to the Problems and Methods of Psycho-Analysis*, London: Hogarth Press (1955), pp. 77–86.

Firestein, S.K. (1980) 'Terminaison de l'analyse (revue générale de la littérature)', *Revue Française de Psychanalyse*, 44: 319–28.

Flournoy, O. (1979) *Le Temps d'une psychanalyse*, Paris: Belford.

Freud, A. (1936) *The Ego and the Mechanisms of Defence*, London: Hogarth Press.

—— (1960) 'Discussion of Dr John Bowlby's paper', *The Psycho-Analytic Study of the Child*, 15: 53–62.

—— (1965) *Normality and Pathology in Childhood*, London: Hogarth Press.

Freud, A. and Burlingham, D. (1943) *War and Children*, New York: International Universities Press.

Freud, S. (1892–99) Extracts from letters to Fliess, in *The Origins of Psycho-Analysis* (1950a), *Standard Edition of the Complete Psychological Works of Sigmund Freud*, SE 1.

—— (1895) 'A project for a scientific psychology', in *The Origins of Psycho-Analysis* (1950a), SE 1.

—— (1900a) *The Interpretation of Dreams*, SE 4–5.

—— (1905d) *Three Essays on the Theory of Sexuality*, SE 7.

—— (1909b) 'Analysis of a phobia in a five-year-old boy', SE 10.

—— (1913c) 'On beginning the treatment', SE 12.

—— (1914c) 'On narcissism: an introduction', SE 14.

—— (1914g) 'Remembering, repeating and working through', SE 12.

—— (1915c) 'Instincts and their vicissitudes', SE 14.
—— (1915d) 'Repression', SE 14.
—— (1915e) 'The unconscious', SE 14.
—— (1916a) 'On transience', SE 14.
—— (1916–17) *Introductory Lectures on Psycho-analysis*, SE 15–16.
—— (1917e [1915]) 'Mourning and melancholia', SE 14.
—— (1920g) *Beyond the Pleasure Principle*, SE 18.
—— (1921c) *Group Psychology and the Analysis of the Ego*, SE 18.
—— (1923b) *The Ego and the Id*, SE 19.
—— (1924b [1923]) 'The loss of reality in neurosis and psychosis', SE 19.
—— (1924c) 'The economic problem of masochism', SE 19.
—— (1925h) 'Negation', SE 19.
—— (1926d) *Inhibitions, Symptoms and Anxiety*, SE 20.
—— (1927e) 'Fetishism', SE 21.
—— (1930a) *Civilization and its Discontents*, SE 21.
—— (1933a) *New Introductory Lectures on Psycho-analysis*, SE 22.
—— (1937a) 'Analysis terminable and interminable', SE 23.
—— (1940a [1938]) *An Outline of Psycho-analysis*, SE 23.
—— (1940e [1938]) 'Splitting of the ego in the defensive process', SE 23.
—— (1941 [1938]) 'Findings, ideas, problems', SE 23.
Gaddini, E. (1982) 'Early defensive fantasies and the psychoanalytic process', *International Journal of Psycho-Analysis*, 63(3): 379–88.
Gibeault, A. (1989) 'Destins de la symbolisation', *Revue Française de Psychanalyse*, 53: 1517–618.
Glover, E. (1955) 'Termination', in *The Technique of Psycho-Analysis*, New York: International Universities Press (1971), pp. 627–40.
Green, A. (1975) 'The analyst, symbolization and absence in the analytic setting (on changes in analytic practice and analytic experience)', *International Journal of Psycho-Analysis*, 56: 1–22.
—— (1979) 'L'Angoisse et le narcissisme', *Revue Française de Psychanalyse*, 43: 45–87.
—— (1983) *Narcissisme de vie et narcissisme de mort*, Paris: Editions de Minuit.
Greenson, R.R. (1967) *The Technique and Practice of Psycho-Analysis*, New York: International Universities Press; London: Hogarth Press and the Institute of Psycho-Analysis.
Gressot, M. (1963 [1979]) *Le Royaume intermédiaire*, Paris: PUF.
Grinberg, L. (1962) 'On a specific aspect of countertransference due to the patient's projective identification', *International Journal of Psycho-Analysis*, 43: 2.
—— (1964) *Guilt and Depression*, London: Karnac (1992).
—— (1968) 'On acting out and its role in the psychoanalytical process', *International Journal of Psycho-Analysis*, 49: 172–9.

—— (1980) 'The closing phase of the psychoanalytic treatment of adults and the goals of psychoanalysis: the search for truth about one's self', *International Journal of Psycho-Analysis*, 61: 25–37.

—— (1981) 'Los Sueños del día lunes', in *Psicoanálisis: aspectos teóricos y clínicos*, Barcelona: Paidos.

Grunberger, B. (1971) *Narcissism: Psychoanalytic Essays*, New York: International Universities Press (1979).

Grunert, U. (1981) 'The negative therapeutic reaction as a reactivation of a disturbed process of separation in the transference', *Bulletin of the FEP*, 16: 5–19.

Guex, G. (1950) *La Névrose d'abandon*, Paris: PUF.

Guillaumin, J. (1989) 'L'Objet de la perte dans la pensée de Freud', report on the 48th Congrès des Psychanalystes de Langue française des Pays romans, Geneva, 1988, *Revue Française de Psychanalyse*, 53: 162–85.

Haynal, A. (1977) 'Le Sens de Désespoir', report on the 36th Congrès des Psychanalystes de Langues romanes, Geneva, 1976, *Revue Française de Psychanalyse*, 41: 17–186.

—— (1985) *Depression and Creativity*, New York: International Universities Press.

—— (1989) 'L'Affect, cet inconnu, et son intrication dans la cure', *Revue Française de Psychanalyse*, 53: 491–3.

International Psychoanalytical Association (1983) 'IPA standards and criteria for qualification and admission to membership of a component society of the IPA', *IPA Newsletter*, XV: 3.

—— (1985) 'IPA minimum requirements for acquiring and maintaining the function of training analyst', *IPA Newsletter*, XVII: 3.

—— (1987) *IPA Brochure*, London.

Joseph, B. (1985) 'Transference: the total situation', *International Journal of Psycho-Analysis*, 66: 447–54.

Kernberg, O. (1975) *Borderline Conditions and Pathological Narcissism*, New York: Jason Aronson.

—— (1984) *Severe Personality Disorders: Therapeutic Strategies*, New Haven, CT: Yale University Press.

Klein, M. (1935) 'A contribution to the psychogenesis of manic–depressive states', in *Love, Guilt and Reparation*, London: Hogarth Press (1975).

—— (1940) 'Mourning and its relation to manic–depressive states', in *Love, Guilt and Reparation*, London: Hogarth Press (1975).

—— (1946) 'Notes on some schizoid mechanisms', in *Envy and Gratitude*, London: Hogarth Press (1975).

—— (1950) 'On the criteria for the termination of a psychoanalysis', *International Journal of Psycho-Analysis*, 31: 78–80.

—— (1952) 'The origins of transference', *International Journal of Psycho-Analysis*, 33: 433–8.

—— (1957) *Envy and Gratitude*, London: Hogarth Press (1975).

—— (1963) 'On the sense of loneliness', in *Envy and Gratitude*, London: Hogarth Press (1975).

Kohut, H. (1971) *The Analysis of Self*, New York: International Universities Press.

Kris, E. (1956) 'The recovery of childhood memories in psycho-analysis', *The Psycho-Analytic Study of the Child*, 11: 54–88.

Ladame, F. (1987) *Les Tentatives de suicide chez les adolescents*, 2nd edn, Paris: Masson.

Laplanche, J. (1980) *Problématique, I: l'angoisse*, Paris: PUF.

—— (1987) 'La Séduction généralisée aux fondements de la théorie et à l'horizon de la pratique psychanalytique', conference at the Raymond de Saussure Centre, Geneva, 9 May, account by J-M. Quinodoz, *Bulletin Société Suisse de Psychanalyse*, 24: 98–9.

Laplanche, J. and Pontalis, J-B. (1967) *The Language of Psycho-analysis*, London: Hogarth Press (1973).

Lax, R.F., Bach, S. and Burland, A.J. (1986) *Self and Object Constancy: Clinical and Theoretical Perspectives*, New York and London: Guilford Press.

Lebovici, S. (1980) 'La Fin de la psychanalyse et ses modes de terminaison', *Revue Française de Psychanalyse*, 44: 236–63.

Liberman, D. (1967) 'Entropía y información en el proceso terapéutico', *Revista de Psicoanálisis*, 24: 1.

Limentani, A. (1981) 'On some positive aspects of the negative therapeutic reaction', *International Journal of Psycho-Analysis*, 62: 379–90.

Luquet, P. (1964) 'Early identification and structuration of the ego', *International Journal of Psycho-Analysis*, 45: 263–9.

Mahler, M., Pine, F. and Bergman, A. (1975) *The Psychological Birth of the Human Infant*, New York: Basic Books; London: Maresfield Library (1985).

Maldonado, J.L. (1989) 'On negative and positive therapeutic reaction', *International Journal of Psycho-Analysis*, 70: 327–39.

Manzano, J. (1989) 'La Séparation et la perte d'objet chez l'enfant, une introduction', report on the 48th Congrès des Psychanalystes de Langue française des Pays romans, Geneva, 1988, *Revue Française de Psychanalyse*, 53: 241–72.

Meltzer, D. (1966) 'The relation of anal masturbation to projective identification', *International Journal of Psycho-Analysis*, 47: 335–42.

—— (1967) *The Psycho-analytical Process*, London: Heinemann.

—— (1975) 'Adhesive identification', *Contemporary Psycho-Analysis*, 11(3): 289–310.

—— (1978) *The Kleinian Development*, Strath Tay, Perthshire: Clunie Press.

—— (1988) 'Aesthetic conflict: its place in the developmental process', in D. Meltzer and M.H. Williams *The Apprehension of Beauty*, Strath Tay, Perthshire: Clunie Press.

Meltzer, D., Bremmer, J., Hoxter, S., Weddell, D. and Wittemberg, L. (1975) *Explorations into Autism*, Strath Tay, Perthshire: Clunie Press.

Padel, J. (1973) 'The contribution of W.R.D. Fairbairn (1889–1965) to psycho-analytic theory and practice', *Bulletin of the FEP*, 2: 13–26.

Palacio Espasa, F. (1988) 'Considérations sur le narcissisme à la lumière de l'agressivité et de la destructivité de la vie psychique', *Bulletin Société Suisse de Psychanalyse*, 26: 4–9.

Pine, F. (1979) 'On the pathology of the separation-individuation process as manifested in later clinical work: an attempt at delineation', *International Journal of Psycho-Analysis*, 60: 225–42.

Pontalis, J-B. (1974) 'A propos de Fairbairn: le psychisme comme métaphore du corps', *Nouvelle Revue de Psychanalyse*, 10: 56–9.

—— (1981) 'Non, deux fois non', *Nouvelle Revue de Psychanalyse*, 24: 53–73.

Quinodoz, D. (1984) 'The accident as it reveals the death instinct', FEP symposium on the death instinct, Marseilles, 1984, *Bulletin of the FEP*, 25: 103–7.

—— (1987) '"J'ai peur de tuer mon enfant" ou: "Oedipe abandonné, Oedipe adopté"', *Revue Française de Psychanalyse*, 6: 1579–93.

—— (1989) 'Les "Interprétations dans la projection"', *Revue Française de Psychanalyse*, 53: 103–10.

—— (1990) 'Vertigo and object relationship', *International Journal of Psycho-Analysis*, 72: 53–63.

—— (1992) 'The psychoanalytical setting as the instrument of the container function', *International Journal of Psycho-Analysis*, 73: 627–36.

Quinodoz, J-M. (1984) 'Formes primitives de communication dans le transfert et relation d'objet', *Revue Française de Psychanalyse*, 48: 571–80.

—— (1985) 'Somatic manifestations, meloncholic object relationship and the death instinct in the course of the analytic process', FEP symposium on the death instinct, Marseilles, 1984, *Bulletin of the FEP*, 25: 109–14.

—— (1986) 'Identifizierung und Identität in der weiblichen Homosexualität', *Zeitschrift für psychoanalytische Theorie und Praxis*, 1: 82–94.

—— (1987) 'Des "Rêves qui tournent la page"', *Revue Française de Psychanalyse*, 51: 837–8.

—— (1989a) 'Female homosexual patients in psychoanalysis', *International Journal of Psycho-Analysis*, 70: 55–63.

—— (1989b) 'Les Interprétations de l'angoisse de séparation dans la cure psychanalytique', report on the 48th Congrès des Psychanalystes de Langue française des Pays romans, Geneva, 1988, *Revue Française de Psychanalyse*, 53: 5–67.

—— (1989c) 'Implications cliniques du concept psychanalytique de pulsion de mort', *Revue Française de Psychanalyse*, 53: 737–49.

Quinodoz, J-M., Bähler, V., Charbonnier, G., Delaite, F., Grabowska, M-J.,

Nicollier, D. and von Siebenthal Rodriguez, A. (1989) 'Contributions des psychanalystes de Suisse romande aux problèmes de l'angoisse de la séparation, de la perte de l'objet et de deuil', *Revue Française de Psychanalyse*, 53: 111–17.

Rank, O. (1924) *The Trauma of Birth*, London: Routledge (1929).

Reich, A. (1950) 'On the termination of analysis', in *Psychoanalytic Contributions*, New York: International Universities Press, pp. 121–35.

Rentschnick, P. (1975) *Les Orphelins mènent le monde*, Geneva: Médecine et Hygiène.

Resnik, S. (1967) 'La experiencia del espacio en el "setting" analítico', *Revista Urugayana de Psicoanálisis*, 9: 293–308.

Rickman, J. (1950) 'On the criteria for the termination of an analysis', *International Journal of Psycho-Analysis*, 31: 200–1.

Rosenfeld, H.A. (1947) 'Analysis of a schizophrenic state with depersonalization', *International Journal of Psycho-Analysis*, 28: 130–9; also in *Psychotic States*, London: Hogarth Press (1965).

—— (1964a) 'On the psychopathology of narcissism: a clinical approach', *International Journal of Psycho-Analysis*, 45: 332–7; also in *Psychotic States*, London: Hogarth Press (1965).

—— (1964b) 'An investigation into the need of neurotic and psychotic patients to act out during analysis', in *Psychotic States*, London: Hogarth Press (1965).

—— (1971) 'A clinical approach to the psychoanalytic theory of the life and death instincts: an investigation into the aggressive aspects of narcissism', *International Journal of Psycho-Analysis*, 52(2): 169–78.

—— (1983) 'Primitive object relations and mechanisms', *International Journal of Psycho-Analysis*, 64(3): 261–7.

Roustang, F. (1976) *Dire Mastery*, Baltimore, MD: Johns Hopkins University Press.

Saint-Exupéry, A. de (1946) *Le Petit Prince*, Paris: Gallimard.

Sandler, J., Kennedy, H. and Tyson, R.L. (1980) *The Technique of Child Psychoanalysis: Discussions with Anna Freud*, London: Hogarth Press. [Reprinted London: Karnac Books and the Institute of Psycho-Analysis, 1990.]

Saussure, J. de (1987) 'Comments on the IPS's training standards and minimum requirements', *Bulletin of the FEP*, 29: 27–52.

Segal, H. (1956) 'Depression in the schizophrenic', *International Journal of Psycho-Analysis*, 37: 339–43.

—— (1957) 'Notes on symbol formation', *International Journal of Psycho-Analysis*, 38: 391–7.

—— (1962) 'The curative factors in psycho-analysis', *International Journal of Psycho-Analysis*, 43: 212–17.

—— (1964) *Introduction to the Work of Melanie Klein*, London; Hogarth Press.

—— (1967) 'Melanie Klein's technique', in B.B. Wolman (ed.) *Psychoanalytic Techniques*, New York: Basic Books.

—— (1978) 'On symbolism', *International Journal of Psycho-Analysis*, 59: 315–19.

—— (1979) *Klein*, London: Fontana/Collins.

—— (1983) 'Some clinical implications of Melanie Klein's work: emergence from narcissism', *International Journal of Psycho-Analysis*, 64: 269–76.

—— (1987) 'On the clinical usefulness of the concept of the death instinct', *Bulletin of the British Psycho-Analytical Society*, 2: 1–12.

—— (1988) 'Sweating it out', *The Psycho Analytic Study of the Child*, 43: 167–75.

Segal, H. and Bell, D. (1991) 'The theory of narcissism in the work of Freud and Klein', in J. Sandler, E. Person and P. Fonagy (eds) *Freud's 'On narcissism – an introduction'*, Yale University Press.

Spira, M. (1985) *Créativité et liberté psychique*, Lyons: Editions Césura Lyon.

Spitz, R.A. (1957) *No and Yes: On the Genesis of Human Communication*, New York: International Universities Press.

—— (1965) *The First Year of Life*, New York: International Universities Press.

Strachey, J. (1957) Editor's introduction to Freud, S. 'Mourning and melancholia', SE 14, pp. 239–42.

—— (1959) Editor's introduction to *Inhibitions, Symptoms and Anxiety*, SE 20.

Tomassini, M. (1989) 'Portance et identification introjective', *Revue Française de Psychanalyse*, 53: 119–23.

Tustin, F. (1981) *Autistic States in Children*, London and Boston: Routledge & Kegan Paul.

Valcarce-Avello, M. (1987) 'Significado y función del juego infantil: el punto de vista del psicoanálisis', *Psiquis*, 8: 11–23.

Wallerstein, R.S. (1985) 'How does self psychology differ in practice?', *International Journal of Psycho-Analysis*, 66: 391–404.

—— (1987) Foreword, *Brochure of the International Psychoanalytical Association*, London: IPA.

—— (1988) 'One psychoanalysis or many?', *International Journal of Psycho-Analysis*, 69: 5–21.

Wender, L., Cvik, J., Cvik, N. and Stein, G. (1966) 'Comienza y final del sesión: dinámica de ciertos aspectos transferenciales y contratrans-ferenciales', *Actas* (Buenos Aires).

Wiener, P. (1985) 'Attachement et perte, vol. 3: La perte, de John Bowlby', *Revue Française de Psychanalyse*, 49: 1598–600.

Winnicott, D.W. (1945) 'Primitive emotional development', in *Collected Papers: Through Paediatrics to Psycho-analysis*, London: Tavistock (1958).

—— (1953) 'Transitional objects and transitional phenomena', in *Collected Papers: Through Paediatrics to Psycho-analysis*, London: Tavistock (1958).

—— (1955) 'Metapsychological and clinical aspects of regression within the psycho-analytical set-up', in *Collected Papers: Through Paediatrics to Psycho-analysis*, London: Tavistock (1958).

—— (1956) 'Clinical varieties of transference', in *Collected Papers: Through Paediatrics to Psycho-analysis*, London: Tavistock (1958), pp. 295–9.

—— (1958) 'The capacity to be alone', in *The Maturational Processes and the Facilitating Environment*, London: Hogarth Press and the Institute of Psycho-Analysis (1965).

—— (1960) 'Ego distortion in terms of true and false self', in *The Maturational Processes and the Facilitating Environment*, London: Hogarth Press and the Institute of Psycho-Analysis (1965).

—— (1971) *Playing and Reality*, London: Tavistock.

Zac, J. (1968) 'Encuadre y acting out: relación semana – fin de semana', *Revista de Psicoanálisis*, 25: 27–64.

—— (1971) 'Un enfoque metodológico del establecimento del encuadre', *Revista de Psicoanálisis*, 28: 593–610.

Name index

Abraham, K. 12, 51, 57, 61, 86
Abraham, N. 29
Andréoli, A. 139
Anzieu, D. 82
Athanassiou, C. 179, 186

Balint, M. 91, 159
Balint, E. 91
Baranger, M. 139
Baranger, W. 66, 139
Bayle, G. 177
Bégoin, F. 135–6
Bégoin, J. 29, 135–6, 164
Bell, D. 67, 73
Bick, E. 82, 83
Bion, W.R. 40, 48, 75–80, 129, 146, 170
Bleger, J. 83
Bowlby, J. 60, 92, 101–3
Brenman, E. 145–6
Brousselle, A. 178
Burlingham, D. 92, 101

Chasseguet-Smirgel, J. 108
Cramer, B. 98

Delaite, F. 130
Diatkine, R. 163
Dolto, F. 168

Ellonen-Jéquier, M. 117
Eskelinen de Folch, T. 122

Etchegoyen, R.H. 45, 51, 121, 122, 123

Faimberg, H. 29
Fairbairn, W.R.D. 26, 29, 86–8, 177
Ferenczi, S. 12, 159
Firestein, S.K. 157, 162, 163
Flournoy, O. 159
Freud, A. 60, 92–3, 100, 101, 103
Freud, S. 5, 6, 7, 11, 12, 18, 26, 29, 30, 34, 39–60, 61, 72, 87, 92, 109, 116, 118, 126, 129, 130, 132, 138, 158, 164, 167, 170, 173, 174–5, 180, 182, 183

Gaddini, E. 136
Gibeault, A. 129
Glover, E. 163
Green, A. 35, 129, 161, 183
Greenson, R.R. 110, 131
Gressot, M. 37
Grinberg, L. 30, 33, 118, 121, 131, 146–7, 148, 160, 163, 187
Grunberger, B. 34, 100
Grunert, U. 136
Guex, G. 135
Guillaumin, J. 139

Haynal, A. 13, 28, 126

International Psychoanalytical Association 108, 152, 191

204

Subject index

accident 137, 145

acting-out 16–18, 143–9; clinical manifestations 144–6; forced re-introjection 147; interpretations 143–9; and psychic containment 146–8; session times and fees 148

aggression 131; turned back against oneself 43, 45, 49–51, 131, 138, 175; *see also* ambivalence; hate.

ambivalence 43, 63, 129; integration of 21, 128–30, 131, 168, 178; pregenital and genital 130; *see also* hate; love

anxiety: affect of 58; of annihilation 55, 60, 62, 63, 73, 116, 129; capacity to tolerate 76–8; 'eight-month' 94; Freud's first theory of 41, 51; Freud's second theory of 7, 51–9, 116; Freud's third theory of 59–60; and infantile helplessness 40, 53; Klein's theory of 61; lack of maternal care and early 88; origin of 8; origin of infantile 41, 54, 62; persecutory and depressive 62; response to the working of the death instinct 61, 62–4; reawakened at the end of analysis 161

attachment and loss 26, 101–3

autism 84

birth 66; danger-situation 54; psychological 94; trauma of 52–3

buoyancy 33, 80, 166–87; broken down in depression and melancholia 174; capacity for reverie and 179; counter-transference and 183; dependence 172; distinct from *holding* 178, 183; dreams and 183–7; dynamic equilibrium of 175–6; identification with a good, containing object 178; identity and 177, 185; independence and 172, 186; Oedipus complex 183; from separation anxiety to 172; solitude and 166; space and time 180

capacity for reverie 77–8; and buoyancy 179

castration anxiety 31; characteristic of Oedipus complex 57; and danger-situation 56

clinical examples: acting-out linked with separation anxiety 145; affects linked with depressive position and buoyancy 173; compulsion to repeat an infantile traumatic situation 139; disavowal of the separation from analyst at the end of the analysis 164; discovery of the feeling of buoyancy 184; feeling of integration at the end of the analysis 170; interpretation of the positive concealed behind the negative 132; introjection of the

206